Oxford Shakespeare Topics

# Shakespeare and the Eighteenth Century

OXFORD SHAKESPEARE TOPICS

Published and Forthcoming Titles Include:

Oxford Shakespeare Topics

GENERAL EDITORS: PETER HOLLAND AND STANLEY WELLS

# Shakespeare and the Eighteenth Century

MICHAEL CAINES

# OXFORD
## UNIVERSITY PRESS

Great Clarendon Street, Oxford, ox2 6DP,
United Kingdom

Oxford University Press is a department of the University of Oxford.
It furthers the University's objective of excellence in research, scholarship,
and education by publishing worldwide. Oxford is a registered trade mark of
Oxford University Press in the UK and in certain other countries

First Edition published in 2013

Impression: 1

Published in the United States of America by Oxford University Press
198 Madison Avenue, New York, NY 10016, United States of America

British Library Cataloguing in Publication Data

Data available

ISBN 978-0-19-964238-0 (hbk.)

978-0-19-964237-3 (pbk.)

As printed and bound by
CPI Group (UK) Ltd, Croydon, CR0 4YY

*Garrick.*  Ye ministers of Drury Lane defend us!
　　　　　Be thou a spirit of health, or poet damned,
　　　　　Bring with thee laurel-wreath, or catcalls shrill,
　　　　　Be thy intents wicked or charitable,
　　　　　Thou com'st in so theatrical a shape,
　　　　　That I will speak to thee. I'll call thee SHAKESPEARE,
　　　　　*Warwickshire lad*, sweet *Willy-o!* – O answer me:
　　　　　Let me not burst in ignorance!

　　　　　...

*Ghost.*  I am Shakespeare's ghost,
　　　　　For my foul sins, done in my days of nature,
　　　　　Doomed for a certain term to leave my works
　　　　　Obscure and uncorrected; to endure
　　　　　The ignorance of players; the barbarous hand
　　　　　Of Gothic editors; the ponderous weight
　　　　　Of leaden commentator; fast confined
　　　　　In critic fires, till errors, not my own,
　　　　　Are done away, and sorely I the while
　　　　　Wished I had blotted for myself before:
　　　　　But that I am forbid to tell the pangs,
　　　　　Which genius feels from ev'ry blockhead's pen,
　　　　　I could a tale unfold . . . .

Arthur Murphy, 'Hamlet, with Alterations; a Tragedy in Three Acts', from *The Life of Arthur Murphy, Esq.* by Jesse Foot (London: J. Faulder, 1811), 268, 270.

# Acknowledgements

Many friends and colleagues have helped me to write this book. For support, advice, comments on various sections of this book, and assistance in libraries and archives, I am grateful to the following: the general editors of the Oxford Shakespeare Topics series, Stanley Wells and Peter Holland; many at Oxford University Press, including Jacqueline Baker, Ariane Petit, Rachel Platt, Rosie Chambers, Anne Halliday, Sarah Barnes, and the anonymous reader of my initial proposal for the book; current and former colleagues at the *Times Literary Supplement*, including Lucy Dallas, Rozalind Dineen, Lindsay Duguid, and Will Eaves; in the English Department at King's College London, Hannah August, Anne Isherwood, and Harriet Tait, as well as Elizabeth Eger, John Lavagnino, and Sonia Massai; Tony Trowles at Westminster Abbey Library; the staff of the British Library and the Theatre Museum in London, and the Huntington Library in San Marino, California; Jonathan Barnes, A. S. G. Edwards, Gerard Kilroy, Gill Perry, Fiona Ritchie, Kate Rumbold, Brian Vickers, and finally the Bardolatrous dedicatee of this book: Laura Baggaley.

If it has any merit in it at all, it is thanks to them. Its shortcomings are certainly all mine.

# Contents

# A Note on Texts and Abbreviations

Most references to the text of Shakespeare's plays in this book are to eighteenth-century editions. All other references to Shakespeare are to *The Complete Works*, ed. Stanley Wells and Gary Taylor (Oxford: Clarendon Press, second edition 2005). Quotations have been modernized unless the argument requires the old spelling.

The following abbreviations are used in the endnotes:

| | |
|---|---|
| Bate | Jonathan Bate, *Shakespearean Constitutions: Politics, Theatre, Criticism, 1730–1830* (Oxford: Clarendon Press, 1989) |
| BD | Philip H. Highfill, Jr., et al., eds., *A Biographical Dictionary of Actors, Actresses, Musicians, Dancers, Managers, and Other Stage Personnel in London, 1660–1800*, 16 vols. (Carbondale: Southern Illinois University Press, 1973–93) |
| De Grazia | Margreta de Grazia, *Shakespeare Verbatim: The Reproduction of Authenticity and the 1790 Apparatus* (Oxford: Clarendon Press, 1991) |
| Dobson | Michael Dobson, *The Making of the National Poet: Shakespeare, Adaptation and Authorship, 1660–1769* (Oxford: Clarendon Press, 1992) |
| ESTC | English Short Title Catalogue |
| Garrick, Letters | David M. Little and George M. Kahrl, eds., *The Letters of David Garrick*, 3 vols. (London: Oxford University Press, 1963) |
| Garrick, Plays | Harry William Pedicord and Fredrick Louis Bergmann, eds., *The Plays of David Garrick*, 7 vols. (Carbondale: Southern Illinois University Press, 1980–2) |

| | |
|---|---|
| Hume, 'Bard' | Robert D. Hume, *'Before the Bard: "Shakespeare" in Early Eighteenth-Century London'*, English Literary History, vol. 64 no. 1 (Spring 1997) |
| Jarvis | Simon Jarvis, *Scholars and Gentlemen: Shakespearian Textual Criticism and Representations of Scholarly Labour, 1725–1765* (Oxford: Clarendon Press, 1995) |
| Johnson | Samuel Johnson, ed., *The Plays of William Shakespeare*, 8 vols. (London: J. and R. Tonson et al., 1765) |
| LS | William van Lennep et al., eds., *The London Stage, 1660–1800: A Calendar of Plays, Entertainments and Afterpieces Together with Casts, Box-Receipts and Contemporary Comment Compiled from the Playbills, Newspapers and Theatrical Diaries of the Period*, 11 vols. (Carbondale: Southern Illinois University Press, 1960–8) |
| Malone | Edmond Malone, *The Plays and Poems of William Shakspeare*, 10 vols. (London: J. Rivington et al., 1790) |
| *ODNB* | *The Oxford Dictionary of National Biography* (Oxford: Oxford University Press, 2004) |
| Pope | Alexander Pope, ed., *The Works of Mr. William Shakespear*, 6 vols. (London: Jacob Tonson, 1725) |
| Rowe | Nicholas Rowe, ed., *The Works of Mr. William Shakespear*, 6 vols. (London: Jacob Tonson, 1709) |
| Seary | Peter Seary, *Lewis Theobald and the Editing of Shakespeare* (Oxford: Clarendon Press, 1990) |
| Taylor | Gary Taylor, *Reinventing Shakespeare: A Cultural History from the Restoration to the Present* (New York: Grove Press, 1989) |
| Theobald | Lewis Theobald, ed., *The Works of Shakespeare*, 7 vols. (London: J. Tonson et al., 1733) |
| Vickers | Brian Vickers, ed., *Shakespeare: The Critical Heritage* (London: Routledge & Kegan Paul, 1974–81) |

The eighteenth century, at least as far as two female friends were concerned, began with Caliban on the throne. The evidence for this curious situation may be found in the coded correspondence of a certain 'Mrs Morley' and 'Mrs Freeman', dating from the 1690s, and in the subsequently published histories of the real women behind these aliases—namely, Princess Anne, Caliban's heir, and Sarah Churchill, Lady Marlborough.

At the time, Lady Marlborough was Anne's closest friend and political confidante. She was also her social inferior; and adopting the plain *noms de plume* 'Morley' and 'Freeman' provided the two women with a means for corresponding as equals. But theirs was not an intimacy of which William III, Anne's Dutch brother-in-law, and Mary II, his wife and her sister, could approve.

During the Glorious Revolution of 1688, which had brought William and Mary to the throne of England, Scotland, and Ireland, Lady Marlborough's soldier husband John Churchill, Lord Marlborough, had defected from the side of Anne and Mary's father, James II, to join with William. But England's new rulers had since come to suspect Marlborough of plotting with their enemies on the Continent—the overthrown James and his great ally, Louis XIV of France—and working to turn the Army against the newly crowned co-regents. The Marlboroughs found themselves banned from Court, while further steps were taken to limit their political influence.

Anne obstinately refused to give up her association with Lady Marlborough. Under intense pressure to break with her friend, Mrs Morley told Mrs Freeman that she was determined to 'keep her in spite of their teeth and . . . by the Grace of God I will go to the utmost verge of the earth rather than live with such Calibans'.[1]

'Calibans'? Was the Court an isle full of noises?

As old resentments, partly caused by William's difficult manner and coolness towards all but a small inner circle of trusted advisors, stirred to the surface, relationships between William and Anne deteriorated further: 'can you believe', Mrs Morley wrote, 'we will ever truckle to that monster who from the first moment of his coming has used us at that rate as we are sensible he had done and that all the world can witness... Suppose I did submit and that the King could change his nature so much as to use me with humanity, how would all reasonable people despise me, how would that Dutch abortive laugh at me and please himself with having got the better [of me]'? 'Mr Caliban has some inclinations towards a reconcilement', she reported to Mrs Freeman, early in 1693, 'but if I ever make the least step, may I be as great a slave as he would make me, if it were in his power'.

Mary died in 1694, and, while gestures towards reconciliation would follow, William could still be described as 'Mr Caliban', a creature capable of 'ill-natured, cruel proceedings' as late as 1701, when he refused to allow Anne to put her household at St James's Palace in London into full mourning on the death of her father, James II.[2] The following year, William himself died, and Anne, the last of England's Stuart monarchs, succeeded him. The year was 1702, and, as this summary of dynastic manoeuvring and name-calling might suggest, Caliban's creator, the poet and playwright William Shakespeare, played a very different role in English culture to the central, canonical role which the coming century would decisively assign him.

Caliban gets into the *Oxford English Dictionary*, too. 'We'll visit *Caliban*, my slave, who never yields us kind answer.' The *Oxford English Dictionary* offers Prospero's line from *The Tempest* as the first quotation in its entry for 'Caliban'; the second is dated to 1678, and Samuel Butler's *Hudibras*: 'I found th'infernal cunning-man, | And th'under-witch his Caliban, | With scourges... armed.' But then the *OED* skips forward to 1876, when George Eliot used the name in *Daniel Deronda*.[3] The further quotations given reflect the increasingly common use of the name over the nineteenth and twentieth centuries, usefully showing how 'Caliban' grew into a familiar monster once Shakespeare had become a household name—or into a man, not a monster at all. The much-vaunted universality of his creator might have something to do with that.

Between Samuel Butler and George Eliot, however, the *OED* fails to mention that at least one other person attached significance to the name, and her name was Anne. Perhaps it was really Lady Marlborough's idea. Perhaps for both correspondents, the name recalled the King's unprepossessing personal appearance as well as the absence of 'humanity' in his behaviour. But assuming for now that the nickname was Anne's: I begin this book with *her* Caliban, the one who once ruled England, precisely because it is an allusion that has been overlooked by literary critics, yet has been hiding, in plain sight, for many years now. Anybody who cared to open a biography of Anne might have seen the name in print; but no historical study that I know of draws a connection with, say, the performance history of *The Tempest*. Students of the Restoration theatre, on the other hand, will know all about the adaptation of Shakespeare's play by John Dryden and Sir William Davenant, first staged at the Duke's Theatre in Lincoln's Inn Fields in 1667. This *Tempest* would remain a popular part of the repertoire, seeing off several rival versions, for the next 170 years, and until John Gay produced *The Beggar's Opera* in 1728, it would remain the most popular work of all on the London stage.[4] There was also the adaptation of the adaptation, in 1674, seemingly reworked by Thomas Shadwell, that turned what was already a highly musical and spectacular show into an even more operatic affair.[5] It is possible to imagine the music-loving Anne enjoying such *Tempests*, in contrast to William. He 'does not care for plays', she had heard.[6]

From the point of view of considering the relationship between a writer (in this instance, Shakespeare, when the name stands for his works, too) and a particular time period (in this instance, the eighteenth century, not the writer's own period but a later one), it seems to me to be crucial to consider this kind of connection, to assess how the past shapes the present—and how the present reshapes the past. If the Restoration stage conception of Caliban hardly accords with Shakespeare's own, for example, it also sounds as if Anne might not have had in mind any deep correspondence between William, as she saw him, and the Restoration Caliban, but simply the character's theatrical appearance. He is, after all, 'not honoured with | A human shape',[7] the Dryden-Davenant Prospero says, much as Shakespeare's Prospero does, while Trincalo asks, on first seeing him:

> What have we here, a man, or a fish?
> This is some monster of the isle; were I in England,
> As once I was, and had him painted,
> Not a Holy-day fool there but would give me
> Six-pence for the sight of him....[8]

As Christine Dymkowski has observed, *The Tempest*'s rewriters succeeded in reducing the character to 'essentially a comic creature, a good-natured being who does not plot against Prospero, is happy to serve his new master Trincalo and does not become embroiled in the ducal faction-fighting'. Caliban and his newly invented sister, Sycorax, are 'natural innocents' rather than 'sophisticated degenerates'; the various omissions and additions to the part take him 'firmly out of the human realm, making him a literal monster whose good nature is all the more appealing'.[9] It might be a mistake, then, given that 'good nature' is probably not what Anne has in mind when she describes William as 'that Dutch abortive', to assume too close a connection between the Restoration adaptations of the play and her own, private use of the name.

Dryden and Davenant do not give Caliban especial prominence in their reworking of the play, and it is telling that in Thomas Duffett's parody of the Shadwell version, called *The Mock-Tempest: Or The Enchanted Castle* (performed in 1674; published the following year), Caliban barely figures at all. The association in Anne's mind between William and the supposed monster remains intriguing, all the same, when considered as an implied comment on both the source of the allusion and its subject. As the source (which version of *The Tempest*) cannot be certainly identified, exactly what Anne is saying about the subject (William as Caliban) remains unclear; but it might help to know that he was 'cold and taciturn' when sober but apparently became quite a different character when drunk (just as Caliban's mental condition is transformed by first contact with alcohol):

William detested all frivolity. He did not suffer fools at all. He accepted contradiction of his opinion only with bad grace, and kept a small group of intimates to which outsiders could not gain easy access.... The only cracks in the austere façade came on the occasions when William got drunk. Then, unfortunately, he was as likely to disgrace himself with wild behaviour as impress with alcohol-induced conviviality.[10]

In the same way, it *may* be some use to learn that Anne's hereditary claim to the throne was stronger than William's—as he knew and resented—since *The Tempest* is, apart from anything else, a play about the problem of succession. If Anne could not rule England yet, she looked forward to the day—the 'sunshine day'—when she would, and when the monster was gone. 'She hopes England will flourish again.'[11] Only it is curious to think that at the outset of this decisive period in the forging of a new polite vernacular culture in England, the highest ranking members of society were to be found unwittingly enacting, and even casting themselves, in a Shakespearian drama...

Princess Anne's choice of one particular character name from what was, for her, possibly a modern opera rather than an old play seems to me to be representative of the sort of contemporary connections between literature and history that the passing of time and the orthodox division of scholarly labour have rendered obscure or ambivalent. To historians of the late seventeenth century and biographers of Anne and Sarah, the future Duchess of Marlborough (as Anne later made her), this clutch of private, passing allusions to *The Tempest* has perhaps appeared to be both self-explanatory and unworthy of any deeper investigation. For literary scholars, it seems likewise to have had little appeal—so it remains unclear not only what exactly the name would have meant to Anne (or whether she even associated it with *The Tempest* in any form, or thought it just sounded exotic and a bit like that other fine scare-word, 'cannibal'), but it is also unclear why she thought it so appropriate a name to apply to her enemy, the King.

The apparently neglected case of Princess Anne's Caliban seems to me to be an example, from the beginning of the period, of a phenomenon that recurs, persistently, throughout the ensuing century. On the one hand, here is something familiar to somebody with a little knowledge about Shakespeare in the twenty-first century: that a play called *The Tempest* featured a character called Caliban, and here he is, naturally enough, some years after that play's composition, performance, and publication, his name a byword for monstrosity. But this is also, on the other hand, quite possibly the Caliban of Shakespeare's Restoration dramatist-successors, or simply a name that seems vaguely fit for the purpose of writing insultingly about a drunken Dutchman, without reference to any play. As an allusion, this 'Mr Caliban' is about as trustworthy as those common words that crop up in eighteenth-century English as they do in its modern equivalent ('generous', 'main', 'virtuoso'), but to varying degrees mean different things. (To quote from Samuel Johnson's *Dictionary* of 1755, the words just given may mean, respectively: 'Not of mean birth'; 'The ocean'; 'A man skilled in antique or natural curiosities.')[12] Shakespeare's cultural afterlife is full of such 'false friends'—celebrated incidents, such as theatrical performances, or publications—and they form a central concern in the chapters that follow.

## Remains of Shakespeare

On the death of William Shakespeare in 1616, a process of division ensued. His 'remains' took several forms: there were the play scripts that belonged to his company, the King's Men, and the living tradition of performance that they represented; there were the published versions of those plays that could circulate widely, as books often do; and there were the physical remains of the man Shakespeare, buried at Holy Trinity in Stratford-upon-Avon in Warwickshire. A fourth form of survival lay in the memory of Shakespeare carried by those who knew him and survived him: family, friends, fellow actors and writers. Ben Jonson, to take one important example, paid homage to his old friend as late as 1640, when his *Timber: or, Discoveries; Made upon Men and Matter* appeared. Here Jonson testified that Shakespeare had 'an excellent *Phantsie*; brave notions, and gentle expressions'; he was 'honest, and of an open, and free nature'. Indeed, Jonson could say that he 'loved the man, and doe honour his memory (on this side idolatry) as much as any'.[13] Through such recollections, Shakespeare 'remained' a presence, albeit a dwindling one, until the middle of the seventeenth century, and even after the Restoration in 1660. The eighteenth century, tantalizingly, caught the last whispers of this tradition.

John Aubrey had his information about Shakespeare from William Beeston, the son of Christopher Beeston, Shakespeare's contemporary, including details about Shakespeare being a schoolmaster at some point, and that 'the humour of the constable in *Midsummer Night's Dream*'—probably meaning Dogberry in *Much Ado about Nothing*—had been drawn from life.[14] Aubrey's account did not circulate widely until the early nineteenth century, but his fellow antiquaries did read his notes in manuscript; and, in the meantime, readers and playgoers had learned to become fascinated by such colourful testimony, only to find that it was unreliable (was Shakespeare really a deer-poacher in his youth, as the actor Thomas Betterton was told?) or suspect in some way (jealousy became the usual reason given for Jonson's criticisms of Shakespeare's prolixity and lack of learning). Betterton was not only the leading actor of the Restoration theatre, but an active researcher into the life of Shakespeare—a writer, *pace* Jonson, whom he idolized. As a founder member of the Duke's Company, Betterton had worked under Sir William Davenant, Shakespeare's supposed godson, from 1660 until Davenant's death in 1668; it was Betterton who supplied Nicholas Rowe with biographical information for his edition of Shakespeare's *Works* published in 1709.

While this oversimplifies matters a little, as will be seen in the following chapters, the performance and republication of Shakespeare in the eighteenth century, as well as his transformation into a cultural icon that Jonson would have found quite perplexing, depended on similar transformations in the course of the preceding hundred years. The Restoration had decisively reshaped the theatrical environment: now there were actresses, who soon came to replace boy actors in female roles; there was moveable scenery and an increasing emphasis on stage spectacle and machinery (although a trap-door continued to be a useful and simple device in any theatre); and there was a new repertoire to reflect changed times, new fashions, shifts in the language itself. Under these circumstances, Davenant chose to cut and clarify *Hamlet*, failed to persuade the audience to like *King Lear* (that would have to wait until Nahum Tate gave it a happy ending in 1681), and—as we have seen—turned *The Tempest* into an opera. Such stage adaptations also made it into print, providing a foil to the heavy tale of *Mr William Shakspear's Comedies, Histories, and Tragedies* as they appeared in new editions, in 1623, 1632, 1663 (with a second impression the following year that incorporated a further seven plays, the so-called Shakespeare Apocrypha, to add to the preceding folios' thirty-six), and 1685. It was this final collection of forty-three plays that Rowe edited in 1709, another form of renewal, in print, for the new century. But there was a long way to go yet.

## The specifics....

'It is impossible to imagine the study of Shakespeare without authentic texts for his works, historical accounts defining his period, facts about his life, chartings of his artistic and psychological development, and determinations of his meanings.' This, the opening sentence of Margreta de Grazia's *Shakespeare Verbatim*, draws attention to what, she argues, would only be adopted as the essential attributes of Shakespeare studies towards the end of the eighteenth century, under the influence of a broad intellectual movement: the Enlightenment. 'Authentic' texts, facts about Shakespeare's life and the rest should not be taken for granted—these are not 'timeless necessities' but the 'determinate needs of a specific historical situation'; that de Grazia finds it possible to question them, two centuries later, indicates that their 'transparency' can no longer be taken for granted, 'after the recent challenges, founded primarily on the work of Foucault and Barthes, to the modern notions of author and work, after the Oxford Shakespeare's re-characterization of the Shakespearian text as malleable, permeable, and even multiple, and after the new-historicist and cultural-materialist emphasis on the production and reproduction of Shakespeare as performance and as text within institutional, ideological, and political contexts'.[15] De Grazia concentrates on the late eighteenth-century edition of Shakespeare that she sees as seminal in this regard: *The Plays and Poems of William Shakspeare* of 1790, edited by Edmond Malone. But there is no shortage of potential subjects for this kind of sceptical re-examination of the cultural products of the past, both before and after Malone, that, despite appearances, must be assigned to their 'specific historical situation'. And although the eighteenth-century Shakespeare has long been an object of study for Shakespearian scholars, it is in the past thirty years that some of the most fruitful work has been done to expose that specificity.

Writing a few years after de Grazia, for example, Robert D. Hume took her initial observation about the impossibility of imagining textual scholarship under radically different circumstances and applied it to the age of Queen Anne's Caliban. It might be impossible for us now to imagine Shakespeare studies without 'authentic texts for his works, historical accounts defining his period, facts about his life, chartings of his artistic and psychological development, and determinations of his meanings', Hume argues, but:

This is precisely the situation in which literate and interested Londoners found themselves at the beginning of the eighteenth century—and what we now need to try to imagine.... Until well into the eighteenth century 'Shakespeare' was a much more inaccessible writer and (from our point of view) a more distorted one than most of his later champions have understood or wished to admit.[16]

When it comes to the eighteenth century, that is, both de Grazia and Hume take note of historiographical and ideological challenges. It is clear that the eighteenth century transformed Shakespeare—not just in terms of how it edited his plays, but how it staged them, appropriated them for use in other contexts, and exalted their creator. But when and how did this happen? Was the transformation gradual, played out through a series of key moments—or, as *Shakespeare Verbatim* argues, really a matter of an abrupt epistemological turning point, late in the century? These questions seem to be worth asking because, many years on from *Shakespeare Verbatim*, the 'afterlife' of Shakespeare, in the eighteenth century and beyond, remains a subject of critical debate. As one scholar put it, writing in the same year that Hume published 'Before the Bard', and considering, among other recently published books, Peter Martin's *Edmond Malone: Shakespearean Scholar*, Gary Taylor's *Reinventing Shakespeare: A Cultural History from the Restoration to the Present*, and Arthur Sherbo's studies of two eighteenth-century Shakespearians, Richard Farmer and Isaac Reed: 'All this work is a way of asking—it is an appropriate question for us to ask—where our critical approaches to Shakespeare have come from and what cultural agendas they have served.'[17] Likewise, in the broader context of the history of Shakespeare's works and his reputation, I suggest that the story of an angry princess and her (seemingly unintended) allusion to Shakespeare at a moment of political crisis invites us to consider how Shakespeare became 'Shakespeare'—how the 'specific historical situation' described by Hume was replaced by that described by de Grazia. Allusion is appropriation: words, phrases, lines of poetry, the characters who speak them, the scenes they inhabit, the plays to which those scenes belong, the corpus of literary works to which those plays belong, all may be purloined, appropriated, re-deployed, to suit new designs and new purposes. In this sense, the eighteenth century redesigned Shakespeare—there is no evidence that the name meant anything to Anne, certainly not what it meant to, say, Malone. Truly she belongs to an age 'Before the Bard'.

Crucially, however, some of Anne's contemporaries did hold Shakespeare in very high regard. In the drawing of maps of the past, the division of the kingdoms into distinctive eras, the discovery of the roads that led from one event to the next, cause and effect, one after the other, it is sometimes forgotten that each moment can contain contradictions. Teleology is a constant temptation when you know the end of the story: we know, for example, that there is a Royal Shakespeare Company based in Stratford-upon-Avon, that his plays are taught at school, that a great deal has been written about him; we know 'If music be the food of love, play on', we know 'Once more unto the breach, dear friends, once more', and we know, of course, 'To be or not to be'. Shakespeare is the god of our idolatry, as he was for a certain eighteenth-century actor. But can 'we', whoever 'we' are, also be certain that it was always going to turn out this way?

At this point, maybe Princess Anne's Caliban can make himself useful again: this time round, as the exemplary counterweight to the late seventeenth century's better-known critical discourse about Shakespeare and to the anachronistic notion that readers and play-goers of that time shared our own historically determined assumptions about his overall cultural significance. Compare that bare, elusive allusion, for example, to Dryden's extensive analysis in his preface to *Troilus and Cressida*, where he offers the same character as an instance of the 'copiousness' of Shakespeare's 'invention':

He seems there to have created a person which was not in nature, a boldness which at first sight would appear intolerable: for he makes him a species of himself, begotten by an *Incubus* on a *Witch*; but this as I have elsewhere proved, is not wholly beyond the bounds of credibility, at least the vulgar still believe it.... Whether or no his generation can be defended, I leave to philosophy; but of this I am certain, that the poet has most judiciously furnished him with a person, a language, and a character, which will suit him, both by father's and mother's side: he has all the discontents, and malice of a witch, and of a devil; besides a convenient proportion of the deadly sins; Gluttony, Sloth, and Lust are manifest; the dejectedness of a slave is likewise given him, and the ignorance of one bred up in a desert island. His person is monstrous, as he is the product of unnatural lust; and his language is as hobgoblin as his person: in all things he is distinguished from other mortals. The characters of Fletcher are poor and narrow, in comparison of Shakespeare's....[18]

It might seem jarring to contrast Anne's plain monster with Dryden's authoritative and considered account of the character. But in the longer-term context of the cultural metamorphosis that is the subject of this book—the transformation in how Shakespeare was read, staged, understood, and represented across the following century—it might serve as a way of representing the diversity of uses to which 'Shakespeare', in a broad sense, could be put, not only from one decade to another, as generations, tastes, political circumstances have changed, but at virtually the same point in time. For what Dryden wrote about Caliban in 1679 would be selectively repeated in 1691, while Anne was making a monster of William III, by Gerard Langbaine in *An Account of the English Dramatick Poets*—a seminal survey of English dramatic literature up to that time.

*The untidy Bard.* Here is a reminder that cultural change does not come about in one uniform movement across the years. Considering the final decades of the eighteenth century, in *Shakespeare: The Critical Heritage*, an extensive collection of 'contemporary documents' relating to the 'critical and theatrical interpretation of Shakespeare', Brian Vickers noted that 'Shakespeare is celebrated for his consistency in "preserving" or "supporting" character'—but 'no sooner do we note a positive appreciation of him than we must record its opposite'.

Rather than tidy schemes, according to which one critical trend neatly replaces another, I have found the existence, side by side, of critical systems which are supposed to have annihilated or displaced earlier ones, but which did not. No major change in the way we think about literature, or anything else, is effected quickly.[19]

The same might be said of the preceding century—and it may be relevant to recall here that the agents propagating these rival critical systems, consciously or not, are themselves a heterodox and untidy lot. In the early 1700s, it would be the playwright and civil servant Nicholas Rowe who would edit the first collection of Shakespeare's plays to be prestigiously given the title *Works*, while the actor and dramatist Colley Cibber concocted the classic stage version of *Richard III*—a version that would influence productions of the play well into the twentieth century. Go forward forty years: another actor and dramatist, Charles Macklin, sensationally reinterprets Shylock in *The Merchant of Venice* as a serious character rather than a buffoon, while various figures, including the poet Alexander Pope, anti-government patriots, and theatre managers temporarily joined forces to raise money for a monument to Shakespeare in Westminster Abbey. Several prominent Shakespeare editors and critics of the eighteenth century had a legal or ecclesiastical background. Samuel Johnson wrote for a living; Edmond Malone didn't need to.

The untidiness seems to me to be largely resistant to neat critical lines of interpretation, but that has not prevented later critics from trying to draw such lines through the century. The contradictions and (sometimes surprising) connections between rival versions of Shakespeare are therefore what I have tried to tease out here, in various ways. For example: both Dryden, the professional poet-playwright-critic, conventionally seen as one of the most important Shakespeare critics of the later seventeenth century, and Princess Anne, a code-writing correspondent, belong to an age that was 'Before the Bard'. Writing over a decade before Anne, Dryden could write knowledgeably about Caliban as a creature of Shakespeare's invention: he has a sense of Shakespeare's oeuvre as a whole; he has compared it with the work of another canonical English dramatist of the early seventeenth century, John Fletcher; and alludes here to the fact that he has written about Shakespeare before ('as I have elsewhere proved...'). Yet this deep interest is idiosyncratically Dryden's. Anne, by contrast, dubs William a Caliban without mentioning Shakespeare by name. Why should she? It is quite likely that, unlike Dryden, she does not think of Caliban as Shakespeare's at all. And in this respect, she may be more representative of the late seventeenth century than Dryden is. As Hume's essay argues, there were many to whom the name Shakespeare meant little at the end of the seventeenth century—or if it did mean something, it meant nothing like the all-pervasive image of the universal genius that would loom later into view. It might mean the author of *King Lear* with a happy ending—the *Lear* familiar to playgoers of the period.

Such strange things are commonplace in the afterlife of Elizabethan and Jacobean plays. Like *The Tempest* in rewritten form, for example, Tate's much-maligned *King Lear* proved to be popular with generation after generation of theatregoers, long surviving the moment of its inception, during the Exclusion Crisis of the 1680s—yet what might be called the Restoration's influence on Shakespeare is visible in Tate's *Lear*, with its hopes for a nation united by strong, virtuous leaders and the righteous punishment meted out to the traitors in their midst. And not every subsequent critic has felt that influence to be a benign one.

For Hazelton Spencer, writing in the 1920s, such 'alterations' of Shakespeare were themselves monstrosities. 'It is, I think, impossible to exaggerate the harm these versions have done, not only in the long career of some of them on the stage, but also because they inaugurated the fashion of adaptation.... It is an amusing whirligig of literary time that the chief satisfaction to be derived from reading these stage versions of Shakespeare is the new beauty they lead us to recognize in their originals.' The Restoration could best please Spencer by staging *Othello* without excessive textual tampering, and he grandly found the cuts to *1 Henry IV* 'unobjectionable'.[20]

There is limited critical value in such belated judgements. More pertinent to understanding why these old plays had to be abridged (sometimes cut in two), given happy endings, verbally clarified, and relieved of their burden of puns, supposed errors, and vulgar language (undoubtedly the fault not of that noble genius Shakespeare but of those low players he had to associate with) are perceptive, historicized accounts by later critics. Exemplary in this respect is Sonia Massai's account of George Lillo's adaptation of *Pericles* as *Marina* in 1738 in relation to 'current medical discourse on prostitution' and an accompanying middle-class ethos of 'reformatory zeal'.[21] Garrick's addition of a dying speech for Macbeth was not just an actor's extravagance but the necessary completion of a moral tale, so that, to the audience's horror, the usurper dies by crying out that his soul is lost forever. In Russia, Catherine the Great translated *The Merry Wives of Windsor* to comment on the dangers of Francophilia, and banned *Julius Caesar* in the time of the French Revolution.

Furthermore, the supposedly misguided activities of Shakespeare's later adaptors begin to make more sense in the context of his increasing visibility beyond the theatre and the library. His home town, Stratford-upon-Avon, became a place of pilgrimage; painters took to Shakespearian scenes as suitably dignified subjects for major exhibition pieces. The bluestocking Elizabeth Montagu argued with the biographer James Boswell over who was the greater poet, Milton or Shakespeare. 'Shakespeare's Head' was a sign adorning not only printers' and booksellers' shops in London, Edinburgh, Dublin, and beyond, but a notorious public house in Covent Garden.

There are further curious connections between the participants in the making of a new Shakespearian culture that should remind us about the irreducible oddity of the past. Queen Anne may be the only monarch to have touched a future Shakespeare editor, Samuel Johnson, for the disease known as scrofula, or the King's Evil. Another editor, Nicholas Rowe, served Anne as undersecretary to the Duke of Queensberry in 1707, when he negotiated the Treaty of Union between England and Scotland, finally uniting the two countries, along with Ireland, under a single government and monarch. (In Shakespeare's time, the time of his patron James VI of Scotland who was also James I of England, the Scots had their own parliament, and the union was personal rather than constitutional.) Anne's latter-day Secretary of War and a Privy Councillor, George Granville, whom she made Baron Lansdowne, had earlier adapted *The Merchant of Venice* as *The Jew of Venice*, reducing Shylock to a buffoon, much as Caliban had been reduced to a comic sidekick in the Restoration adaptations of *The Tempest*. The past century has seen the creation of not only an extensive and increasingly sophisticated body of useful works for studying the theatrical culture of the eighteenth century (such as *The London Stage* and the *Biographical Dictionary of Actors, Actresses, Musicians, Dancers* etc.) and its scholarly activities (such as Arthur Sherbo's studies of individual editors and textual critics, Simon Jarvis's *Scholars and Gentlemen*, and Andrew Murphy's *Shakespeare in Print*), but cultural studies that consider other developments and connections: between Shakespeare and the eighteenth-century culture of sensibility, for example, or even as narrow a case as the link between William Dodd, the 'Macaroni Parson' and the compiler of the most popular Shakespeare anthology of all time, *The Beauties of Shakespeare*, and the campaign in England against the death penalty. Such studies are intimations of infinite riches where dismissals such as Spencer's suggest only philistinism.

### Reinventing, authenticating, making, constituting

For all of these reasons, it can be rewarding to trace the course of Shakespeare's changing reputation through the eighteenth century, including the transformations of his plays on the stage and (with the poems) in the study, and the reflections of those works and their author. This book therefore offers an account of what the eighteenth century did to Shakespeare—and vice versa. While the book does trace a rough progression from 1700 to 1800, however, it seems worth pointing out that this progression was a decidedly uneven one. Were this the Grand Tour of the cultural landscape of the eighteenth century, its itinerary would be seen to include many of the period's most celebrated landmarks—the Shakespeare Jubilee in Stratford-upon-Avon, the home of Samuel Ireland and his forger-son William Henry, in Norfolk Street in London. There are scholarly battlefields and the theatrical 'temples' to Shakespeare, in which celebrities such as David Garrick, John Philip Kemble, and Sarah Siddons are the high priests. But between these, the more predictable sites, lie lesser known by-ways. In fact, my intention here is to emphasize contradictions and tensions between rival constructions of Shakespeare as national poet, natural poet, or anything else, and how contemporaneous developments articulated these tensions. The chapter titles are, in this respect, shorthand for wider debates and disguises for digression: 'Pope versus Theobald' is not just about an unseemly squabble between two early eighteenth-century men of letters, but the incompatible ideas that underlie their approaches to editing Shakespeare's *Works*, as well as further implications of these ideas. 'Unreal Shakespeare' considers the question of 'authenticity' in Edmond Malone's edition of Shakespeare in combination with his decisive involvement in the Ireland forgery controversy of the mid-1790s, and the place of William Henry Ireland's 'discovery' of a whole play by Shakespeare, *Vortigern*, in late eighteenth-century performance history.

Taken as a whole, the subject is vast, and neither in my revisiting of well-trodden paths, nor the digressive turns away from them do I intend this book to be read as a narrowly prescriptive course in eighteenth-century Shakespeare studies. It is rather a series of explorations on a theme of this period and its contradictions—not the least of which is that the Shakespeare it created has inspired such diverse reactions among both contemporaries and later critics.

Particularly since the 1980s, several important critical and historical studies have appeared to break new ground, offering compelling, theoretically sophisticated reassessments of what the eighteenth century did to Shakespeare and how it did it: how it edited his works; how it idolized him and marked him out not just as a great writer but as an exemplary Englishman, an ancestral worthy; how it staged and rewrote his plays. From study to study, however, the emphasis changes, and the process has to be described in different terms. For Gary Taylor, the key process is one of 'reinventing' Shakespeare. For Margreta de Grazia, it is a case of 'authenticating' him, something which only happened at the end of the century, in 1790, when Edmond Malone published *The Plays and Poems of William Shakspeare*. Michael Dobson has traced a paradoxical process that he calls the 'making of the national poet', that granted Shakespeare cultural authority at the same time as it suppressed aspects of his plays that it could not condone. Peter Seary has acclaimed Lewis Theobald's editing of Shakespeare, and shown how personal hostility towards him has had a lasting effect on his scholarly reputation. Simon Jarvis, noting that de Grazia's work was in many ways 'diametrically opposed' to Seary's, set out himself to consider the relationship between two 'discontinuous strands in the history of eighteenth-century textual criticism': contradictory ideas about the role of the textual editor, 'intimately bound up with division of intellectual labour and with representations of such divisions'.[22] Jonathan Bate has argued that between 'Renaissance Shakespeare' and 'modern Shakespeare', a critical bridge was needed—'our century has not been the first to make him contemporary'—and argued that, in the eighteenth and early nineteenth centuries, 'Shakespeare was constituted in England . . . and how cultural life during that period was by constitution Shakespearean'.[23]

Reinventing, authenticating, making, constituting: while these studies share common ground, recognizing the need to understand and explain the eighteenth-century Shakespeare (or *Shakespeares*), each emphasizes a different aspect of a large-scale cultural metamorphosis, and concentrates on a different point in time or different areas of activity. And the critical dialogue that they represent shows little sign of abating in the twenty-first century (see the 'Further Reading' section of this book for some examples). Perhaps this is because the study of the eighteenth century's Shakespeare can also serve as a means of reconsidering some of our own basic assumptions about the study, celebration, and restaging of the works of this one exceptional dramatist and poet—as well as how to account for his current, seemingly unassailable position of supremacy in Western culture. But to revisit Shakespeare in this period is also a plunge into the past that is neither Shakespeare's nor our own: with the eighteenth century, we are *in medias res*. And this book's revisiting of the encounters between rival Shakespearians, contradictory approaches to the text, and the connections between editors, critics, performers, writers, and others is an attempt to catch a glimpse of a metamorphosis—Caliban into Ariel—in progress.

# *Cibber's* Richard III, *Rowe's* Works

Richard's himself again.

> (Colley Cibber, *The Tragical History of King Richard III*)[1]

The notion of Shakespeare entertained by any age affords an index to its thought in general.

> (Hazelton Spencer, *Shakespeare Improved*)[2]

As he tries to sleep, alone in his tent, on the night before the Battle of Bosworth Field, King Richard III is tormented by bad dreams. The ghosts of his victims appear to him, including those of the two Princes he had murdered in the Tower of London. 'O! 'twas a cruel deed!', the spirits of those boys tell him, 'therefore alone, | Unpitying, unpitied shalt thou fall.' His 'wretched' wife, Lady Anne, encourages him to remember her in battle: 'edgeless fall thy sword – despair and die'. And with the dawn, the spirit of the king he stabbed, Henry VI, condemns him to 'all the hells of guilt':

> And let that wild despair, which now does prey
> Upon thy mangled thoughts, alarm the world.
> Awake, Richard, awake, to guilty minds,
> A terrible example.[3]

Richard's conscious remorse, however, is swiftly driven away by Catesby, who brings him news of the preparations for battle, and, seeing Richard so shaken by his 'horrid dreams', implores him to 'Be more yourself ': 'Were it but known a dream had frighted you, | How would your animated foes presume on't?'[4] Richard responds well to that:

> Perish that thought—No, never be it said
> That fate itself could awe the soul of Richard.
> Hence babbling dreams, you threaten here in vain;
> Conscience avant, Richard's himself again.[5]

In significant ways, then, this blustering Richard III is nothing like his original, Shakespeare's Richard III, whose dreams last longer, include repeated invocations to 'despair and die', and are also shared with his enemy, Henry, Earl of Richmond, who receives contrasting messages of blessing and encouragement from the same ghosts. (Cibber has Richmond briefly report in the following scene that Richard's victims appeared to him in his sleep.) When Shakespeare's Richard does awake, his torment continues for much longer, and when Ratcliffe (not Catesby) appears, he hardly brings about a drastic improvement in the King's state of mind; instead, he continues to be plagued by the remembrance of those bad dreams, even when he is meant to be rousingly addressing his men.

For eighteenth-century audiences, the 'Richard's himself again' sequence represented a defining moment for one of their most familiar stage villains: thanks to Colley Cibber, the actor-playwright who adapted the role to suit his own purposes, and would still be performing it forty years later, they knew Richard III as a character who could shrug off guilt in the space of a few lines. In this respect, this short sequence is also representative of Cibber's 'alteration' of *Richard III* as a whole, as well as the pragmatic tendencies of many earlier and later rewritings of Shakespeare for the stage: this *Richard III* is Shakespeare simplified. Two-thirds of the length of the original play, it explains the historical context concisely, removes poetical ambiguities, and concentrates on the figure of Richard himself, who now appears in fifteen scenes out of twenty in total, rather than fifteen out of twenty-five, and speaks 39.9 per cent of the total number of lines, rather than 31.2 per cent—an increase due in part to the addition of seven soliloquies.[6]

Simplification could, in many respects, bring about a dramaturgical improvement, if only in a historically contingent sense—but in this regard Cibber excelled himself. His *Richard III* was the most enduringly popular of all adaptations of Shakespeare, its influence stretching from its beneficial effects on his own acting career (Cibber performed the title role over eighty times before 1739), to its crucial place in the repertoire of actors such as David Garrick, George Frederick Cooke, and Edmund Kean, and eventually even some influence on Laurence Olivier's film version of 1955. On stage, it was still being performed in the early twentieth century (as late as 1930 in Boston, without acknowledgement to Cibber, according to A. C. Sprague).[7]

Like Cibber's 'Off with his head. So much for Buckingham'[8], the line 'Richard's himself again' alone (perhaps inspired by Shakespeare's line 'Richard loves Richard; that is, I am I', 5.5.137) has acquired its own afterlife. Sir Walter Scott adapted it for an epigraph in the extremely popular novel *Ivanhoe* (1820), with reference to another king of England: 'Shadows avaunt!—Richard's himself again', while, a few years earlier, in 1815, Andrew Becket had adapted it for a more abstruse work of textual commentary, *Shakspeare's Himself Again: or The Language of the Poet Asserted: being a Full but Dispassionate Examen of the Readings and Interpretations of Several of the Editors*. Here, as if to offer support to Michael Dobson's argument for the profound connection between adaptation and canonization, an allusion to Cibber's *Richard III* comes to stand for a book that claims to conjecture its way into asserting the 'language of the poet'. Becket crowns his 'adoration of a writer, perhaps the most distinguished that England can be said to boast'[9] with an allusion to Cibber. What was the secret of this alteration's success? And did it have more to do with the skill of the much-maligned Cibber than Shakespeare 'himself'?

## An improvement on Shakespeare

It seems unlikely that Cibber expected Shakespeare's name to be a superior selling point in 1700—at least as far as the theatre was concerned. Although a few of Shakespeare's plays, some in adapted form, were in the repertoire at the end of the seventeenth century, 'In all probability, no play of Shakespeare's was performed in the seventeenth century with the playwright's name attached'.[10] Booksellers, meanwhile, did not give their reissues of Shakespeare's plays special treatment; in fact, they tended to advertise the full range of what printed plays they had in stock (or what was soon to be available) without authorial attribution at all. And those critics who did write about Shakespeare did not deem him to be above criticism—far from it. Cibber would have been aware of the recent example of Thomas Rymer, whose *Short View of Tragedy* had initiated a debate in 1693 about the many defects of *Othello*, including the hero's garrulity ('His words flow in abundance, no butter-queen can be more lavish'), the playwright's folly in mixing the serious business of tragedy with the low stuff of comedy ('Thereby un-hallowing the theatre, profaning the name of tragedy, and...turning all morality, good sense, and humanity into mockery and derision'), and the play's ludicrous dependence on the trifling device of Desdemona losing her handkerchief and Iago using it to trick Othello into believing her guilty of infidelity ('So much ado, so much stress, so much passion and repetition about an handkerchief!').[11] Even a more sympathetic critic, and a practising dramatist, Charles Gildon, could praise Shakespeare for 'drawing' Othello 'so finely' but finds that he had 'made but a scurvy piece' of Desdemona—there was no doubt in Gildon's mind that Thomas Otway was the best English writer of tragedy.[12] Like others before and after him, Gildon therefore attempted to emulate Otway, the author of *The Orphan* (1680) and *Venice Preserved* (1682), in his own tragedies, while finding room for improvement in Shakespeare's comedies: his *Measure for Measure: or, Beauty the Best Advocate* was performed at Lincoln's Inn Fields in February 1700.

By Rymer's neoclassical criteria, *Othello* was an irregular and unsatisfactory play, and no contemporary could come up with a very good reply to his *Short View*, being more or less bound by the same aesthetic preoccupations. Yet this critical condemnation clashed with theatrical practice: *Othello* had been a mainstay of the Restoration repertoire since the early 1660s. *Richard III* was a different matter, since it was not an established repertory piece in its unwieldy original form. Some later remarks by Gildon demonstrate the persistence of principles such as Rymer's into the early decades of the eighteenth century.

For all their supposed faults, Shakespeare's plays, as we shall see, would soon prove to be a valuable asset to the right bookseller—namely, in 1709, the astute Jacob Tonson. The innovative edition of Shakespeare Tonson published that year, in six octavo volumes, might have been intended as part of a series of 'vernacular classics',[13] but the swift production of a second issue within 12 months and a further edition in 1714 suggest that Shakespeare did better business than Tonson had anticipated—that this was not a writer without readers. Tonson's competitors paid him the compliment of trying to cash in. The most audacious among them, Edmund Curll, produced a 'seventh' volume to match the design of Tonson's six: it included the poems by Shakespeare that Tonson's edition omitted, and an essay and a critical commentary on Shakespeare by Gildon.

Richard is 'not a fit character for the stage', Gildon wrote here, 'being shocking in all he does, and ... Providence is too slow and too mild in his punishment'. His liking for a 'long soliloquy' is 'highly unnatural, for as the Duke of Buckingham has observed they ought to be few, and short'. 'Years add authority to a name', which was a dangerous development, Gildon thought: 'Our young poets should never imitate our Shakespeare in this', his general love of allowing characters to have 'near fourscore lines of calm reflections, nay narrations to myself'.[14] Cibber was therefore committing no textual sin by reworking *Richard III* so drastically, but improving it, as best he could, to suit contemporary ideals. Although his Richard dominates the play, his soliloquies tend to be much shorter than the ones Shakespeare gives him. Gildon thought the original too long; Cibber's *Richard III* is considerably shorter, and in speeding up the visitation of the ghosts before the Battle of Bosworth, perhaps had in mind something of the same climactic efficiency advised by *The Whole Art of the Stage* (1684): 'the poet must not ... add to the *catastrophe* superfluous discourses and actions, of no use as to the concluding the play, which the spectators neither look for, nor are willing to hear.'[15]

While other dramatists and critics, such as John Dryden, might at times take a more admiring line in their comments on Shakespeare, there is little evidence to suggest that the majority of theatregoers of Cibber's time cared deeply about such specialist debates. And a general indifference to Shakespeare's name at the turn of the century is one reason why, on the title page of the first edition, it was possible to attribute *The Tragical History of King Richard III* merely to '*C. Cibber*'.[16] But Cibber had also earned himself this place beneath the play's title by the extent of his improvements, and was being entirely conventional for his time by relegating his acknowledgement of Shakespeare's contribution to a preface. Surveying the title pages, prefaces, and so forth for all such adaptations from 1670 to 1730, Robert D. Hume concludes that 'most adapters regarded the plays as their own . . . but that they were if anything pleased and proud to tout the Shakespeare connection' (sometimes in a preface, sometimes in a prologue or epilogue). Only the odd 'textual purist' would have thrown up their arms in disgust at the sight of any textual interventions: '"Altered" implies horrors to us, but probably signified "improved and helpfully corrected" to the early eighteenth-century buyer of quartos.'[17] In the case of Cibber's *Richard III*, it also seems that the explicit acknowledgement of Shakespeare on the title page only came with the two-volume collection of his plays published in 1721, in which it appears as 'altered' from him; as late as 1736, it was still possible to find the play newly reissued as 'Revived, with alterations, by Mr Cibber', as it had been in 1718.[18]

Cibber's achievement was to turn one of Shakespeare's longest plays into what would now be called a star vehicle: the portrait of a 'complete monster', as Hazelton Spencer calls it in *Shakespeare Improved*, albeit one who lacks the 'intellectual malignity' of Shakespeare's Richard.[19] Cibber's 'altered' Richard dominates a play in which there are about a dozen speaking parts, instead of forty-odd, as in the original; and he begins more violently, not by speaking a soliloquy concerning the winter of our discontent and this son of York, but (after other characters have done some useful scene-setting) by stabbing Henry VI to death in the Tower. Cibber cuts out scene after scene, and omits the Duke of Clarence and Queen Margaret altogether—in fact, although it is customary to think of this *Richard III* as an adaptation of a single play, Cibber supplied 1,069 lines himself, just over half of its 2,053 lines, while Shakespeare's *Richard III* supplies another 795, and the rest come from a further seven of Shakespeare's history plays.

Quoting those figures in the *Oxford Dictionary of National Biography*, however, Eric Salmon disparages the text as a 'curious farrago', and goes on to argue that Cibber's *Richard III* is 'so radically different from the Shakespeare play that it must surely be reckoned as an original play by Cibber'. 'Actors often claim that the result is a piece that is theatrically more playable than Shakespeare's original text and one which an audience would find easier to follow.'[20] In the same way, while admitting that this *Richard III* is 'a fair acting version, here and there touched up with extremely effective theatrical flourishes', Hazelton Spencer condemns it as 'a thing of patches, if not of shreds'.[21] There seem to be the makings of a revealing contradiction in such remarks: Cibber may be praised for his theatrical flourishes but not for his textual patchwork, as if these are unrelated phenomena.

More positively, Scott Colley praises it as the 'inspired product of a remarkable theatrical intelligence': Cibber 'largely embellishes hints and suggestions from Shakespeare's portrait of Richard', making a 'well-structured, coherent, and psychologically convincing play out of the sprawling, mysterious, and ambiguously archetypal original'. Cibber is 'always more economical than Shakespeare'.[22] Perhaps the strength of Cibber's *Richard III* as a script for performance actually lies in its textual 'hybridity', in which respect it might be seen to exemplify an often overlooked but significant subgenre of the Restoration and early eighteenth-century stage—a subject to which I will return later in this book.

### A risky business

Cibber's theatrical career had begun in the early 1690s with minor roles in the United Company at the Theatre Royal in Drury Lane, although he demonstrated his skill at creating a comic part for himself with *Love's Last Shift* in 1696, in which he played the foppish Sir Novelty Fashion. John Vanbrugh helped him to confirm that reputation later in the same year with *The Relapse*, in which Sir Novelty returns in the ennobled guise of Lord Foppington. Before Richard, his sole Shakespearian role appears to have been as 'Gloster' in Nahum Tate's alteration of *King Lear*. Behind the scenes, he was making himself useful to his manager, Christopher Rich. But Cibber's progress would not be easy. The end of the seventeenth century was, according to Judith Milhous, the 'darkest period for the English theatre since the Commonwealth'.[23] Disputes between actors and managers, the uneasy political climate, and a moral crusade that only intensified after the publication of Jeremy Collier's polemic *A Short View of the Immorality and Profaneness of the English Stage* in

1698: these problematic circumstances affected everybody in the business. There was talk of closing both of London's licensed theatres, at Drury Lane and Lincoln's Inn Fields.

Around 1700, reflecting these challenges, the theatre lost some of its best actors, as they either retired or sought work elsewhere. It must have been uncertain how long the veteran 'triumvirate' who led the so-called Actors Company—Thomas Betterton, Elizabeth Barry, and Anne Bracegirdle—would continue to perform, while the manager at Drury Lane, Christopher Rich, struggled to put the theatre on a stable financial footing. Long a specialty of Betterton's, spectacular devices such as the masques inserted into Shakespeare adaptations (Gildon's *Measure for Measure* and *The Jew of Venice* by George Granville, Lord Lansdowne, for example) could be essential to a production's success or the means to make it financially disastrous. Indeed, it should be noted now that the question of theatrical spectacle was the cause of abiding disagreement and critical anxiety throughout the eighteenth century, from the first theatrical season to the last. But it was also a necessity.

Cibber wrote a masque called *Venus and Adonis* in 1715, complete with a chorus of huntsmen and a Mars who dismisses his rival with the line, 'Adonis, hence; but range these woods no more', only to sing, as an aside: 'I'll leave my vengeance to the boar'.[24] But this was not Cibber's tribute to the author of an antiquated and then little-known poem; it was a counter to the rival attractions of opera at the King's Theatre in the Haymarket and similarly strong attractions at Lincoln's Inn Fields. There would be similar occasions on which the simplest explanation for the alteration of a play by Shakespeare—professional survival—would appear to be the best.

Trying to prove his versatility, Cibber wrote a lurid tragedy called *Xerxes*, which possibly only played for one night.[25] If so, its theatrical appearance earned Cibber nothing, since a play had to reach a third night for its author to receive the profits of an all-important 'benefit' night. (He might have made something from its publication.) It is also possible that Cibber was later rather ashamed of *Xerxes*, since he failed to include it in a collection of his plays, and does not mention it in his *Apology for the Life of Mr Colley Cibber, Comedian*.[26]

*Richard III* was not only an artistic improvement, then, on Cibber's previous effort, but, in the short term, might have given him a desultory increase in his earnings because, on its first run, it did reach its third night. The adaptation's first performances are sometimes dated to late 1699, although Cibber's modern editors, Timothy J. Viator and William J. Burling, suggest that it was a little later in the same season, in February or March 1700;[27] either way, it is a period for which there is relatively little reliable information for what was performed in each theatre, and with what success. In his *Apology*, however, Cibber tells how his tragedy was ingeniously ruined by the Master of the Revels, Charles Killigrew, who, in a fit of over-sensitivity to potential political readings of the play, demanded that the first act be cut entirely: 'all the reason I could get for its being refused', Cibber wrote in his preface to the first edition of the play, 'was, that Henry the Sixth being a character unfortunate and pitied, would put the audience in mind of the late King James'.

Cibber thought this was the 'best act in the whole'; hoping to make up for its omission, he added a scene in which the princes are murdered. But that, too, it has been suggested, was a wrong move: Princess Anne's ten-year-old son William died in the summer of 1700, and the potentially offensive scene, although it appeared in the first edition of the play, is absent from the editions published later in Cibber's lifetime.[28] Hopelessly compromised by that point in time, if not before, *Richard III* made Cibber, he later claimed, just five pounds on benefit night.[29]

Those subsequent editions of the play seem to reflect improved fortunes, as Cibber revised it and saw it gradually becoming established in the Drury Lane repertory (and eventually becoming a fixture at other London theatres, too). According to his modern biographer, Helene Koon, he played 'his original version' of *Richard III* 'without objections' from the Lord Chamberlain's office, after a change of policy and personnel, for his benefit night (as an actor, that is) in 1704.[30] A newspaper advertises a performance for 27 March 1710 with a 'Henry VI' in the list of characters—showing that the first act could certainly be performed by then, and that audiences had either forgotten about the late King James or stopped pitying him.[31]

Cibber's idiosyncratic acting style would always attract adverse commentary, but, looking at his later career, with his controversial comedy *The Non-Juror* (adapted from Molière's *Tartuffe*) in 1717 and his appointment as Poet Laureate in 1730, it is not always easy to disentangle genuine criticism from political point-scoring. All the same, Cibber's enemies sometimes scored hits that depend on a rejection of both his acting and his habits as a 'great plagiary', albeit one who 'frequently altered for the better what he borrowed'.[32] (Later adaptations included *The Rival Fools*, 1709, based on Fletcher's *Wit without Money*, and *Papal Tyranny in the Reign of King John*, 1745, based on Shakespeare's *King John*, as well as adaptations of Corneille, Dryden, Molière, and Vanbrugh.)

Aware of his limitations as an actor, Cibber had taken a 'characteristically pragmatic' approach to tragedy:

It was painfully obvious he could never play a traditional tragic hero, but a villain with a touch of the grotesque might be within his range. As he had created a type for himself in comedy, so now he must create a tragic figure that would fit him. He found his inspiration in what was then one of Shakespeare's least popular plays, *Richard III*. . . . Richard was a character he could tailor to his own style. . . . The deep-dyed villainy of Richard lent itself to his kind of exaggeration, the ironic speeches were ideal for the sort of comic inflection he had heard [Edward] Kynaston use in serious roles.[33]

If Cibber played Richard the same way throughout his career—as a form of impersonation, with the veteran Kynaston as his model—that would explain some of the diatribes against him from critics of a younger generation, who thought him absurd. By the end of it, Koon remarks, he was 'an anachronism, his grimaces and gestures out of place in this new era'.[34] Of his wooing scenes with Lady Anne, the *Grub Street Journal* (rumoured at the time to be the creation of Cibber's enemy Alexander Pope) could report in 1734 that 'he looks like a pickpocket, with his shrugs and grimaces, that has more design on her purse than her heart'. During the final battle, 'he appears no more like King Richard than King Richard was like Falstaff, he foams, struts, and bellows with the voice and cadence of a watchman rather than a hero and a prince'.[35] He played Richard with 'the distorted heavings of an unjointed caterpillar', Aaron Hill wrote around the same time.[36] And by the end of his career, the anonymous author of *The Laureat*, in 1740, could insinuate Cibber's hypocrisy in first botching a script out of Shakespeare, and then taking the principal role, in which he haplessly exposed his inability to distinguish tragedy from comedy:

...being invested with the purple robe, he screamed thro' four acts without dignity or decency.... in the fifth act, he degenerated all at once into Sir Novelty; and when in the heart of the Battle at Bosworth Field, the King is dismounted, our comic-tragedian came on the Stage, really breathless, and in a seeming panic, screaming out this line thus—*A Harse, a Harse, my Kingdom for a Harse.* This highly delighted some, and disgusted others of his Auditors; and when he was killed by *Richmond,* one might plainly perceive that the good people were not better pleased that so *execrable a Tyrant* was destroyed, than that so *execrable an Actor* was silent.[37]

The author of *The Laureat* also implies that the textual hybridity of Cibber's *Richard III* is critically, if not ethically, unacceptable:

The play of Richard the third was altered, as the phrase is, from *Shakespeare;* that is, a play of *Shakespeare* is vamped up by some modern *poetical botcher* for his own benefit; for this entitled him then to the profits of a third night etc, as if he were really the author. This was *Shakespeare's* misfortune here. The *botcher* indeed had, besides mangling and leaving out many beautiful and just images in the original, made him full amends, as he thought, by ransacking all his works, and pillaging almost all the fine images he could find in this great poet's plays, to enrich this *one.*[38]

Cibber's misfortune in receiving such harsh treatment may be due in some measure to his political allegiance, but the longevity of his career also meant that he lived to perform his Richard for an audience with a greatly increased awareness of the 'original'—or rather, the originals. In accusing Cibber of not only mangling *Richard III* but ransacking 'all his works', *The Laureat* recognizes the hybridity of *Richard III* and condemns it for precisely that quality.

### Sandford and Shakespeare

Later still, looking back on his career, Cibber offers another signifi-cant insight into the play's heterogeneous origins, when he claims in his *Apology* that he conceived the part of Richard not just in terms of reviving or interpreting Shakespeare's original, but as the sort of thing that he thought a much-admired older actor, not Kynaston this time but Samuel Sandford, might have played perfectly. (Mil-hous suspects Sandford did play Shakespeare's Richard III from time to time, without great success, and Koon speculates that he might have seen Sandford attempt the role during the 1692–3 season.)[39]

Although the accuracy of Cibber's recollections of Sandford is open to debate,[40] it is interesting that he chooses to remember this talented supporting actor as 'not the stage-villain by choice, but from necessity; for having a low and crooked person, such bodily defects were too strong to be admitted into great, or amiable characters'. Whereas Cibber found himself typecast as a fop, 'whenever, in any new or revived play, there was a hateful or mischievous Person, *Sandford* was sure to have no competitor for it'. It is due to the 'defects' of Sandford's appearance, Cibber suggests, that 'inferior actors' began to make their own appearances 'as frightful and as inhuman . . . as possible' when they were cast in similar roles.[41] His own imitation of Sandford in *Richard III* he sets apart as something quite different:

> Had *Sandford* lived in *Shakespeare's* time, I am confident his judgment must have chose[n] him, above all other actors, to have played his *Richard the Third*: I leave his person out of the question, which, though naturally made for it, yet that would have been the least part of his recommendation; *Sandford* had stronger claims to it; he had sometimes an uncouth stateliness in his motion, a harsh and sullen pride of speech, a meditating brow, a stern aspect, occasionally changing into an almost ludicrous triumph over all goodness and virtue: From thence falling into the most assuasive gentleness, and soothing candour of a designing heart. These, I say, must have preferred him to it; these would have been colours so essentially shining in that character, that it will be no dispraise to that great author [i.e., Shakespeare], to say, *Sandford* must have shown as many masterly strokes in it (had he ever acted it) as are visible in the writing it.
>
> When I first brought *Richard the Third* (with such alterations as I thought not improper) to the stage. . . . I imagined I knew how *Sandford* would have spoken every line of it: if therefore, in any part of it, I succeeded, let the merit be given to him. . . . the late *Sir John Vanbrugh*, who was an admirer of *Sandford*, after he had seen me act it, assured me, that he never knew any one actor so particularly profit by another, as I had done by *Sandford* in *Richard the Third: You have*, said he, *his very look, gesture, gait, speech, and every motion of him, and have borrowed them all, only to serve you in that character.*[42]

There are interesting hints here about how Cibber saw Richard, and how he imagined his performance to be virtually a physical quotation of another actor—one who just happened to have a 'low and crooked person', perfect for the portrayal of the 'deformed' usurper Richard.

Bringing the character on stage, Cibber borrowed from Sandford, just as he had borrowed lines as he wished from Shakespeare's history plays. Viator and Burling rightly warn against too readily conflating 'Cibber as author with Cibber as performer',[43] but in this case, they seem to have adopted parallel if not thoroughly imbricated approaches to writing and performing. In both respects, Cibber was reaching into the theatrical past, and striving for continuity by per-petuating it in adapted form. And the mimicking or imaginary casting of Sandford here seems even more peculiarly apt given his early success in the title role of Malignii in *The Villain* by Thomas Porter, one of the first favourites of the Restoration theatre, first staged in 1662: for *The Villain* also drew on Shakespeare, in its *Othello*-like characters and structure. (For Malignii, read Iago.)[44]

A further suggestive aspect of Cibber's comments about Sandford in his *Apology* is their opening gambit, in which Cibber imaginatively transports Sandford back in time by sixty years, to make him a member of Shakespeare's company. The *Richard III* in question now is 'his', Shakespeare's, not Cibber's, 'with such alterations as I thought not improper'—and in imitating Sandford when he acts Richard III himself, Cibber implicitly aligns himself with both of them. And as imagined as Shakespeare's contemporary, Sandford also becomes his equal: as Richard, he would have shown 'as many masterly strokes . . . as are visible in the writing it'. This is high praise, but there is also an intriguing irony here: for if Cibber's *Richard III*, which it would seem that he also envisaged, in performance, as Sandford's (or indeed Kynaston's), contributed significantly to the creation of a Shakespeare cult during the eighteenth century, as it remained one of the most popular of all stage plays long after Cibber's death in 1757, then it helped to create a new mode of admiration for the writer that would lead to the denial that any actor could be the equal of the author, Shakespeare himself.

Such a separation between the status of writing and acting would seem to be potentially a consequence of the 'mutually reinforcing' processes of 'adaptation and canonization' described by Michael Dobson in *The Making of the National Poet*.[45] In the middle of the eighteenth century, it was possible for Cibber in his *Apology*, to write of Sandford as the ideal Richard III, while David Garrick, who made his sensational London debut in the same role the following year, could profitably propagate an image of himself as Shakespeare's representative on earth, his greatest living interpreter. James Boaden could still voice such an opinion in 1827: 'If nature wrote through Shakespeare, the poet in his turn spoke best through Garrick.'[46] But not everybody agreed. For Charles Lamb, writing in 1811, there could be no such equality between the literary and the performing arts. To him, Garrick as apotheosized in the form of his statue in Poets' Corner, in Westminster Abbey, appeared to be a 'harlequin figure'. The monument's claims that 'A Shakespeare rose; then, to expand his fame | Wide o'er this breathing world, a Garrick came', and that 'Shakespeare and Garrick like twin-stars shall shine' forever, are a 'farrago of false thoughts and nonsense'. Not even Garrick could equal Shakespeare, and it had always been a way of complimenting such an actor, Lamb found, by saying that he had a '*mind congenial with the poet's*'. How could people 'confound the power of originating poetical images and conceptions with the faculty of being able to read or recite the same when put into words'? What connection could there possibly be between 'that absolute mastery over the heart and soul of man which a great dramatic poet possesses' and 'those low tricks upon the eye and ear, which a player... can so easily compass'?[47]

Lamb's Romantic, elitist views help to bring into focus the strength of Cibber's antithetical rendering of *Richard III*: as a 'wonderfully playable' stage melodrama,[48] its strength lies in its simplicity. Lamb treasures a poetic complexity, a sheer richness that means the great Shakespearian dramas could not be acted at all.

Cibber, operating a century earlier under very different circumstances, can see an obvious solution to that problem. Unhampered by canonical concerns, he takes what he wants from Shakespeare's history plays, adapting them just as he adapts the performance style of a fellow actor. And just as he would be generous in his acknowledgement of Sandford's example for him as an actor, so in his preface to the first edition of his *Richard III*, published in 1700, he appears to be humble in the presence of a superior writer:

Though there was no great danger of the readers mistaking any of my lines for Shakespeare's; yet, to satisfy the curious, and unwilling to assume more praise than is really my due, I have caused those entirely Shakespeare's to be printed in this italic character; and those lines with this mark (') before 'em, are generally his thoughts, in the best dress I could afford 'em: What is not so marked, or in a different character is entirely my own.[49]

The first edition of Cibber's *Richard III* was the only one in which the extra marks appear, and while the system might occasionally go awry, it does succeed in giving clearly the general impression of a busily reworked, hybrid text—and one that shows how 'simplicity' on stage was hard won.

The following extract from the end of the fourth act, for instance, combines a few lines by Cibber with some of Shakespeare's *Richard III*, and a reworked speech from *2 Henry IV*. A single speech by Catesby is split in two by the interpolated instruction to have Buckingham executed (usually identified as Cibber's invention but italicized here, presumably because the first half of the line is lifted from Shakespeare's third act; there is a similar outburst from Queen Margaret in *3 Henry VI*).[50] Cibber then skips back a couple of speeches to add, in severely abbreviated form, the Fourth Messenger's news from Yorkshire, followed by a couple more lines of his own, including a 'horse' reference anticipating Richard's famous line from the end of the play, and finally six lines from *2 Henry IV* reworked and expanded to seven:

> *Cat.*   My liege, the Duke of Buckingham *is taken.*
> *Rich.*  Off with his head. So much for Buckingham.
> *Cat.*   My Lord, I'm sorry I must tell more news.
> *Rich.*  Out with it.
> *Cat.*   *The Earl of* Richmond *with a mighty power*
>      *Is landed, Sir, at* Milford:
>      *And, to confirm the news, Lord Marquess* Dorset,
>      *And* Sir Thomas Lovewel *are up in* Yorkshire.
> *Rich.*  Why aye, this looks rebellion. Ho! My horse!
>      By Heaven, the news alarms my stirring soul.
>      'And as the wretch, whose favour weakened joints,
>      'Like strengthless hinges buckle under life;
>      'Impatient of his fit, breaks like a fire
>      'From his fond keeper's arms, and starts away:
>      'Even so these war-worn limbs grown weak
>      'From wars disuse, being now enraged with war,
>      'Feel a new fury, and are thrice themselves.
>      Come forth my honest sword. . . .[51]

Such an intricate piece of stitching gives the lie to Hazelton Spencer's dismissal of the whole business as Shakespeare merely 'mangled';[52] a modern reader who dislikes the final effect of the passage ought to be able to admit, nonetheless, that it has not been indifferently flattened out so much as cunningly dismantled and reassembled. Clumsy opprobrium like Spencer's speaks unflatteringly of its own historical moment, the early twentieth century, and can hardly help us now to understand the theatrical culture of the 1700s. If we are to appreciate that, we have to admire, if we can, Cibber's deft handiwork: the innovative 'mangling' that directly gives the play its straightforward theatricality.

## The playwright and the essayist

The mediation of Shakespeare in both print and performance, at the close of the seventeenth century, was seemingly in the hands of men of the theatre, as it had been when John Heminges and Henry Condell took responsibility for the First Folio of 1623. Not long after the first performance of Cibber's *Richard III*, around December 1700, a younger writer (and another future Poet Laureate), Nicholas Rowe, had his first play performed at London's other licensed theatre, in Lincoln's Inn Fields: *The Ambitious Stepmother*, an 'intrigue play with an oriental setting in the old [Elkanah] Settle manner'.[53] While Cibber's talent, his *Richard III* aside, was for comic writing, Rowe specialized in tragedy; his *Tamerlane* (1701; a very different beast from Marlowe's *Tamburlaine*) and *The Fair Penitent* (1703) would eventually become eighteenth-century mainstays. With its emphasis on female suffering, *The Fair Penitent* in particular foreshadows the shape of Rowe's dramatic response to *Richard III*: in 1714, he had a great success with what he termed a 'she-tragedy', 'Written in Imitation of Shakespeare's Style', about the repentant mistress of Edward IV: *The Tragedy of Jane Shore*. As with Vanbrugh's *Relapse*, here another playwright took a leaf out of Cibber's book—only *Jane Shore* was a prequel rather than a sequel, and the imitated playwright could easily have been said to be Otway. *Jane Shore* strengthened Cibber's association with the character of Richard, Duke of Gloucester, who is seen here already plotting his way to the throne and bringing about Jane's downfall, while also consolidating a connection between Rowe and Shakespeare already in existence.

Some might have remembered this in 1714, but Rowe's Scriblerian friends Jonathan Swift and Alexander Pope were among those who frowned over his claim that *Jane Shore* was written in a Shakespearian style (as, later, would Samuel Johnson). The play contains numerous allusions to Shakespeare which, presumably, his contemporaries missed, and, apparently following Cibber's *Richard III*, it draws its inspiration from English history. (Rowe would attempt to repeat the trick with his last play, *The Tragedy of Lady Jane Gray*, in 1715.) But it is also an orderly, well-structured piece of work, with none of the profuse irregularities that so vexed the likes of Rymer and Gildon, and it plays out some of the period's distinctly current concerns in a historical setting. 'There are more ways of wickedness than one', the epilogue notes, and hopes that the poets of a 'reforming stage' might 'move compassion | And with she-tragedies o'errun the nation'.[54] That explains Rowe's sympathetic focus on Jane Shore's repentance and suffering. But the play also reflects on the unresolved issues of loyalty to the throne—those non-juring clergymen who inspired Cibber to write *The Non-Juror*, here described as 'meddling priests'—and the 'order of succession'. Both of those references were cut from the play's first performance, but found their way into print in 1714, in both an edition of the play published at the Hague and an opportunistic collection of Rowe's work, *Poems on Various Occasions*, put out by Edmund Curll.[55] On the question of the succession in particular, Rowe had to tread carefully, since Queen Anne, being without a direct heir, looked likely to be followed by a foreign prince, George, Elector of Hanover; and, unlike Cibber lamenting a much clumsier act of censorship in 1700, he offered no outcry in defence of the few lines that had to be dropped from *Jane Shore* in performance.[56]

Such minor cuts could hardly damage *Jane Shore* in the way the Master of the Revels had damaged Cibber's *Richard III*, but both cases show how adapting English history as material for a play, regardless of the innocence of a playwright's declared intentions, could be taken as a form of topical commentary. The sufferings of Jane Shore, for example, are the consequences of political oppression, as Brett Wilson argues—Richard 'makes sympathy a capital crime' by declaring acts of charity towards her to be a treasonable offence. The play becomes a kind of 'national she-tragedy',[57] an impression that Rowe's claim to be imitating Shakespeare ('Our humble author... | ... owns he had the mighty bard in view'),[58] could only enhance.

Such sentimental mappings of the present on to the past were not to be confined to the theatre. Five years before *Jane Shore*, Rowe's Whig friend Richard Steele had recorded his patriotically emotional response to reading a scene in Shakespeare's *Richard III* in November 1709:

I came home this evening in a very pensive mood; and to divert me took up a volume of *Shakespeare*, where I chanced to cast my eye upon a part in the tragedy of *Richard III* which filled my mind with a very agreeable horror. It was the scene in which that bold but wicked prince is represented as sleeping in his tent, the night before the battle in which he fell. The poet takes that occasion to set before him in a vision a terrible assembly of apparitions, the ghosts of all those innocent persons whom he is said to have murthered. Prince *Edward, Henry VI*, the Duke of *Clarence, Rivers, Gray*, and *Vaughan*, Lord *Hastings*, the two young Princes, Sons to *Edward* the Fourth, his own Wife, and the Duke of *Buckingham*, rise up in their blood before him, beginning their speeches with that dreadful salutation, *Let me sit heavy on thy soul tomorrow*; and concluding with that dismal sentence, *Despair and die*. This inspires the tyrant with a dream of his past guilt and of the approaching vengeance. He anticipates the fatal day of Bosworth, fancies himself dis- mounted, weltering in his own blood....

A scene written with so great strength of imagination indisposed me from further reading and threw me into a deep contemplation. I began to reflect upon the different ends of good and bad kings; and as this was the birthday of our late renowned monarch [William III] I could not forbear thinking on the departure of that excellent prince, whose life was crowned with glory, and his death with peace. I let my mind go so far into this thought as to imagine to myself what might have been the vision of his departing slumbers. He might have seen confederate kings applauding him in different languages, slaves that had been bound in fetters lifting up their hands and blessing him, and the persecuted in their several forms of worship imploring comfort on his last moments. The reflection upon this excellent prince's mortality had been a very melancholy entertainment to me had I not been relieved by the consider- ation of the glorious reign which succeeds it.[59]

Steele goes on to praise the virtues of Queen Anne and the triumphs of her reign—his melancholy dissipates in this remembrance of things present—drawing a connection between inner feeling and the patriotic imagination that would have an enduring effect on eighteenth-century literature, as the essays of Steele and his political and literary ally Joseph Addison, especially in *The Tatler* and *The Spectator*, were to set the tone for much of the literary journalism of their successors. Laudatory references to and reflections on Shakespeare were to become part of the fabric of this new essayistic epoch. Returning to the original moment of Steele's essay, however, it also seems significant that the 'volume' Steele takes down in November 1709 might well have been the fourth in an edition of Shakespeare published only a few months earlier—there is perhaps a touch of modish showing-off here on Steele's part.

## 1709

June 1709 had seen the appearance of *The Works of Mr William Shakespeare*, which—as the title page reveals—came in six volumes, was 'Adorned with cuts' (i.e., with illustrations, mostly to the histories and tragedies), and had been 'Revised and corrected, with an account of the life and writings of the author. By *N. ROWE*, Esq.'.[60] It was also a publication in the octavo format, its portable separate sections implying quite different habits of readership from the library-bound folios of the seventeenth century (a gentleman who 'took up' such a volume of Shakespeare would be taking up all the plays at once, whereas Steele just happens to pick one that contains only English history plays). Whereas a monumental folio format was intended to 'embody the cultural prestige of its contents', Robert Hamm suggests, Tonson recognized the attraction of private reading, and accordingly advertised some publications as 'for the pocket'. Shakespeare would be one of the first of many authors whose works Tonson (or rather the Tonsons, for there were now two Jacobs, uncle and nephew, in business together) would republish in a 'vernacular series', created in imitation of the two series of scholarly editions Tonson had already undertaken, over the preceding decade, of Latin and Greek texts. (Hamm argues for the overlooked role of the printer John Watts in designing these elegant books and improving the quality of Tonson volumes all round.) Shakespeare was to be a standard author, then—'a part, but not the central figure' of a literary canon, as in the theatrical repertoire. Eventually, he would have, among others, Beaumont and Fletcher, Jonson, Milton, Otway, Spenser, and *The Spectator* for company in what, for Hamm, 'no doubt . . . comprised a standardized series of titles'.[61]

The timing of *The Works of Mr William Shakespear* is significant, too, as well as the size and shape. By 1709, almost a quarter of a century had elapsed since the publication of the last folio edition of Shakespeare's *Comedies, Histories, and Tragedies*; apart from anything else, the legal situation had changed. With the expiration of the Licensing Act in 1695, the question of what ought to replace it became a persistent subject for parliamentary debate; booksellers such as Tonson sought to retain favourable terms that guaranteed to protect their interests as copyright-holders, while also hoping to limit or end the powers of censorship held by the Stationers' Company, that had restricted their activities under the old act. In most respects, these booksellers got their way, when new legislation, euphemistically called the Act for the Encouragement of Learning (and otherwise known as the Copyright Act or Statute of Anne), was finally passed in 1710, after more than ten attempts, since 1695, to negotiate a truce between the rival factions. As in London's theatres, the publishing business in England had begun the new century in a state of considerable uncertainty.

The copyright in the Shakespeare folio had passed from firm to firm since 1623, when the First Folio had appeared, under the imprint of Isaac Jaggard and Edward Blount; the Tonsons acquired it very cheaply in the late 1700s, through deals in 1707 and 1709. By publishing a new edition of Shakespeare so soon after that (meaning Rowe would have to work fast), they hoped to beat the new legislation: the Copyright Act distinguished between works published before and after 1710, stipulating that copyright could last for a term of 14 years for later works and 21 years for earlier works.[62]

Tonson was therefore seeking to ensure that his right to publish Shakespeare would last as long as it possibly could. That could have been a matter of simply publishing a 'word-for-word reprint of the Fourth Folio without commissioning an editor and more than forty engravings', as Don-John Dugas observes,[63] but clearly there were other considerations. A straightforward reprint did not seem likely to sell well. And the 1685 text was ripe for correction: it looked old-fashioned and seemed to contain numerous errors. If that was all there was to it, it would hardly have been a sound investment on the Tonsons' part. The solution was to turn these desultory conditions to advantage.

The previously anonymous role of whoever had prepared the text for publication was now to become a feature on the title page, stressing its novelty. Hamm suggests that the fee Rowe received, £36 10s., while 'fairly substantial', hardly meant that this was a 'special project' for Tonson, who had paid Dryden £200, ten years earlier, for his translation of Virgil's *Aeneid*.[64] Perhaps the appearance of Rowe's name on the title page was intended as some sort of further compensation, were any needed (or was even something that Rowe insisted on).[65] Opening the first volume, in any case, reveals a name that could not have been easily overlooked at the time, even if it usually has been since: the book was dedicated 'To His Grace, the Duke of Somerset'.[66] For if Rowe's dedication is to be believed, then the Duke in question, Charles Seymour, like the dedicatees of the First Folio in 1623, William Herbert, Earl of Pembroke, and his brother Philip, was not only a power in the land but an admirer of Shakespeare. At the same time, Rowe is careful not to make too great a claim for himself as Shakespeare's editor:

I have sometimes had the honour to hear Your Grace express the particular pleasure you have taken in that greatness of thought, those natural images, those passions finely touched, and that beautiful expression which is every-where to be met with in *Shakespeare*. And that he may still have the honour to entertain Your Grace, I have taken some care to redeem him from the injuries of former impressions. I must not pretend to have restored this work to the exactness of the author's original manuscripts: Those are lost, or, at least, are gone beyond any inquiry I could make; so that there was nothing left, but to compare the several editions, and give the true reading as well as I could from thence. This I have endeavoured to do pretty carefully, and rendered very many places intelligible, that were not so before. In some of the editions, especially the last, there were many lines, (and in *Hamlet* one whole scene) left out together; these are now all supplied....And I believe I shall be thought no unjust disposer of this, the author's estate in wit, by humbly offering it where he would have been proud to have bequeathed it.[67]

The implication of this passage, which is only the second of the five long paragraphs that make up the whole dedication, seems to be that Somerset could be interested in what Rowe has done to the text. But it is no accident, I suggest, that a couple of pages later, Rowe is congratulating Somerset, a highly prominent member of Anne's cabinet, on his successes in office ('Never, certainly, was there a fairer prospect of happiness than that which now rises to our view'), and comparing the 'troublesome condition of those past times'—meaning the reign of James II, when Somerset had lost favour for refusing to see a papal nuncio—with the 'Security of the present'.[68] Implicitly associating an edition that improved the condition of the plays by Somerset's admired Shakespeare, and was now 'bequeathed' to him as an 'estate in wit', with the political activities of a dedicatee who was putting the country itself on a secure footing was no bad move. The patronage system prevailed in England—as it would do for many decades to come—and Tonson, as the organizer of the Kit-Cat Club, was perfectly placed to introduce writers, such as Rowe, to potential patrons, such as Somerset. Writers and patrons, that is, who happened to have compatible political views: if Rowe had hit the mark here, the £36 10*s.* from Tonson could have been just one form of payment for his work on Shakespeare. The dedication, like the edition's engravings and Rowe's attempts to give the 'true reading' of the plays wherever possible, may be regarded as 'part of an effort to modernise Shakespeare's text'.[69]

For the first time, too, Shakespeare's plays were given the dignified title of *Works* (Ben Jonson's plays, by contrast, had been known as *The Workes of Benjamin Jonson* as early as 1616), following the mode of those Latin *Opera* that Tonson and Watts had already published. The 'cuts' denoted the frontispiece illustrations for every play, as well as an engraving of his monument in Stratford-upon-Avon opposite Rowe's reference to it in his biographical introduction to the edition. Then there was that essay itself, 'Some Account of the life, &c. of Mr William Shakespeare', the revision and correction of the play texts (the counterpart to 'altered' as glossed by Hume), the addition of consistent lists of *dramatis personae*, act and scene divisions, the assignment of locations for the action, and the modernization of Shakespeare's spelling and punctuation. This is where comparisons with later editors are valid: Samuel Johnson thought it would take him a year to produce his edition, but it did not appear until nine years after he had started taking subscriptions for it; both Edward Capell and Edmond Malone took decades over their work. Rowe had less weighty editorial theories to slow him down, it seems, and a tighter deadline.

The copyright situation determined certain aspects of Rowe's editorial practice—most significantly, that he was bound to use a copy of the Fourth Folio, published in 1685 by Henry Herringman et al. as his copy text. (Although there is the tantalizing survival, in the British Library, of a folded sheet with the opening of *The Tempest* printed on it, which seems to have been a 'trial run'; it was printed in 1708 and is based on the text of the Second Folio of 1632, a copy of which was in Rowe's library at his death.)[70] The order of the plays in 1709 follows that of 1685, so that they retain their generic groupings, as comedies, tragedies, and histories, in spite of Rowe's observation in his 'Account' that Shakespeare's plays are 'properly to be distinguished only into comedies and tragedies': 'Those which are called histories, and even some of his comedies, are really tragedies, with a run or mixture of comedy amongst 'em.'[71] But this did not mean he was bound to follow the Fourth Folio slavishly in every detail. On the contrary, his changes suggest that this was a theatrically minded text produced by the editor restaging the plays in his mind rather than passively reading and duplicating a received text.

Rowe's *Hamlet*, for example, selectively adopts readings from the quarto of 1676 making the situation less clear-cut than he suggests in his dedication to the Duke of Somerset.[72] He tells the reader that *Antony and Cleopatra* is set in 'several parts of the Roman Empire', and that Timon throws the dishes at the parasites who gather at his final banquet.[73] He reset passages that seemed to his ear to be poetry rather than prose. The play that the Fourth Folio calls *The Tragedy of Richard III: With the Landing of the Earl of Richmond, And the Battel at Bosworth Field*; in 1709 here becomes *The Life and Death of Richard III: With the Landing of the Earl of Richmond, and the Battel at Bosworth Field*, perhaps reflecting Rowe's sense that this was not really a tragedy per se but a mixture of genres.

Overall, these changes speak of a desire to enliven the reading experience, much as do the illustrations that accompany the 1709 *Works*. J. Gavin Paul suggests that they 'carry with them the potential

to ground readers' imaginings of particular incidents, a point that
would have been especially important for those plays that had yet to
enter the eighteenth-century repertory, like *All's Well That Ends Well*
and *The Comedy of Errors*.[74] The illustration to *Hamlet*, meanwhile,
picks out the moment when the prince, seeing his father's ghost for a
second time, leaps back and knocks over his chair (that is, the stage
Hamlet of Betterton rather than the chair-free Hamlet of the Fourth
Folio). A three-cornered hat adorns Macbeth's head as he watches the
visions of a line of kings conjured up for him by the witches. *The
Famous History of the Life of King Henry VIII* is preceded by a
famously ahistorical 'cut' depicting the King challenging Cardinal
Wolsey; in the background are three courtiers in full-bottomed
wigs and early eighteenth-century dress. What could be odder?
And yet, as Stephen Orgel has argued, it is a Shakespearian image
in its fidelity to the present rather than the past: 'Shakespeare apparently saw nothing about history that required any special fidelity to
the chronicler's version of events—he is not, that is, notably
more faithful to his sources in the history plays than he is in the
tragedies or comedies.' If the image of Henry in 1709 constitutes 'an
allusion to Holbein's famous portrait of the monarch', then 'history
lies . . . precisely in the anachronism', and for Orgel this anachronism
therefore can be made to serve a higher purpose:

Henry VIII has to be recognizable as Henry VIII, not simply as a generic
king. . . . But the world of the play is modern. . . . Odd as this looks to us, it is
a reasonable enough conception—people do, after all, sometimes live in old
houses. What such a production says is that the characters are just like us;
Shakespeare is faithful not to history but to nature, and nature is not confined
by historical eras.[75]

Yet this unconstrained approach to 'nature' would be rejected later in
the century, even as Shakespeare became increasingly acclaimed as
nature's great poet.

  The illustrations to two consecutive history plays in the fourth
volume echo moments found in Cibber's *Richard III*. The 'cut' for *The
Third Part of King Henry VI* depicts the moment from the last act of
the play that Cibber took as the beginning of a bloody ascent to the
throne (and which the Master of the Revels initially banned), when a
hunchbacked Richard ('I, that have neither pity, love, nor fear') stabs

King Henry, who, caught in a moment of pious contemplation, looks skyward ('O God, forgive my Sins, and pardon thee'), a book falling from his hand; in the background is a crucifix on the table (a detail that points forward to Hogarth's use of the same piece of religious iconography in his famous painting of Garrick as Richard III, waking in his tent before the Battle of Bosworth). The setting of this scene would seem to be a contradiction of the stage direction indicating that it should really take place 'on the Tower Walls'—but maybe, like Betterton's Hamlet knocking over his chair when he sees the ghost of his father again, it is a remnant of stage practice and Cibber's *Richard III*, in which Richard does dispatch Henry VI in his chamber.[76] The 1709 illustration to *Richard III* itself amplifies the reproach, showing Richard struggling to sleep, sitting at a table in his tent, his sword on the table, his armour on the floor, the open-mouthed ghosts of his victims encircling him. Again, there is an element of Cibber here, for the ghosts' simultaneous messages of reassurance for Richmond have vanished—neither Cibber nor Rowe's illustrator can accommodate the jump-cutting structure of the original.

By making that abridgement, Cibber was sparing his company a staging problem as well as keeping the audience's attention on Richard (played by one Colley Cibber). Rowe makes a subtler alteration at the equivalent point in his edition. The Fourth Folio bisects each spirit's speech according to addressee:

> Enter the Ghost of Lord Hastings.
> *Ghost.* Bloody and guilty: guilty awake,
>      And in a bloody Battel end thy days,
>      Think on Lord *Hastings*; despair, and die.
> *Ghost to Rich.* Quiet untroubled soul,
>      Awake, awake:
>      Arm, fight, and conquer, for fair *Englands* sake.[77]

Rowe, however, imposes a different sense of coherence, converting the change of addressee into a stage direction, although very little else has changed:

> Enter the Ghost of Lord Hastings.
> *Ghost.* Bloody and guilty; guilty awake,   [*To* K. Rich.
>      And in a bloody Battel end thy Days,

> Think on Lord *Hastings*; despair and die.
> Quiet untroubled Soul,                    [ *To* Richm.
> Awake, awake:
> Arm, fight, and conquer, for fair *England*'s sake.[78]

In the 1709 text, then, the identity of the speaker becomes the overriding authority for determining the presentation and integrity of each unit of verse, rather than, as in 1685, the addressee. If that sounds like common sense, that may be because the script of a play does generally work like that, as it did in Rowe's day (although the change in placing the direction for an aside from the end of the line, as he would have found conventional, to the beginning, does suggest that an uninterrupted continuum of practically identical reading habits should not be assumed). But it is not what the Fourth Folio presents, and Rowe's streamlining of the text is in keeping with his general practice as 'a playwright attuned to the realities of the eighteenth-century stage'.[79] This *Richard III* might not be the one that playgoers would have seen in the early 1700s but it was presented to be read as if it was.

Revision and correction meant bringing Shakespeare's *Works* up to this standard of presentation in every respect, however minute. In a deft comparison of the 1709 text with that 1708 trial sheet and the equivalent pages from the seventeenth-century folios, Peter Holland has shown how Rowe edited out the seventeenth century from Shakespeare's texts at the levels of both punctuation and spelling. In that first scene from *The Tempest*, for example, Rowe regularizes the irregular use of 'Ferdinando' for 'Ferdinand', adds a verb where one seems to be lacking, puzzles over 'But' (in the Fourth Folio), and eventually decides it must be a 'Boat'. And his re-punctuation of the scene amounts to a drastic intervention in what Holland calls the 'complex interrelationship of syntax, verse, and voice in Shakespearean drama', in particular by rejecting the seventeenth-century fondness for a colon as an indicator of a breathing space but not a complete semantic break between 'linguistic units'. Following an argument put forward by Bruce R. Smith, Holland emphasizes the difference between the essentially 'ear-driven' punctuation of, say, the First Folio, and the 'eye-driven' punctuation of Rowe's edition.[80] Such interventions in the texts of Shakespeare's plays are indicators of a distinct break with the past at the same time as they derive from a critical activity that ostensibly seeks to preserve it.

## Shakespeare's biographer

Rowe's work on the *Works*, Tonson's high production values and Shakespeare's reputation had to justify a high advertised price of 30s. (10s. could keep a family going for a week;[81] a single new play in quarto might cost as little as 1s. or 1s. 6d.; and later in the century, a novel might cost 7s. 6d.) One of its chief selling points was Rowe's biography of Shakespeare. Here Rowe revealed what few readers would have known about the author already, and affirmed what he saw to be Shakespeare's outstanding qualities as a dramatic poet.

Born in 1564, Rowe's Shakespeare was the son of a 'considerable Dealer in Wool', briefly attended the 'Free-School' in Stratford-upon-Avon, and married young. He fell into 'ill Company'; 'probably the first Essay of his Poetry' was a ballad about Sir Thomas Lucy of Charlecote, who prosecuted him for stealing deer from his park. But it was through fleeing from punishment for this youthful crime that Shakespeare came to London and to his 'first Acquaintance in the Play-house'. It is unclear to Rowe which was Shakespeare's first play, but it does seem that he quickly distinguished himself more as a writer than an actor. 'Queen *Elizabeth* had several of his Plays Acted before her, and without doubt gave him many gracious Marks of her Favour', and Shakespeare returned it by alluding to 'A fair Vestal, Throned by the West' in *A Midsummer Night's Dream*. She commanded him to write another play about Falstaff, *The Merry Wives of Windsor*, she liked the character so much in the *Henry IV* plays. Spenser wrote a poem about him retiring from town for a while. Jonson owed his career to Shakespeare's spotting the potential of his first play. And so on, through the 'Seven Ages of Man' speech, acknowledgement of the force of Thomas Rymer's criticisms, of the diversity and power of Shakespeare's writing, the stories of his retirement and death, and a final admission: 'There is a book of poems, published in 1640 ... but as I have but very lately seen it, without an opportunity of making any judgment upon it, I won't pretend to determine, whether it be his or no.'[82]

If that seems a frankly open way to end 'Some Account', it is in keeping with the relaxed voice of the rest of the essay. As the other elements of the edition would seem to suggest, Rowe writes here for the present moment, referring casually to Dryden and Rymer, to *The Jew of Venice* by Granville; he is interested to know which play is Shakespeare's first but does not force a theory on to the available evidence. Being a classicist himself (Rowe translated Lucan's *De Bello Civili* and wrote a play inspired by Homer, *Ulysses*) does not stop him arguing of Shakespeare and the 'ancient poets' that the 'delicacy of his taste, and the natural bent of his own great genius' were 'equal, if not superior to some of the best of theirs'—and here is the first eighteenth-century reiteration of the idea that Shakespeare was possibly better off not knowing too much about the classics:

> ...though the knowledge of 'em might have made him more correct, yet it is not improbable but that the regularity and deference for them, which would have attended that correctness, might have restrained some of that fire, impetuosity, and even beautiful extravagance which we admire in *Shakespeare*....[83]

Although in retrospect Rowe's praise here does not look especially bold, it clearly signals his position in the aesthetic debates of the day: not everybody admired Shakespeare's 'beautiful extravagance'. 'Fire' was the element of heavenly inspiration, but 'regularity' and 'correctness' were, in neoclassical terms, nature codified and perfected—deviations from the unities of time, place, and action were difficult to justify, as many had agreed.

When Charles Gildon produced *The Laws of Poetry* in 1721, he could draw on the combined authority of three peers to create a composite neoclassical statement about the proper way to write. These were *The Laws of Poetry, As laid down by the Duke of Buckinghamshire in his Essay on Poetry, by the Earl of Roscommon in his Essay on Translated Verse, and by the Lord Lansdowne on Unnatural Flights in Poetry, Explained and Illustrated*. According to these collective authorities, 'a true poet must be inspired by nature, must have a great imagination, or pregnant fancy, which to be truly beautiful must be regulated by judgment or learning'; nature and art had united in the works of Homer, Virgil, Sophocles, Euripides, 'and many more who are lost', but 'for want of this conjunction, *Shakespeare* has been able to give us scarce anything perfect'. Writing plays about English history, as Shakespeare had supposedly done, in order to educate a 'generally very ignorant' audience was a 'very poor and mean undertaking for a great poet', and it did not help that Shakespeare had 'in some particulars, if not falsified, yet at least not justly represented the characters he has made use of '. This 'great, but very irregular genius' was one of those poets who lived in 'ignorant times, and unpolished nations, which deprived them of the knowledge of art, that would have regulated their exuberant geniuses, and have given them that perfection which the ancients enjoyed'.[84]

Shakespeare could have learned, for example, what Buckingham knew well enough to put into verse: that 'soliloquy had need be few, | Extremely short, and spoke in passion too'. In this respect alone, the extravagant Shakespeare was a serial offender against the laws of poetry:

*Shakespeare* has *frequently* soliloquies of threescore lines, and those very often, if not always, calm, without any emotion of the passions, or indeed conducive to the business of the play; I mean, where there is any business in the play peculiar to it. That famous *soliloquy*, which has been so much cried up in *Hamlet*, has no more to do there, than a description of the grove and altar of Diana, mentioned by *Horace*. *Hamlet* comes in talking to himself, and very sedately and exactly weighs the several reasons or considerations mentioned in that *soliloquy*,

*To be, or not to be*, & c.

As soon as he has done talking to himself, he sees *Ophelia*, and passes to a conversation with her, entirely different to the subject he had been meditating on with that earnestness, which as it was produced by nothing before, so has it no manner of influence on what follows after, and is therefore a perfectly detached piece, and has nothing to do in the play. . . . To go through all the *soliloquies* of *Shakespeare*, would be to make a volume on this single head. But this I can say in general, that there is not one in all his *works* that can be excused by nature or reason.[85]

These are percipient remarks, since Rowe had already given his readers a 'perfectly detached piece' from a play by Shakespeare, the speech beginning 'All the world's a stage' and ending 'Sans teeth, sans eyes, sans taste, sans ev'rything' from *As You Like It*, in the course of 'Some Account';[86] and such detachment to varying degrees and in different situations would serve as one of the abiding means of appropriating Shakespeare during the coming century. The neoclassical animus against Shakespearian extravagance would have far-reaching effects on his plays in performance and in the eyes of the critics for many years to come. But it seems typical of Rowe that his edition should have gestured towards this process of detachment—a process that leads to Shakespeare anthologies, citation in Johnson's *Dictionary*, allusions in novels, poems, plays, and non-literary arts.

Like that of Cibber's play, the reputation of Rowe's edition of Shakespeare has wavered somewhat over the years. While acknowledging him as a pioneer, later editors did not fail in their duty to point out what Rowe did wrong—or had failed to do altogether, such as tackle questions of attribution. Samuel Johnson at least believed that as an editor Rowe had 'done more than he promised', and that in his edition 'without the pomp of notes or boasts of criticism, many passages are happily restored'.[87] Rowe's edition, in this respect, is of its moment, and unqualified comparisons with the work of his successors can be misleading, implying that he was trying to accomplish exactly the same thing as them—whereas, as Johnson well knew, pompous and boastful attempts to reveal the true texts of Shakespeare's *Works* were precisely what lay in store for them in the years after Rowe.[88]

As reprinted by Edmond Malone in *The Plays and Poems of William Shakspeare*, in 1790, the biographical 'Account' is sometimes driven off the page altogether by the sheer volume of footnotes, correcting or vastly expanding on Rowe's essay, recording discoveries made by other editors or Malone himself. (Malone 'discredited virtually everything Rowe had to say'.)[89] Despite its failings as a historical record, however, Rowe's 'Account' had presented a Shakespeare the eighteenth century could not only esteem but love: in his keeping 'ill Company' and versifying on a theme of Sir Thomas Lucy, he had something of Prince Hal's combination of early erring and promise of greater things; his fellow writers admired him (even envious Jonson), and he got as near as you can get to collaborating with royalty on *The Merry Wives of Windsor*. The reward for his labours lay in a serene retirement to the English countryside. All of this was well calculated to please, and explains why the 'Account' stayed in print, in Pope's abridgement, for the rest of the century.

For Johnson, Rowe could at least be said to have written a Life of Shakespeare 'such as tradition then expiring could supply'.[90] The links in the chain were visible enough, leading from Shakespeare to his alleged godson Sir William Davenant to Thomas Betterton, and to Betterton again from the community of Stratford-upon-Avon. But Rowe was at the end of that chain, and his own situation as a writer bore little resemblance to Shakespeare's. Hence, perhaps, his admiration for the seeming serenity of Shakespeare's retirement to Stratford to spend his last days 'in ease, retirement, and the conversation of his friends' ('as all men of good sense will wish theirs may be'). There may be a touch of man-of-letters wistfulness in this final vision of the playwright rewarded for his labours, with an 'estate equal to his occasion':[91] in contrast, with his financial wellbeing tied to his entailed property in Devon and Cornwall, Rowe had to persuade Parliament to pass a private bill in 1706, that would allow him to sell off his own estate. It was an act that marked the finality of his transition from 'country gentry to bourgeois intellectual, from absentee landlord to civil servant'.[92]

From his 'estate in wit', meanwhile, Rowe still had a Shakespearian harvest to gather—*Jane Shore*—and his tragedy was not the only attempt at an imitation of Shakespeare to emerge in the wake of the 1709 *Works*. In 1715, a future editor of Shakespeare, Lewis Theobald, published *The Cave of Poverty*, an allegorical poem that could have been described as an imitation of Spenser, did it not adopt the stanzaic form of *Venus and Adonis* – presumably Shakespeare seemed to be the more commercially advantageous name to drop. Tonson, meanwhile, although he did not publish *Jane Shore*, reissued what plays he could of Rowe's, with the name of his renamed shop on the title page: '*Shakespeare's* Head over-against *Katherine* Street in the *Strand*', with the image of the playwright Rowe had edited above it.

Tonson had also reprinted the *Works* in 1709, silently creating a second edition. In 1714, a third had emerged, apparently revised by John Hughes, in eight duodecimo volumes—plus the additional volume that Edmund Curll and Egbert Sanger had shrewdly published in 1710 to resemble the original six volumes of plays. Now the dramatic oeuvre could be officially united with the long poems and the Sonnets as they had been re-ordered and given titles by John Benson in 1640 (the 'book of poems' that Rowe claimed to have barely seen), as well as some of Gildon's critical thoughts on the plays and the 'art, rise and progress of the stage in Greece, Rome and England'. But there had been another volume of poems published by Bernard Lintott in 1709, the two selections of plays published by Thomas Johnson in The Hague in 1711 and 1712, and *An Essay on the Genius and Writings of Shakespeare* by John Dennis (also 1712). Noting these responses and more, Don-John Dugas calls the productions of this period 'the most remarkable proliferation of Shakespeare-related material' yet. Turning to the performance of Shakespeare's plays, however, he suggests that the long-term impact of all this activity was 'negligible'—and the next two chapters explore the very different productions of the Shakespeare industry, as it might now be called, between the 1720s and the 1740s.

# *Pope versus Theobald*

Give me another horse—bind up my wounds!
Have mercy, Jesu—soft, I did but dream.
Oh coward Conscience! How dost thou afflict me?
The lights burn blue! Is it not dead midnight?
Cold fearful drops stand on my trembling flesh;
What do I fear? My self! &c.

(*Richard III*, as quoted in *The Tatler*, No. 90,
by Richard Steele)[1]

Establishing a precedent for all those who came after him in the eighteenth century, Nicholas Rowe had made a prudent claim for his edition of Shakespeare's *Works* in 1709, in his Dedication to the Duke of Somerset: that his edition was an improvement on the previous ones. What self-respecting editor could have said otherwise? Rowe's successors would follow suit, stating that they were rescuing Shakespeare from the 'errors' of his predecessors, while often silently borrowing from them or introducing questionable innovations, especially questionable emendations, of their own. Hamlet was not to *comply* with Rosencrantz and Guildenstern on their reunion at Elsinore, Sir Thomas Hanmer suggests; he must *complement* with them.[2] William Warburton decides that Rosalind does not liken the sanctity of Orlando's kissing to the touch of holy *bread* but of holy *beard*.[3] Alexander Pope looks at the following three lines in *Macbeth*, as printed by Rowe:

No, this my hand will rather
The multitudinous sea incarnadine,
Making the green one red.[4]

And he decides that the middle line is so bad it must be banished from the main text of the play to the margin, where it retains Rowe's singular sea, and 'The' becomes 'Thy'. On the same page, also banished to the small print, is the Porter's entire speech.[5]

Such local alterations tend to be symptomatic of an attitude problem. Most of these editors saw it as their duty to do something about defects in the text where they found them, continuing a process of emendation and improvement begun in the seventeenth-century folios. But this process gained a commercial dimension, as Shakespeare's plays became the property of a family business: after Rowe, the Tonsons and their business partners would go on to publish the 'new and improved' editions of Alexander Pope (1725; second edition 1728), Lewis Theobald (1733/4; second edition 1740), and William Warburton (1747); a fourth, that of Sir Thomas Hanmer (1743/4; second edition 1770), was published in Oxford, only to be reprinted the following year by the Tonson 'cartel' with a notice that coolly undercut Hanmer's authority by announcing that it would mark the alterations he had decided not to, and also those taken from the previous edition, by Theobald and his collaborators Warburton and Styan Thirlby. 'The changes in the disposition of the lines for the regulation of the metre are too numerous to be taken particular notice of.'[6] It was around the same time that Samuel Johnson and Edward Cave issued their *Proposals for Printing a New Edition of the Plays of William Shakespeare*; it appears that the Tonsons forced them to abandon their plans for a publication by subscription that would be not only corrected in its text, with 'the various readings remarked', the 'conjectures of former editors examined, and their omissions supplied', but also would sell for £1 5s. in total. The higher prices of its rivals—six guineas for Pope's, two for Theobald's, three for Hanmer's—were duly noted.[7]

In ten years' time, however, when Johnson had published his *Dictionary* and made his name, the Tonsons were more interested in letting him edit Shakespeare. In a second prospectus, *Proposals for Printing, by Subscription, the Dramatick Works of William Shakespeare*, dated 1 June 1756, he tried to explain why this author stood 'in more need of critical assistance than any other of the English writers, and what are the deficiencies of the late attempts, which another editor may hope to supply'. In part, the answer lay in the corruptions of sixteenth- and seventeenth-century intermediaries: 'transcript after transcript' was made, 'vitiated by the blunders of the penman, or changed by the affectation of the player; perhaps enlarged to introduce a jest, or mutilated to shorten the representation; and printed at last without the concurrence of the author, without the consent of the proprietor, from compilations made by change or by stealth out of the separate parts written for the theatre'. Being 'thus thrust into the world surreptitiously and hastily', they suffered from the 'ignorance and negligence' of the printers, too: 'in no other age was the art of printing in such unskilful hands'. In Johnson's eyes, 'all the present editions are apparently and intentionally defective' in correcting these texts; there were 'many restorations' yet to be made. He also promised that his edition, to be published by Christmas 1757, would 'exhibit all the observable varieties of all the copies that can be found, that, if the reader is not satisfied with the editor's determination, he may have the means of choosing better for himself'. Nothing would be 'imposed, as in the Oxford edition, without notice of the alteration'. He could also justifiably point out that while his predecessors had devoted their energies to correcting Shakespeare, 'they had not sufficiently attended to the elucidation of passages obscured by accident or time'.[8] Since they had already done much of the work of emendation for him, for which he was grateful, he was free to concentrate on what they could not:

...Mr. Rowe and Mr. Pope were very ignorant of the ancient English literature; Dr. Warburton was detained by more important studies; and Mr. Theobald, if fame be just to his memory, considered learning only as an instrument of gain, and made no further enquiry after his author's meaning, when once he had notes sufficient to embellish his page with expected decorations.[9]

As it happens, fame was far from being just on this occasion. Theobald was in most respects the most theoretically sophisticated of Shakespeare editors in the first half of the eighteenth century, before the era of Edward Capell, George Steevens, Isaac Reed, and Edmond Malone. No little thanks to his dealings with Pope and Warburton, however, and to Johnson gullibly endorsing their views, his reputation suffered the most, at least before Malone. As Shakespeare scholarship matured, Theobald's achievement became clearer. His is one of several eighteenth-century editions of Shakespeare that have continued to receive attention from later commentators, on account of its combination of ingenious emendations founded in historically and bibliographically informed scholarship. By the same token, Theobald's rivals, Pope, Hanmer, and Warburton, have been criticized for emending Shakespeare as they liked, moulding the texts according to eighteenth-century criteria (although Pope, like Rowe before him, is sometimes given credit for importing certain quarto readings into folio texts). Yet Theobald's antithetical edition, the most often reprinted of the eighteenth century, would not have come into being without Pope's. By attacking Pope in *Shakespeare Restored* (1726), Theobald offered a specimen of his own formidable knowledge of Shakespeare—something that Pope himself acknowledged by silently adopting many of Theobald's readings for his second edition of Shakespeare, published two years later. Pope also made Theobald one of the chief dunces in his mock-epic masterpiece *The Dunciad*—although as the poem developed through its various incarnations, Theobald lost his place of honour to another favourite target of Pope's, Colley Cibber—crediting him with pedantic footnotes, from the title of the poem onwards, mocking his accurate adherence to the letter rather than, as Pope saw it, the spirit of poetry. Even the spelling of the writer's name, 'Shakespear' or 'Shakespeare', became a subject for disagreement between them. '*THE DUNCIAD, sic MS*', reads a supremely sarcastic footnote in *The Dunciad*:

It may well be disputed whether this be a right reading: Ought it not rather to be spelled *Dunceiad*, as the etymology evidently demands? *Dunce* with an *e*, therefore *Dunceiad* with an *e*. That accurate and punctual man of letters, the restorer of *Shakespeare*, constantly observes the preservation of this very letter *e*, in spelling the name of his beloved author, and not like his common careless editors, with the omission of one, nay sometimes of two *ee's*, [as *Shakspear*] which is utterly unpardonable....[10]

In ominous anticipation of the shape of Shakespeare editions to come, and mimicry of the abstruse debates between commentators sometimes to be found in scholarly editions of classical and biblical texts, other voices then join in the debate: 'This is surely a slip...'; 'It is to be noted...'; 'Though I have as just a value for the letter *E*, as any Grammarian living...yet cannot it induce me to agree with

those who would add another *e* to it, and call it the *Dunceiade*.'[11]
Pope's quarrel is not with Theobald alone but the whole school of
pedantry that, for him, loses itself in obscurity and pettiness (revived
in the late eighteenth-century debates over Edmond Malone's
preferred spelling: 'Shakspeare'). How else, however, was the true
text of Shakespeare's plays to be 'restored'?

## Pedantry and punctuation

Recalling his 'very pensive mood' of 4 November 1709 in *The Tatler*,
Steele not only remembered that he had taken down a volume of
Shakespeare and read a scene from *Richard III*, thus sending himself
even further into a 'deep contemplation', he quoted a few lines from
the play, too, as above. These are the first words of the usurper-king
as he wakes after a night in which the conscience-pricking ghosts of
his victims have visited him, and substantially they are the same
words Shakespeare's contemporaries could read in 1597, when the
first quarto of the play appeared (to be followed the next year by
the second of eight quartos before the Civil War, suggesting something of its popularity). But Steele, in quoting this passage, also alters
it. His Richard rhetorically asks himself if it is midnight, instead of
asserting that as a fact: 'it is now dead midnight'. It was the second
quarto's misprint, 'it is not dead midnight', that had been taken up in
the First Folio of 1623, survived into the Fourth Folio of 1685, and into
Rowe's 1709 edition.

Emendation led to emendation: 'is it not dead midnight?', as the
phrase appears in Steele's essay, and in subsequent collected editions
of Shakespeare, up to and including those of Edward Capell, George
Steevens, and Edmond Malone in the second half of the eighteenth
century.[12] Later, realizing his mistake, Malone undid it in time for his
posthumously published edition of *The Plays and Poems of William
Shakspeare* of 1821. But in a long footnote, he stated that 'all the
subsequent editors, including Mr. Steevens' had got this line wrong,
'till my first edition of this work had appeared'. Never mind that his
first edition had got it wrong, too; Malone could hardly turn down
such an opportunity to drive home what he saw as an essential point
of editorial principle:

...here we have a decisive proof of the progress of corruption, and of the licentious and arbitrary manner in which emendations were made, even in the first folio, when a passage in the quarto that was printed from appeared corrupt. Some idle conjecture was formed and adopted, instead of resorting to the original copy, where the true reading would have been found; and, in like manner, when errors were found in the first folio, the revisor of the second endeavoured to amend them, merely by conjecture, without resorting to the earliest quarto copy of these plays, where that aid might have been obtained; and, in the other plays, where there was no quarto, without attempting to find any other manuscript copy than the one which that copy followed. This I have asserted and proved again and again; and it has again and again been denied.[13]

To anybody who is uninterested in such matters as reversing the order of two words or the addition of a question mark, it might sound as if Malone is getting somewhat carried away here. Yet arguing over such minutiae was a venerable component of textual scholarship. At stake here was Malone's belief that the 'earliest quarto copy' of a given Shakespearian text should carry (in the absence of authorial holographs) the ultimate authority—greater authority, certainly, than the tradition of 'idle conjecture' and emendation conducted in a 'licentious and arbitrary manner'. Yet Malone's salutary point of principle stands in sad contrast to the inaccuracy of his account of the phrase in question. It was untrue that 'all subsequent editors' after the First Folio had taken the line as 'Is it not dead midnight?' Rowe, for a start, seems to have taken the phrase as a statement (perhaps a dazed observation, as Richard comes to, whereas the rhetorical question sounds altogether cleverer and composed).

And what if it was not an editor at all, but Steele who, by adopting this reading of the phrase in his *Tatler* essay, had pre-empted and perhaps influenced the fate of this single phrase? For it was not Rowe, but the next two editors of Shakespeare's *Works*, Pope and Theobald, who seem to have followed Steele's reading—a trivial matter of punctuation, perhaps, but one that opens on to an arena of conflict over the texts of Shakespeare's plays, which teem with such ambiguities and signs of disagreement and widely varying modes of interpretation. The rectification of spelling and punctuation offered the active editor opportunities to impose themselves on Shakespeare's text; so did problems of metre and misprinted lines, missing stage directions, the inconsistent use of characters' names. To identify such issues and decide to do something about them was in turn to raise questions of what Shakespeare had intended, and what could be blamed on meddlesome players or negligent printers.

Although ingenious emendations and obvious signs of decisive editorial intervention tend to attract more critical attention, the cumulative impression of the millions of local decisions that went into the making of new editions, by the anonymous annotators of the seventeenth century, by Rowe, Pope, Theobald et al., is one of endemic instability—the mediating hand of the editor is visible at every turn of the page. (To take another example from those few lines from *Richard III*, the collected editions of the seventeenth and eighteenth centuries manage to squeeze a few variations out of the half-line Steele renders as 'What do I fear? My self!'—Rowe, Pope, and Theobald agreeing on 'What? do I fear my self?', while Capell and Malone both prefer 'What do I feare? my selfe [*sic*]?', in keeping with the first quarto, suggesting subtly different thought processes.) The results of such interference might seldom meet with the approval of modern scholarship, but the energy that went into such projects is impressive (not least given that Shakesepare's oeuvre then seemed to consist not of thirty-six but forty-three full-length plays). When Pope complains about 'dull duty of an editor', it is easy to see what he means by that phrase—but also that it was a bad sign for his edition if that was what he thought of editorship.

While Pope had a 'natural horror of pedantry',[14] the devil was always in the detail: by manipulating Shakespeare's texts at the level of spelling and punctuation, the individual word and phrase, that Pope and his successors immersed themselves in an expressive, trans-formative kind of drudgery. And when it was cast in this light, it was not so difficult for the editor to reconcile himself to his task. 'Shakespeare', Pope later wrote, 'For gain, not glory, winged his roving flight, | And grew immortal in his own despite'. A footnote elaborates on the point: 'Shakespeare and Ben. Jonson may truly be said not much to have thought of this immortality, the one in many pieces composed in haste for the stage; the other in his latter works in general, which Dryden called his *Dotages*.' While Jonson lost interest, in other words, it was assumed that Shakespeare took no interest in seeing his plays into print at all, into making them 'immortal'. The ambiguities and errors could therefore be seen as deriving directly from Shakespeare's stage-bent 'fire', a pure, ephemeral form of writing, 'in haste', that had nothing to do with the messy business of booksellers, authors' proofs, and trivial matters like punctuation. The editor, on other hand, becomes the keeper of Shakespeare's flame, the interpreter of heavenly poetry. And Shakespeare himself was safely removed from the messy business of publication. Thus 'dematerialized', he seems all the riper for critical deification.

## Squabbles

In this arena of pedantry, Pope and Theobald make exemplary combatants, in that their battles were conducted multifariously, through their rival editions of Shakespeare, Theobald's attack on Pope's errors in his book *Shakespeare Restored*, and Pope's subsequent poems—but also because of the incompatible ideas about editing Shakespeare that their squabbles expose.

In 1709, Rowe's edition of Shakespeare's *Works* had apparently allowed Jacob Tonson, Sr to tighten his grip on a potentially profitable share of the emerging vernacular literary canon; the success of that initial experiment, as we have already seen, exceeded expectations. But in order to go on making money from Shakespeare, the firm would have to show a new edition was needed—hence, after Rowe's death, the publication of a 'correct edition' was advertised on the basis that Rowe's had been 'very faulty'.[15] By contracting the most acclaimed poet of the day, Pope, to edit Shakespeare again, on a grander scale, the firm was seeking success on a different scale. Rowe's edition had broken with the folio format by putting Shakespeare into the more easily portable form of six octavo volumes (seven with the addition of the Curll-Gildon volume); now, Tonson and Pope would risk publishing Shakespeare's *Works* as an expensive large quarto, while retaining the division into six volumes, which eventually appeared in 1725. The decision was also made to charge £6 6s. per copy—which explains why there were still 140 copies in stock in 1767, when the Tonson stock was sold off. Commercially, this edition was prestigious but seems not to have had the immediate impact of Rowe's edition.

In May 1721, Pope had signed a contract with Jacob Tonson, Jr (the nephew of the Jacob Tonson who commissioned Rowe's edition twelve years earlier) to edit Shakespeare in the aftermath of the South Sea Bubble—the financial crisis of 1720 that saw many investors lose hundreds and in some cases thousands of pounds (Pope was affected but not drastically), and brought to power Sir Robert Walpole and his faction. Pope had his own editorial faction—William Broome and Elijah Fenton—who were, at the same time, collaborating with him on his translation of the *Odyssey* (he had also needed help, over several years, with his translation of the *Iliad*). Despite his dislike of pedantry and dull duties, he was also editing works by Thomas Parnell and John Sheffield, Duke of Buckingham (thus thwarting Theobald from making his own contribution to an edition of Buckingham, which Pope's friends in the House of Lords had scotched, and giving Theobald a motive for revenge).[16] Pope, in other words, was deeply involved in shaping the reception of other writers, and was not just dabbling in editorship when he came to edit Shakespeare. Thanks to these other projects, however, he would not write the preface that would complete his edition until October 1724; advertisements for subscriptions began to appear a few weeks later. When the edition did appear, in March 1725, it was attacked repeatedly in *The Weekly Journal, or Saturday's Post* for its price and its approach to the text.[17]

One aspect of that approach is announced in Pope's preface when he claims that the 'various readings are fairly put in the margin, so that everyone may compare 'em; and those I have preferred into the text are constantly *ex fide Codicum*, upon authority'. Preparing the ground by dwelling on the many interpolations and corruptions he believes the texts have suffered over the course of the seventeenth century, he has 'degraded' the 'excessively bad' passages to the bottom of the page. There are notes on the 'obsolete or unusual words'. And:

Some of the most shining passages are distinguished by commas in the margin; and where the beauty lay not in particulars but in the whole, a star is prefixed to the scene. This seems to me a shorter and less ostentatious method of performing the better half of criticism (namely the pointing out an author's excellencies) than to fill a whole paper with citations of fine passages, with *general applauses*, or *empty exclamations* at the tail of them.[18]

Behind Pope's declared practice as an editor, in other words, lies an impulse towards aesthetic judgement—one that not only allows him to deny that Shakespeare had much of a hand in what he sees as lesser works (namely, *Love's Labour Lost* [sic], *The Winter's Tale*, and *Titus Adronicus* [also sic]), and nothing at all to do with the 'apocryphal' plays (including *Pericles*), but to demarcate, as efficiently as possible, what he regards as the heart of the matter, Shakespeare's most beautiful writing. There is also a dig here at the compilers of poetic commonplace books such as *The Art of Poetry* (1702) by Edward Bysshe and *The Complete Art of Poetry* (1718) by Charles Gildon, with Shakespeare being especially prominent in the second of those two. This discourse of poetic beauties and defects (or faults) would continue to be highly influential for the reception of Shakespeare in subsequent decades.

At once, though, as already noted, critics took exception to Pope's methods. Gildon and Edmund Curll had profited from the first Tonson edition of Shakespeare by publishing the non-dramatic works attributed to Shakespeare that Rowe had not been able to include; and there was also an attempt to cash in on Pope's edition by reproducing a similar 'seventh' volume in May 1725, edited by the doctor and Tory hack George Sewell. In *Shakespeare Restored, or, A Specimen of the Many Errors as well Committed, as Unamended, by Mr. Pope in his Late Edition of This Poet*, Theobald took a different approach: he attacked Pope's edition directly, arguing that he had both intervened egregiously in places, and left many other passages untouched where he ought to have intervened. In fact, the most celebrated instance of Theobald's work demonstrates his willingness to intervene, in the name of restoring Shakespeare, rather than leaving the text untouched.

Pope had considered that an odd line in *Henry V*, 'His nose was as sharp as a pen, and a table of green fields', in Mistress Quickly's description of the dying Falstaff, meant that there was a table on stage ('it being a scene in a tavern where they drink at parting'), and 'Greenfield' must have been the name of the 'Property-man' who brought it on stage: 'A Table of Greenfield's'. It is an imaginatively theatrical solution, informed by Pope's view that the corruption in the text—that is, that the direction to Greenfield has crept into Mistress Quickly's speech—derives from a playhouse copy of the script.

Claiming to be building on the work of a 'gentleman sometime deceased', Theobald suggested that the words are in the right place, but have been printed incorrectly: 'and a' babbled of green Fields' is the emendation a modern editor ought to make.[19] There are emendations suggested in *Shakespeare Restored* that have not won much support, if any—but many readers have agreed with Theobald on this one, beginning with Pope himself, who adopted it in the second edition of his Shakespeare. As the debate over this single phrase has gone on, however, intermittently ever since the 1720s, the issues have remained the same: is the error one of theatrical origin (Pope's initial reading), or a misprint to be corrected by recourse to a sense of the dramatic situation within the play? (Babbling, Theobald argues, is what children do 'that cannot yet talk, or dying Persons when they are losing the Use of Speech'.)[20] Is there a mistake there at all, in fact? Was Theobald really 'like so many English scholars, a sentimentalist at heart' who could not resist the sound-association of green fields and 'babbling brooks'?[21]

The majority of critics would probably vote in Theobald's favour, but it is not simply a matter of being right or wrong. The literary-critical basis of his argument, and the underlying need to vindicate emendation itself, have been sources of enduring disagreement.[22]

The bulk of *Shakespeare Restored* is taken up with a systematic textual commentary on a single play, *Hamlet*, with plenty of commentary on other plays in a lengthy appendix, and his arguments derive from comparisons between different editions of the plays, between different plays, and between Shakespeare and other authors. Does Polonius liken Hamlet's vows, those untrustworthy 'brokers', to Ophelia to 'sanctified and pious bonds'—or 'bawds'? Theobald suggests the latter, despite the former appearing in 'all the impressions that have ever come in my way', and shows that Shakespeare made a similar connection between brokers and bawds in *The Two Gentlemen of Verona*, *All's Well that Ends Well*, and *King John*.[23] Comparing different editions, he is prepared to accept almost any reading instead of Pope's 'A very Peacock', offering the change of a single letter (just the sort of emendation Pope sends up in that first footnote to *The Dunciad*) to 'Meacock' ('a cravenly bird'), 'pajock' (found in two folios and a quarto), 'paddock', and 'puttock' ('a ravenous *kite*, a mere bird of prey; a devourer of the state and people; without any of the excellencies and *defensive* virtues of the royal eagle, [Hamlet's] Father?').[24] And is it possible that Shakespeare could write couplets that were 'bald and poor in the *diction*'? Pope might want to believe that, and so omit them, but Theobald is less reverent: for him, as for the Second Folio, 'How in my words soever she be shent, | To give them seals never my soul consent' is part of *Hamlet*, whether we like it or not.[25]

*Shakespeare Restored* is a highly significant intervention in the history of textual scholarship on vernacular literature, coming at a moment when the texts of very few English authors received the same treatment that was given to those of classical authors. Out of Christ Church, Oxford, had come *The Works of Geoffrey Chaucer* (1721), edited by Thomas Urry (who died before it was complete), and Timothy and William Thomas; the Master of Trinity College, Cambridge, Richard Bentley, produced a controversial edition of Milton's *Paradise Lost* in 1732. The plays and poems of other English authors—even Colley Cibber—might well appear as *Works*, but that nominal claim to some literary standing did not necessarily entail a particular mode of scholarly care over the texts themselves. Yet, Theobald argued in *Shakespeare Restored*, 'the more the editions of any book multiply, the more the errors multiply too'.[26] Pope had denied that he had indulged himself in 'Innovation' by changing the texts according to 'my private sense or conjecture'. But there had to be a middle way between arbitrary alteration and leaving the text exactly as it was, without paying it any critical attention at all. 'For my part', Theobald wrote,

I don't know whether I am mistaken in judgment, but I have always thought, that whenever a *gentleman* and a *scholar* turns *editor* of any book, he at the same time commences critic upon his *author*; and that wherever he finds the reading suspected, manifestly corrupted, deficient in sense, and unintelligible, he ought to exert every power and faculty of the mind to supply such a defect . . . and by a reasonable emendation, to make that satisfactory and consistent with the context. . . .[27]

Pope's response to this challenge was two-sided if not two-faced—he adopted many of Theobald's readings for the second edition of his *Works of Shakespeare*, tacitly accepting his reasoning, while sending him up in *The Dunciad* and elsewhere. Theobald had already done enough, however, to convince the Tonson cartel that he should be the next editor of Shakespeare. Following some drawn-out negotiating over payment, his *Works of Shakespeare* appeared in 1733, then in a second edition in 1740, and would go on to become the most reprinted of all eighteenth-century editions of the *Works*.

Here, in his own edition of Shakespeare, Theobald got to put his emendatory talents to good use—here, Falstaff on his deathbed certainly babbles of green fields. Those sanctified and pious bonds became bawds, and Pope's use of the same emendation was triumphantly noted, as is his opponent's view that he would opt for anything rather than that 'Peacock' (he chooses 'Paddock').[28] And there are other ways in which Theobald's edition speaks of dispute: ironically, in the preface's grateful note to 'my most ingenious and ever-respected friend, the Reverend Mr. *William Warburton* of *Newark* upon *Trent*', for their long correspondence on the subject of editing Shakespeare,[29] since Warburton would soon turn on him, and defect to the side of Pope; and by implication in the list of subscribers to Theobald's edition. Although the list is headed by the Prince and Princess of Wales, and contains many peers and notable individuals, whose preference for a copy printed on 'Royal Paper' is noted, there is also a notable contingent of actors on the list, including the Poet Laureate and Theobald's heir as King of the Dunces, Colley Cibber, his son Theophilus, Dennis Delane, Henry Giffard (of whom more in the following chapter), and James Quin, as well as the composer Johann Christoph Pepusch, the manager (John Rich), and the prompter (John Stede) of Covent Garden, the printer (and later novelist) Samuel Richardson, and several members of the Walpole family, including the most powerful man in the country, Sir Robert himself, who ordered six copies.

This list was itself a mark of Theobald's success, and the avid interest in seeing a new edition of Shakespeare. It also shows how party politics and satirical literature could affect the levels of support that such a project received, and how the enmity between Pope and Theobald was common knowledge—an enmity which was in large measure dictated by their broader allegiances. As Theobald told Warburton, he 'never knew or approached' the Duke of Chandos, but when Pope was thought to satirize him in his 'Epistle to Burlington', the Duke subscribed 'for four sets of my Shakespeare on Royal Paper'—a fairly unambiguous indication of Chandos's feelings on the matter.[30]

### Editors versus actors

Peter Seary suggests that Theobald had another advantage over Pope besides his general sense of the authority of various old editions in relation to modern, derivative editions. Whereas Pope had relatively little sustained involvement in contemporary theatre, Theobald had written tragedies, adapted *Richard II* (it was performed in 1719 without much success), and written essays on Shakespeare for his short-lived periodical *The Censor* (1715). He supplied the libretti for John Rich's operatic pantomimes at Lincoln's Inn Fields and then Covent Garden theatres, including some of the most popular and profitable works of the century, and through his friendship and work as assistant to Rich's prompter, John Stede, he had prepared texts for performance, seen passages deleted, and 'must have learned that as a general rule authors tend to write plays that actors consider too long'.[31] All this must have been thought-provoking 'insider' knowledge for a would-be Shakespeare editor.

Like Rowe before him, Theobald also profited by the close association between his name and Shakespeare's by staging, after *Shakespeare Restored*, a play called *Double Falsehood* that he claimed to be adapted from a play originally by Shakespeare and John Fletcher (Theobald did not draw attention to the collaborative aspect of the case) called *Cardenio*, via three post-Restoration copies in manuscript. These copies might have been destroyed in the fire that consumed Covent Garden in 1808, and the truth about Theobald's claim will probably never be known—but Malone and many others have viewed it as a desperate fraud. There is some evidence that Theobald saw Shakespeare's oeuvre as being larger than it was in Pope's view. Whereas Pope denied that the apocryphal plays had anything to do with Shakespeare at all, Theobald thought that 'beyond all controversy', he could 'prove some touches in every one of them to come from his pen'.[32] If it had been left to him, rather than the booksellers, to decide what made up the text of his edition in 1733, it is possible that this mysterious play would have found its way into the canon of Shakespeare's works long ago. As it was, *Double*

*Falsehood* was acted at Drury Lane in December 1727, with some success, and occasionally thereafter (including in May 1741 as a benefit for 'the last editor of Shakespeare').[33] Brean Hammond's thorough edition of the play, published in 2010, devotes a considerable portion of its introduction to chasing the shadow of a lost copy of a lost play, and building a cautious case in Theobald's defence. It is possible that in taking pot-shots at specific lines in *Double Falsehood*, as he does twice in *Peri Bathous: or, Martinus Scriblerus His Treatise on the Art of Sinking in Poetry*, first published in March 1728, Pope was instead attacking some well-disguised lines by Shakespeare.

In 1725, Pope's edition had exhibited a dismissive attitude to the theatre that was not allowed to pass without criticism. The Elizabethan audience was 'generally composed of the meaner sort of people', he had found, so it followed that Shakespeare had to write about them from time to time: 'Yet even in these, our author's wit buoys up, and is born above his subject...like some prince of a romance in the disguise of a shepherd or peasant.'[34] The actors, meanwhile, knew 'no rule but that of pleasing the present humour, and complying with the wit in fashion', and are 'just such judges of what is right, as tailors are of what is graceful'. Shakespeare's faults may therefore be ascribed to this unfortunate association.[35] Although it has received less critical attention than the clash between Pope and Theobald, in redeeming Shakespeare, Pope seeks to remove his *Works* from the theatrical context altogether, another key battle for eighteenth-century Shakespearians.

*An Answer to Mr. Pope's Preface to Shakespeare...Being a Vindication of the Old Actors who were the Publishers and Performers of the Author's Plays* (1729), attributed on the title page to a 'strolling player', later supposed to be a certain John Roberts, offers a defence of the stage, fought on several fronts. In response to Pope's comparison between actors and tailors, he writes:

...the difference of judgment between the poet and the player, is no more than betwixt one tailor who cuts out the cloth according to rule and measure, and t'other that makes it up, and fits it to the body, according to that cutting out.[36]

Quoting Pope's compliments to the modern '*Gentlemen of the stage*' who enjoy 'the familiar conversation of our nobility, and an *intimacy*

(not to say dearness) with people of the first Condition' and denigra-
tion of the '*mere* players' of Shakespeare's day, he proceeds to list
thirteen of the most prominent men of the Elizabethan and Jacobean
theatre (reclaiming a couple of playwrights as players along the way,
and vice versa), including: Edward Alleyn, Robert Armin ('I find he
made a shift to appear as an *author*...'), Richard Burbage, Nathaniel
Field ('he was very much esteemed by Chapman, and other...con-
temporary writers'), Thomas Heywood ('This *actor* was the most
voluminous *author*'), William Kempe ('the PINKETHMAN of
that age', comparing Shakespeare's clown with William Pinkethman,
a greatly admired comic actor of the late seventeenth century), and
Christopher Marlowe ('He trod the stage with applause, both from
Q. *Elizabeth* and K. *James*'; applause from the latter is quite an
achievement, given that Marlowe died in 1593).[37]

The author of *An Answer* then digresses to remark on Theobald's
emendation of that 'Table of green Fields' to offer an alternative
suggestion that maybe the names of two players have been inserted
by accident—it is an instruction for Green and Field to 'strike'
the table ('TABLE OFF'). Failing that, he prefers Theobald's
emendation to Pope's explanation of the line, and endorses Theobald
as being a gentleman of superior 'capacity...to every *former editor*'.[38] But
the alternative emendation is a strikingly theatrical one, which would
never have occurred to Pope and apparently did not occur to Theobald
either, despite his first-hand experience of the theatre.

Finally, *An Answer to Mr. Pope's Preface to Shakespeare* suggests that
'*Two* large *Chests* full of this GREAT MAN's *loose papers* and *manuscripts*' had been 'carelessly scattered and thrown about' by a Warwick
baker, 'till they were all consumed in the general fire and destruction
of that town', which prompts the chimerical thought of lost plays and
a vision of Shakespeare's later life:

These [the contents of the two chests] were perhaps the labours of his retired
years, which he spent at his native *Stratford*, in a calm retreat from the stage,
from town and business: As his judgment with his years advanced, and as he
wrote not here, for pecuniary advantage or popular applause, no doubt but
these were his *superior productions*, and the want of them, therefore much
more to be deplored![39]

And just as deplorable would be the fate of these 'purer works' if they had 'escaped the flames', only to fall into the hands of Shakespeare's 'native neighbours', on whose ineptitude Roberts blames the 'notoriously false spelt' inscription for Shakespeare's grave. The locals are to blame for that, just as the printers are to blame for the 'imperfections of the press'.[40] So the actors are in the clear there, too.

## United in Newtonianism?

On the basis of their politics, literary practices, and editorial approaches, then, Pope and Theobald would seem to be absolute opposites, and bound to edit Shakespeare in completely different ways. The intriguing suggestion comes from Gefen Ben-On Santor, however, that both editors belong to a culture of 'Newtonianism' in the eighteenth century—beyond a fascination with the genius of Isaac Newton himself, that is, and his achievements in so many aspects of 'natural philosophy', his example inspired a 'broad search for truth', for the laws of Nature, not least the 'hidden laws of human nature'. This, Santor argues, has been a 'missing context' for the study of Shakespeare's plays in the period.[41] And I wonder if the relevance of Newton to the history of Shakespeare's reception has been disguised somewhat by the deceptive continuity between eighteenth-century praise for Shakespeare the poet of Nature and the invocations that predate the birth of Newton himself.

Editors and critics were not simply custodians of old plays but quasi-Newtonian investigators into the world around them, via the medium of Shakespeare. Santor duly points out the contrast between modern praise for Shakespeare's 'linguistic and theatrical skill' and the sense that emerges from the prefaces written by Shakespeare's eighteenth-century editors of the principal reason for admiring him being his 'incomparable understanding of the hidden principles of human behaviour'.[42] 'Knowledge of human nature', Theobald writes, is 'our author's masterpiece.'[43] Pope had preceded him: '*Homer* himself drew not his art so immediately from the fountains of Nature. . . . The Poetry of *Shakespeare* was inspiration indeed: he is not so much an imitator, as an instrument, of Nature; and 'tis not so just to say that he speaks from her, as that she speaks thro' him.'[44]

This reading also accounts for the rivals' consistent praise for Shakespeare's diverse characters ('What draughts of Nature! What variety of originals, and how differing each from the other!' 'every single character in *Shakespeare* is as much an individual, as those in life itself ').[45] This variety is evidence of his 'close engagement with the particular details of reality' that are the clues to 'underlying principles'; they might be regarded as 'requisites for true knowledge'.[46] This approach can be profitably read alongside older essays by Brian Vickers and John Bligh that between them trace the emergence of 'character criticism' out of 'character study'—older habits of commenting on characters as part of a wider-ranging, Aristotelian discourse on dramatic writing, and how they gave way, in the last quarter of the eighteenth century, according to Vickers, to a newfound and exclusive interest in character, resulting in a spate of 'essays and whole books...devoted to individual characters, and those alone'.[47]

The conclusion to Santor's argument is that while Pope and Theobald are remembered as 'opponents', it is possible to see affinities between their approaches 'on a basic conceptual level'.[48] While Theobald's practice as an editor might be seen as more obviously 'scientific', with his methodical and cautious approach, Pope's can be viewed in the same light once it is accepted that he is serious about taking the principle of taste that guides him to make his heavier interventions to the text to be a 'truth-revealing mechanism':

In today's conceptual universe, taste is a subjective term, but in eighteenth-century culture people did not oppose taste to objective truth to the extent we do today; and the scientific spirit of the period involved a quest to define aesthetic value objectively. . . . In the same way that Newton had a special connection with nature, Pope believed that his own taste and natural poetic talent afforded him privileged access to the hidden truth of Shakespeare. While that conviction fails to exonerate Pope from the charge of sloppy editing, the rhetoric of truth and objectivity that he employs is not a strategy of deception; instead, it reflects methodological self-consciousness that links Pope's understanding of editing to the scientific discourses of his age.[49]

There are objections one could make to this argument—that it too easily lumps all mid-century editors together, with Pope and Theobald as the extreme examples of antithetical tendencies, or that Theobald's approach perhaps has intellectual roots that are not exactly Newtonian but have a related source in the textual scholarship of Newton's friend Richard Bentley. But Santor's suggestion is an intriguing one, not only as an attempt to reconcile these two antagonists but as an exercise in trying to place them in the contemporary intellectual scene. Seeing Theobald's edition in this context perhaps suggests an explanation for what has always seemed an odd inconsistency on his part: his use of a second edition of Pope's *Works of Shakespeare* as the basis of his own text.

For Peter Seary, it seems that the decision to use the 1728 text could have been imposed on Theobald by the Tonsons, as they sought to extend the duration of their rights to Shakespeare's plays—as editor, he was fulfilling a legal function for them by renewing their claim to the work of his immediate predecessor, who happened to be Pope.[50] Andrew Murphy, in *Shakespeare in Print*, instead follows Simon Jarvis in putting down this choice of text to 'a certain essential lack of clarity' in Theobald's approach to textual criticism, perhaps deriving from his 'general feeling of respect for inherited notions of the centrality of the "received" text (i.e., the text moulded by and inherited from the editorial tradition)'.[51] Not that these are mutually exclusive propositions: Theobald could have respected the received text and therefore have had no qualms about meeting the booksellers' requirements. And it should be added that Theobald had already made himself part of that tradition with the corrections from *Shakespeare Restored* that Pope adopted for the second edition.

Murphy also notes Thomas Lounsbury's view that Theobald respected Pope's 'unassailable supremacy as a master of verse, and in the propriety of applying his superior skill to the rectification of Shakespeare's text',[52] and there is therefore a distinction to be made between different ways in which Theobald treated Pope's text, since, despite his general resistance to emendations unfounded on quarto or folio readings, and his protests about the omission of words for the sake of metre (something that Rowe had done as well as Pope), Theobald could retain Pope's transpositions and expansions of words unless they clashed with his sense of the Shakespearian pronunciation of words such as 'hour' or 'fire':

It was the meter for which [Pope] specially cared, not the matter.... In the text of Shakespeare, as it has come down to us, there are defective lines, there are redundant lines, there are lines that do not read smoothly. It was an object which Pope kept steadily in view to remove these irregularities, to reduce everything to the measured monotony of eighteenth-century versification. To bring about this result, words were inserted in the verse, words were thrown out, or the order of words was changed. To these three classes belonged the vast majority of Pope's emendations. Nor were they few in the number. On the contrary, they mounted into the thousands.[53]

Lounsbury offers a useful test case in *The Text of Shakespeare*, in an efficient statistical comparison between the successive texts of *Measure for Measure*. He finds that Pope removed a total of fifty words from the play; Theobald restored twenty-nine of them. Pope made fifty-seven 'substitutions' of one word for another; Theobald retained thirty-eight. But when Pope 'transposed' six words, Theobald retained four of those transpositions; and when Pope 'contracted or expanded' seventeen 'words or syllables', Theobald allowed all but one of these changes to stand.[54] The transpositions, contractions, and expansions may be minute changes, but they also contribute to the general smoothing out of the text Pope inherited from Rowe and Hughes. Lounsbury offers the striking example of Isabella's lines informing the Duke of her appointment to meet Angelo in his garden, as printed by Rowe:

> There have I made my promise, upon the
> Heavy middle of the night, to call upon him.[55]

Theobald acknowledges Pope has improved this (in his first edition as well as his second):

> There on the heavy middle of the night
> Have I my promise made to call upon him.[56]

In silently following Pope in imposing such expressions of his 'passion for mechanical regularity', as Lounsbury calls it,[57] on the play texts, Theobald was ensuring that Shakespeare would remain a prescient master of eighteenth-century versification in the new edition of 1733, as he had been in Rowe's edition and Pope's. But Theobald's passivity on this score, if that was what it was, might not be inconsistent with a belief in taste as a guide to 'objective truth', as suggested by Santor.

Pope's metrical alterations to Shakespeare were not the subject of the main thrust of Theobald's criticisms, so it may be that Theobald could have thought that 'taste and natural poetic talent' had indeed led his rival to the 'hidden truth' of Shakespeare. Theobald, that is to say, could benefit from Pope's skill at versification in his own edition just as Pope had (albeit unwillingly) benefitted from *Shakespeare Restored*; in a 'Newtonian' view of these seemingly incompatible approaches to textual editing, there may be an affinity between historically informed emendation and a modern poet's regularizing of Shakespeare's verse. Theobald announces in his preface that he has 'religiously adhered to' the 'genuine text' of Shakespeare, in order to show up the 'numerous faults and blemishes' that are 'purely his own', as well as the beauties.[58] But the 1733 text of Shakespeare was at least as much a collaboration between enemies with complementary talents as it was a faults-and-all 'restoration'.

In the wake of Pope and Theobald's efforts to produce the definitive edition of Shakespeare's *Works* came many more, following a similar pattern of interaction and 'improvement'. The 1740s brought the editions (and the bickering) of Hanmer and Warburton. There was Johnson's ambitious proposal and the gradual labours of Edward Capell. As with the rival editions of Pope and Theobald, however, it seems that much of this activity was driven by conflicting urges that would find alternative forms of expression: in the alteration for performance, the critical essay, the anthology, the work of reference. And if one of those urges was to venerate Shakespeare, then, as the following chapter suggests, it would soon be expressing itself in marble, too—with a little help from Pope and his friends.

# Macklin's Shylock, Shakespeare's Statue

This is the Jew
Which Shakespeare drew.

(Attributed to Alexander Pope.)

'What a number of poets are reposited beneath this noble structure!' said I—'by their own merits entitled to a resting-place in this sacred building, consecrated to the royal, illustrious, great, and celebrated dead! What multitudes are indiscriminately mixed beneath the earth we tread! They who were once rivals for fame, are now no longer so. Ambition has here dropt her plume. Pride, folly, and enmity are no more. Beauty has here ended her triumph...'

(Elizabeth Bonhote, *The Rambles of Mr. Frankly*)[1]

It was on 14 February 1741, that the actor Charles Macklin 'restored to its native lustre' the character of Shylock in *The Merchant of Venice*.[2] In both that seven-word rhyme sometimes attributed to Alexander Pope and the biographies that appeared not long after Macklin's death in 1797 (possibly his ninety-eighth or ninety-ninth year), the performance could be acclaimed as a watershed in theatrical history. In 1701, George Granville, Lord Lansdowne, had turned *The Merchant of Venice* into *The Jew of Venice*, a vehicle for the comic talents of Thomas Doggett. Unlike its contemporary, Cibber's *Richard III*, this would not still be an acceptable alteration in a hundred years' time. Francis Aspry Congreve, one of those biographers of

Macklin, could write of the 'comic' Shylock: 'we are prompted to laughter instead of detestation'; 'the alterations rather lessen than improve the beauty and effect of the matchless original'; and the 'musical masque...profusely decorated with dancing and singing' would surely have conspired to 'disgrace the order of our modern theatres'.[3] Never mind that Granville's *Jew of Venice* was hardly a repertory piece, with only one performance in the five seasons before Macklin's revival[4]—the task of restoring Shakespeare's 'Jew' here takes on a kind of moral, patriotic lustre of its own. Pope, or whoever came up with that apparently impromptu rhyme, must have remembered their reading in Rowe's edition of Shakespeare's *Works*, when Granville's adaptation was a fresher memory:

> ...though we have seen that play received and acted as a comedy, and the part of the *Jew* performed by an excellent comedian, yet I cannot but think it was designed tragically by the author. There appears in it such a deadly spirit of revenge, such a savage fierceness and fellness, and such a bloody designation of cruelty and mischief, as cannot agree either with the style or characters of comedy.[5]

What Shakespeare 'designed' and what Shakespeare 'drew' were therefore what the audience saw on 14 February, and Macklin's interpretation of Shylock was to be portrayed in this approving light. It is the first of three classic reasons why 1741 is often portrayed as a turning point in Shakespeare's eighteenth-century afterlife—the other two being the installation of a statue of Shakespeare in Westminster Abbey, in Poets' Corner, and the London stage debut, during the following season, of Macklin's friend—friend for the time being, at least—David Garrick. Was this the beginning of a new, monumentally Shakespearian age? What had come before?

As his barrister-friend and biographer William Cooke retold the story, after Macklin's death, the Irish actor could claim a heroic, individual role in rescuing Shakespeare, and in particular Shylock, from 'broad farce':

> ...the celebrated Doggett performed the *Jew* almost in the style of broad farce. Macklin saw this part with other eyes; and, very much to the credit of his taste and understanding, as well as a proper estimation of his own powers, he found he could build a reputation by reviving the original of Shakespeare, and playing the character of Shylock in a different manner. The attempt

was arduous, and subject to many miscarriages, and in particular to public prejudice; but a consciousness of being right will generally give great confidence—Macklin felt this consciousness, and was determined on the trial.[6]

Cooke's account of this episode is fascinating and sometimes even credible, but, as Arthur H. Scouten later proved, both Macklin and Garrick were in fact lucky to be able to take advantage of a relatively new but firmly established taste for Shakespeare in London's theatres—an appreciative spirit that seems to have influenced the campaign for a Shakespeare monument, too. Scouten, taking a statistical approach to the available data for theatrical performances at all London theatres during the first half of the eighteenth century, shows that only a few of Shakespeare's plays had not been staged in London during the decade prior to Garrick's debut, the 1730s—and that actually fewer plays by Shakespeare were stock pieces at the end of Garrick's time as manager of Drury Lane than at the beginning. How he went from having twenty-two Shakespeare plays in the repertory in 1747 to thirteen by 1776, yet still maintained a reputation as the pre-eminent Shakespearian actor of his day is a question for the next chapter.

Macklin's 'arduous' attempt to revive *The Merchant of Venice* may be better understood in the context of the season to which it belonged, 1740–1. As information presented by Robert D. Hume makes clear, this was a season when a steep rise took place in advertising a play as Shakespeare's, suggesting that it had suddenly become a valuable piece of information.[7] Macklin and his manager at Drury Lane, Charles Fleetwood, had already overseen revivals of *As You Like It* (20 December 1740) and *Twelfth Night* (15 January 1741), while at Goodman's Fields, Henry Giffard revived *The Winter's Tale* (on the same night as Drury Lane's *Twelfth Night*) and *All's Well That Ends Well* (17 March 1741). Not long after Garrick's debut as Richard III at Goodman's Fields the following season, Macklin and Fleetwood would revive *The Comedy of Errors* (11 November 1741).[8]

Here were a few comedies—albeit, like *The Merchant of Venice*, comedies with more than a hint of tragedy about them—to complement the tragedies and histories that were already stock pieces at Drury Lane, as well as *The Merry Wives of Windsor* and *Much Ado about Nothing*. 'The [Drury Lane] company performed little but

Shakespeare for more than two months (unprecedented in the recorded history of the British theatre)', Hume observes of this period, 'and touted his name for all it was worth'. Goodman's Fields 'had not bothered' to mention Shakespeare's name in its earlier advertisements; now 'written by Shakespeare' seemed to be something worth mentioning. For both theatres, that is, Shakespeare had become a means for competing with Covent Garden's latest attraction: 'Peg Woffington's legs in breeches-roles'[9] (both roles were in plays by George Farquhar: Silvia in *The Recruiting Officer* and Sir Harry Wildair in *The Constant Couple*).

Commercial competition, then, is one reason why Fleetwood, who increasingly relied on Macklin to manage the artistic side of the business,[10] was happy for him to stage *The Merchant of Venice*, as Cooke says, 'merely as a revived piece, which might bring money to the treasury'. If the production seemed to have curiosity value, it was not because Shakespeare was an unknown name; and those who apparently went to Fleetwood to complain about Macklin's intended approach to the role of Shylock ('His best friends shook their heads at the attempt; whilst his rivals chuckled in secret'), prompting the manager to ask the actor to 'give up the part', missed the point. Macklin clearly relished the 'opportunity' to make the part his own, to recover Shakespeare's play—and he had recent experience of trying to revive similarly complex, serious Shakespearian comedies at Drury Lane.[11] *The Merchant of Venice* was duly advertised as being a comedy 'never acted there before' and 'written by Shakespeare'.[12]

## Before 1741

During the 1720s and 1730s, while Pope and Theobald were at war over Shakespeare's plays in collected form, Shakespeare had made numerous appearances in periodicals, pamphlets (including the anonymous *Some Remarks on the Tragedy of Hamlet, Prince of Denmark*, 1736), and even in William Hogarth's pioneering paintings inspired by *The Tempest* (Ferdinand's first sight of Miranda) and *2 Henry IV* (Falstaff inspecting his troops).[13] Assuming a readership deeply familiar with *Othello*, John Hervey had couched an attack on Sir Robert Walpole, Britain's first 'prime minister', as *Iago Displayed* in 1731. In 1734, the bookseller Robert Walker had declared war on the Tonsons by issuing a series of cheap editions of Shakespeare's plays, to which the Tonsons had responded by issuing their own copies—with statements declaring the invalidity of their rivals' products. Walker began to trade under the sign of Shakespeare's Head in several locations, including one on the Strand, not far from the Tonsons. This intense combat over the Shakespeare 'brand' flooded the market with cheap reprints, offering readers rival versions of the whole range of Shakespeare's work (which then still included apocryphal plays such as *Locrine* and *The London Prodigal*). There are signs of discontent with established styles of performance, too. In *The Prompter*, Aaron Hill criticized the actress Sarah Thurmond (whose major Shakespearian roles had included Desdemona, Lady Macduff, and Portia in *The Jew of Venice*) for 'whining out good verses, in a drawl so unpleasantly extended'.[14] The attacks on Cibber's acting by Hill and others have been quoted already, in the first chapter.

Against these scattered signs of interest in Shakespeare, however, might be set some contrary evidence from the records of theatrical activity in London over the same period. In his examination of the surviving account books for John Rich's company, during the 1720s and the early 1730s, Paul Sawyer reaches the conclusion that demand for Shakespeare's plays in performance was actually declining. Excluding benefit nights (when the most important factor was perhaps performers' individual popularity and personal ability to sell tickets) and afterpieces (such as *The Cobbler of Preston*, abridged by Christopher Bullock from the induction to *The Taming of the Shrew*), Sawyer finds that over a run of thirteen seasons, there were 142 performances of Shakespeare's plays alone, in virtually original form or as altered by Tate, Cibber et al.; the average proceeds of £37 per performance were slightly outdone by the £40 taken, on average, by non-Shakespearian plays presented alone over the same period. When a Shakespeare play shared the bill with a pantomime at Lincoln's Inn Fields (for which the price of entry went up), things improved considerably, and the takings increased by 25 per cent.

Thanks largely to the 'extraordinary success' of *The Beggar's Opera* by John Gay (of which more shortly), ballad operas could claim average takings of £77 per night; other non-Shakespearian nights earned £64. When Shakespeare was on the bill, it was most often in the comic form of *The Merry Wives of Windsor*, with James Quin giving his farcical Falstaff, as the following table shows:

| Play | Total number of (non-benefit) performances |
|------|:--:|
| *The Merry Wives of Windsor* | 76 |
| *King Lear* (Tate) | 28 |
| *Measure for Measure* | 27 |
| *1 Henry IV* | 27 |
| *Macbeth* (Davenant) | 26 |
| *Hamlet* | 26 |

The other Shakespearian plays staged by Rich's company over this period were *Othello*, *Julius Caesar*, *Henry VIII*, *Much Ado about Nothing*, *Coriolanus*, *The Jew of Venice* (Granville's adaptation of *The Merchant of Venice*), *Richard III* (Cibber's version), *Troilus and Cressida* (Dryden's version), and *Titus Andronicus* (Ravenscroft's version)—fifteen in total, six of them adaptations, plus a couple more that, for various reasons, fall outside Sawyer's remit. It seems that Rich saw the advantage in staging old plays that did not come with the cost of paying for authors' nights; actors liked them, and they did not absolutely demand heavy investment in new props, costumes, or scenery. But he had an understandable preference for the more profitable alternatives: over this period, the number of Shakespearian performances dropped from twenty-three nights in 1720–1 to an average of twelve in later seasons.[15]

Such figures have to be treated cautiously.[16] Although Sawyer excludes actors' benefit nights from his analysis, there were other factors that contributed to the popularity of Shakespeare's plays in this period, and show that any intrinsic qualities those plays might have, or attraction that Shakespeare's name might have for regular theatregoers, cannot easily be set apart from outside influences.

Quin's presence in Rich's company explains the frequency with which *Merry Wives* was performed. But there was also a formidable Falstaff at Drury Lane, John Harper, and the generally stronger cast there could apparently expect to attract 'crowded audiences'. Such competition did not depend primarily on the power of Shakespeare's name to draw a crowd, but on the combination of particular performers and in particular roles. 'Comparisons will always be made when capital characters are exhibited at the same time at different theatres', Benjamin Victor writes in his *History of the Theatres of London and Dublin*. Due to that generally superior attraction of Drury Lane, Quin's rival as Falstaff, the 'jolly, facetious, low-comedian' Harper, was 'more seen . . . though less admired', and some did prefer him in the part. Although he lacked 'wanted the marking eye, and some other judicious strokes of *Quin*, yet he had what *Quin* at that time wanted, *that jollity and natural propensity to excite laughter*, which *Shakespeare* has apparently given to *Falstaff*'.[17] (Harper also has the distinction of having been arrested in costume as Falstaff, at the Haymarket, on 12 November 1733, under the Vagrant Act of 1713, by one of the patentees of Drury Lane, John Highmore; Falstaff was therefore taken to Bridewell prison, although he was later released when it was proven that he was no vagrant.)[18]

Perhaps it was on account of this theatrical competition that Hogarth painted Falstaff examining his recruits, which seems to draw on Harper's performance and contemporary stage production even as it adds a few telling embellishments (the painting-within-a-painting, for example, contrasting the superhuman figure of 'Gloucester Giant' with Falstaff's less impressive specimens). A reading of Hogarth's painting suggests, furthermore, another reason for the popularity of Falstaff on stage. In the figure of the fat, corrupt knight, for his 'neglect of the British army and for the vast fortune he amassed through corrupt practices', it satirizes Walpole, who is once again the target of a 'Shakespearian' attack, aligning him with a character who is, at the end of the play, dismissed by the new king.[19]

The primary motive for staging *Merry Wives* and the *Henry IV* plays cannot be speculated into existence backwards, as it were, via Hogarth's idiosyncratic re-creation of a single scene. But some might have felt the hope for Walpole's dismissal was dynamically expressed in the spectacular production of *Henry VIII* that Drury Lane mounted to celebrate the accession of George II, following his coronation on 11 October 1727. Here is a clearer case of external factors shaping theatrical production: as George immediately faced calls for him to get rid of Walpole,[20] *Henry VIII* became the hit of the new season; the King, Queen, the Princess Royal, and Princess Caroline all attended a performance, complete with an enactment of the 'magnificent coronation of Queen Anna Bullen', within a month of George's own coronation. They would therefore have seen, played out for them, a scene in which a strong English monarch deprives an over-powerful minister, Cardinal Wolsey, of his power. With the spectacle of the stage-coronation contributing greatly to its attraction, this timely *Henry VIII* continued to draw 'numerous audiences'—'which is owing to the excellency of the performance, and the extraordinary grandeur of the decorations', according to the *Daily Post*—while Rich struggled to find an answer. But it is interesting to see what he turned to, in vain: a low version of Shakespeare, in the form of *The Jew of Venice*; Quin in *Macbeth*, which did even worse than *The Jew of Venice*; and a topical pantomime, *Harlequin Anna Bullen*.[21] Yet Drury Lane's triumph would have unexpected repercussions for the coming decade.

### From *The Beggar's Opera* to the Licensing Act

Giffard, Macklin, and Fleetwood had embarked on their theatrical careers in the decades preceding the Licensing Act of 1737—the much-despised Walpole's enduring legacy to English theatre. There was already, in the 1730s, a campaign to curb the theatre's excesses (as John Loftis stresses in *The Politics of Drama in Augustan England*, 'the Act...gave legal reality to the recommendations of a long series of commentators on theatrical affairs'), dating back to the Collier controversy of the late 1690s. Yet it was only under 'strong provocation' that Walpole took the decisive action.[22]

Colley Cibber and his fellow managers at Drury Lane had known how to respond when the writer John Gay brought them an odd play for production—'too out-of-the-way, too experimental, too nonstandard for commercial success', as Winton guesses they might have seen it[23]—and refused it. The result was that while Drury Lane enjoyed its moment of glory (*Henry VIII*) and then an immodest encore (Cibber's alteration of *The Provoked Husband* by Vanbrugh, which had a run of twenty-eight successive nights), Gay took his new 'what'd'ye call it' (you can call it a ballad opera) to Rich. It opened at Lincoln's Inn Fields on 29 January 1728, and would run for an unprecedented sixty-two consecutive nights.

This was in large measure due to its 'dazzling originality'[24]—its innovative form, a brilliant travesty of Italian opera combined with a 'low' setting and familiar melodies. In its setting alone, in London's criminal underworld, it commented abrasively on the political machinations of the Whig faction in power since the South Sea Bubble—including both Walpole and his principal political ally, Charles, Viscount Townshend—and it provided Walpole's opponents with an enduring means of ridiculing them. 'Bob Booty' stuck as a name for Walpole himself. The highwayman Macheath's involvement in a love triangle with Polly Peachum and Lucy Lockit, as well as his general pursuit of 'free-hearted ladies', echoed the rumours about Walpole's private life. (Macheath, incidentally, alludes to *Twelfth Night*—'If music be the food, play on'—as he settles into the company of Jenny Diver, Betty Doxy, Mrs Slammekin et al.)[25] And the scene that finds the 'fence' and thief-taker Peachum and the Newgate jailer Lockit at one another's throats seemed to sum up the vexed relationship between Walpole and Townshend all too well ('like great statesmen, we encourage those who betray their friends . . .').[26]

Gay's victim must have put on an impressive show of equanimity if he really did attend a performance of *The Beggar's Opera* in its first season. During the performance, Macklin would later tell Cooke, Walpole became conscious of being the object of the audience's attention as Lockit sang, in the middle of that sharp scene with Peachum: 'When you censure the age, | Be cautious and sage, | Lest the courtiers offended should be . . .'[27] Drawing on his 'fund of good humour', however, Walpole apparently managed to encore the song himself; he then 'joined in the general applause', and earned himself 'a general huzza from all parts of the house'.[28]

Regardless of the truth of that sporting story, it was an ill omen for the theatre of the future that, as Macklin also recollected, Walpole 'never could with any satisfaction be present at [a performance of *The Beggar's Opera*], on account of the many allusions which the audience thought referred to his character'.[29] In the short term, the business was flourishing, thanks to *The Beggar's Opera* and another success of the same year, *The Provoked Husband* (Cibber had turned down *The Beggar's Opera*, incidentally, but, with this consolation prize, he still managed to make Drury Lane 'more money . . . than any work produced there over the previous 50 years').[30] A city that could support a season including such long runs of single plays, as London did in the 1727–8 season, was ripe for more. Within a couple of seasons, there were five theatre companies in operation, where before there had been only two. Through subscriptions (not all of which were realized) and the profits from *The Beggar's Opera*, Rich could open a glorious new theatre in Covent Garden in 1732.

The relatively new genre of pantomime, meanwhile, as devised by Rich and Theobald, continued to thrive, despite the hostility of the critics. The 1730s would prove to be a time of expansion and experimentation all round: 'the drama in the 1730's was still the most popular form of literature, and the London audiences were being continually regaled with new performances of all sorts, including not only the legitimate forms of tragedy, comedy, and farce, but also pantomimes, operas, and nondescript entertainments'.[31] In the summer of 1731, George Lillo provided Drury Lane with 'almost a new species of tragedy', a pathetic tragedy about a London apprentice, a bourgeois counterpart to Gay's (political) criminals, *The London Merchant, or, The History of George Barnwell*, that would remain a fixture on the London stage, traditionally being performed on an apprentices' holiday, every 27 December, until well into the 1800s. Giffard ran his company at Goodman's Fields from 1731 onwards (with a season at Lincoln's Inn Fields), and made Shakespeare's plays a significant element in his repertory.[32]

Henry Fielding, meanwhile, after courting Walpole as a patron for several years, switched sides, and by 1736, had become a dangerously popular voice for the opposition. Fielding operated 'The Great Mogul's Company of Comedians' out of the Little Theatre in the Haymarket—which Eliza Haywood, the novelist and sometime member of Fielding's company, would later describe as 'F—g's scandal shop': 'because he frequently exhibited there certain drolls, or, more properly, invectives against the ministry'. Her imputation there is that, besides financial profit, Fielding also hoped that his theatrical activities would secure him some official post from 'those whom he had abused, in order to silence his dramatic talent'.[33] With *Pasquin* in March 1736, he certainly scored a hit comparable to *The Beggar's Opera*: it ran for more than sixty performances, and played blatantly on the theme of political corruption.

Walpole's solution, and revenge, was the Licensing Act of 1737. With this legislation, passed under highly suspicious circumstances, he inaugurated a new age of theatrical censorship, in which all new plays would have to be submitted to the Lord Chamberlain's office for approval and possibly abridgement. It also re-established Drury Lane and Covent Garden as the only two theatres which could legitimately perform spoken drama. Giffard and others would find ingenious ways around the Act, but its implications for the performance of Shakespeare were clear: 'From this point onwards his plays become safe choices, low-risk theatre, vehicles in which each new performer can make (or lose) a reputation.'[34]

It helped that many Shakespeare plays were already in the repertoire, but if there were more to revive, like *The Merchant of Venice*, now was the time to revive them; and they could be cost-effective, next to the expense of giving a living playwright a benefit on every third night of a successful run. Relatively few new plays were banned outright, but the two patent theatres had every encouragement to play it safe and protect their privileges. The damage was really done, as Loftis argues, by the limitation on the number of theatres rather than the licensing side of things. Now Fleetwood at Drury Lane and Rich at Covent Garden had their pick of both experienced dramatists and ambitious young tyros. Fleetwood was losing interest, and Rich was a Harlequin, so, from the dramatists' point of view, this was not exactly good news.[35] With its 'inhibiting effect' on new drama, the Act was an important contributing factor to the Shakespeare 'revolution' of 1740–1—the logical, albeit abrupt culmination of developments in the 1730s—and, for Loftis, it arrested English drama's long-term 'movement away from formalization in plots, characterization, and dialogue', and towards a more 'novelistic' complexity.[36] Assuming demand for that mature mode of dramatic writing did not entirely mutate into a demand for novels, its continued existence after 1737 might well be answered by revivals such as *The Merchant of Venice*, featuring the restored, serious Shylock of Macklin.

The explosion of 1741 had been a long time in the making—and depending on which theatre historian you ask, it might be better described as the continuation of a process begun in the mid-1730s by a group of specific theatregoers. Around 1736, a group of women who became known as the Shakespeare Ladies Club 'began a movement which restored many of Shakespeare's neglected plays to the boards, increased the frequency with which many of the familiar ones were presented, brought his works a great deal of publicity in an exceedingly short time, and became a model to later groups which similarly wished to improve the stage'.[37] Emmett L. Avery had to admit that he had been unable to find out who any of them were. But he could point to evidence of 'Shakespeare's Ladies' persuading the theatres to revive, for example, *Cymbeline* for the first time since 1720, and *King John* for the first time in the eighteenth century. In January 1737, every performance of a Shakespeare play bar one, a royal command performance of *Hamlet*, was 'at the desire of several ladies of quality', according to the playbills. Over a year later, the Shakespeare Ladies Club was still active, and it could be mentioned in a prologue in August 1738 as a 'sacred band, determined, wise, and good', who 'strove to wake, by Shakespeare's nervous lays, | The manly genius of Eliza's days'.[38]

Only in 1992, in *The Making of the National Poet*, did Michael Dobson offer the identities of three members of the Club: Susanna Ashley-Cooper, Countess of Shaftesbury (making her the wife of one of Walpole's opponents), Mary Cowper (who wrote a poem on 'the Revival of Shakespeare's Plays by the Ladies in 1738'), and the writer Elizabeth Boyd,[39] with Fiona Ritchie subsequently suggesting that, rather than an 'official club with a distinct body of members', these ladies formed 'a more fluid organization with a key core of supporters but open to the participation of other female playgoers who supported their aims'.[40] Ritchie also suggests, with qualifications, that the 'chronicle plays' were in demand, and quotes the striking statistic that out of thirty-four performances of Shakespeare at Covent Garden, in the 1737–8 season, twenty-four were of the histories, including *Richard II* and *Henry V* (both claimed to be 'not acted these forty years'), and *1 Henry VI* ('not acted these fifty years'). It was stressed that the *2 Henry IV* to be acted on 16 February 1738, 'at the desire of several ladies of quality', was 'the genuine play of Shakespeare, and not that altered by Mr Betterton, and so frequently acted at the other theatre'.[41] Not long before Garrick, that is, nor Macklin's Shylock, the 'genuine' Shakespeare was making himself useful in the competition between theatres.

Something that Dobson and Ritchie both emphasize, in different ways, is that this female campaign to rescue 'the admirable, yet almost forgotten Shakespeare', as Haywood called him, had ramifications beyond the theatre. 'They have generously contributed to raise a monument to his memory', Haywood wrote of the Shakespeare Ladies Club.[42] Elizabeth Boyd, in her play *Don Sancho: or, The Students' Whim*, imagines a statue appearing instead of Shakespeare's ghost, to take its place in a literary Temple of British Worthies.[43] Something of this nature was indeed soon to take place.

## Shakespeare in Poets' Corner

Barely a fortnight before Macklin's night of triumph at Drury Lane, a different venue had witnessed a different kind of triumph: the installation of a statue of Shakespeare, designed by William Kent and executed by Peter Scheemakers, in Westminster Abbey on 29 January 1741. 'Arguably', Ritchie argues, 'the commissioning of this monument was only possible or desirable as a result of the efforts of the Shakespeare Ladies in popularizing Shakespeare in the contemporary theatre'.[44] But this had also been a campaign in which Pope, the Earl of Burlington, and Dr Richard Mead, as well as the Shakespeare Ladies Club, had apparently played leading roles, while both Fleetwood (with a performance of *Julius Caesar* on 28 April 1738) and John Rich (with a performance of *Hamlet* on 10 April 1739) had participated in the fund-raising process, too. The editors of Garrick's correspondence suggest that he was involved, before his stage career had taken off, although they give no source for this information.[45] As far as Shakespeare's reputation was concerned, the campaign was the grandest public gesture yet made towards affirming his central place in the English canon, although the irony is that, if Theobald was being serious in his dedication to *Shakespeare Restored* (1727), it was his friend and employer, the Harlequin, Rich, who had first raised the idea, long before anything was actually done about it:

... however you may have been a sinner against SHAKESPEARE, you are not an impenitent one. And as King *Henry* IV erected a chapel to expiate the injuries which he had done to his predecessor, King *Richard*; so, the Town at least say, you intend to appease the *Manes* [i.e., the soul] of our POET by *erecting* a MONUMENT to him. Go on in that pious, that reputable intention; and, while the taste of the public demands it of you, continue to sacrifice fresh *pantomimes* to his memory; when their palates alter, convince them that you are provided to entertain them with an elegance suitable to their expectations.[46]

Theobald's allusion to the relationship between the historical Richard II and Henry IV is apt: as discussed in the previous chapter, his adaptation of *Richard II* had not proved popular, unlike the pantomimes he devised for Rich. It was not only Rich who needed to appease Shakespeare's spirit by erecting a monument to him. In the end, however, it was through a collective effort that, in the south transept of the Abbey, known already as Poets' Corner, a statue of Shakespeare assumed a place of honour among monuments to his fellow English writers—Chaucer, Spenser, Cowley, and Dryden were among the poets already buried there.

Until the early eighteenth century, the development of Poets' Corner as a posthumous clustering of illustrious names had been a haphazard affair. Chaucer had been buried there, for example, for non-literary reasons, because he was a former Clerk of Works and an Abbey tenant; a sixteenth-century admirer had him moved to a tomb that was grander than the original in 1556.[47] Spenser had apparently wanted to be buried near Chaucer. Seventeenth-century successor-poets were likely to have been inhabitants of the City of Westminster in their lifetimes, and maybe friends, such as Abraham Cowley and John Denham, who chose to be buried in neighbouring plots as a mark of friendship rather than just poetic kinship. In the First Folio, both William Basse and Ben Jonson touch on this combined sense of canonicity and community when they pay tribute to Shakespeare, although both ultimately decide that he ought to be set apart from the others. In Jonson's words: 'I will not lodge thee by | Chaucer or Spenser, or bid Beaumont lie | A little further to make thee a room.'[48]

But burial in Poets' Corner would eventually acquire a greater significance, and again Walpole became a source of back-handed inspiration: commemorating and boosting the status of England's deceased writers was a means of condemning the dearth of government patronage for the living.

In the eighteenth century, the literary world itself was still a neighbour to the ecclesiastical world; the formidable Francis Atterbury, as Dean of Westminster, buried at least two of his friends in the south transept, Joseph Addison and (pompously, with all the details worked out in advance by the deceased) Matthew Prior. Burial was not necessarily permanent, though: the republican mid-seventeenth-century poet Thomas May had been disinterred and removed from the Abbey after the Restoration.[49]

Pope and Burlington took a more programmatic and political interest in the Abbey. Pope had already contributed to it by supplying epitaphs for Samuel Butler and Nicholas Rowe, for instance (although the latter was soon published in a newspaper, it would only appear in the Abbey in adapted form, when the Rowe monument was erected around 1742).[50] In the extensive gardens of Stowe, in Buckinghamshire, Richard Temple, Viscount Cobham, had shown how to create an ornamental show of opposition to Walpole, and included—as in Boyd's play—a Temple of British Worthies, designed by Kent, in which one of the busts was of Shakespeare. (Frederick, Prince of Wales, and a figurehead for the opposition to Walpole's long reign, paid a symbolically loaded visit to Stowe in 1739.) Much like a Shakespeare play in the hands of a Cibber or a Tate, Poets' Corner showed potential as a venue for a Stowe-like show of opposition, and renovation according to modern taste—an opportunity to create an English pantheon in marble, in which Shakespeare deserved a prominent position.

The only snag was that his bones belonged to Stratford-upon-Avon, where they resided in Holy Trinity Church. But this did not stop visitors to the Abbey apostrophizing Shakespeare on this spot, moved by the sight of Scheemakers's statue, and the recollection of those plays they had seen at Drury Lane or Covent Garden (or maybe even read). In so doing, they were contributing towards what became virtually a site-specific genre, in both verse and prose, of tributes to Shakespeare.

After 1741, that is to say, Poets' Corner, with the statue of Shakespeare at its heart, came to serve metropolitan *littérateurs* as a welcome source of inspiration, for both celebrating the achievements of the past and condemning the present. And to survey such responses to Westminster Abbey is to see, for one thing, how amenable to mid-eighteenth-century taste could be the melancholy or effusive appreciation of the literary achievements of the past.

A catch-all patriotic pride characterizes some of the writings from (or inspired by) the Abbey, which take in Shakespeare much as they would, say, Henry VIII or some nearby divines. Other commentators draw crucial distinctions between princes and poets. 'The poet's name can strike a pale a-round', John Dart could claim in *Westminster-Abbey: A Poem*, in 1721, 'And where he rests, he consecrates the ground'. The thought came to mind, Dart claimed, as he had walked around the Abbey and 'fixed my eyes' on the floor where '*Addison* near great *Eliza* lies'; 'Thus *Virgil*'s tomb attracts the trav'ler's eyes, | While none can tell where great *Augustus* lies'.[51] Worldly power fades; Addison is all but a saint.

Writing about forty years later, however, well after the erection of the Shakespeare monument, Reginald Heber dwelt on the indifference of 'obdurate Death' to individuals' qualities of 'genius, innocence [or] truth', noting the abasement of Milton with a piquant allusion to Shakespeare's *Henry V* ('Quenched in the dust is *Milton*'s muse of fire'), and that Dryden's 'once harmonious tongue' was 'mute', as were those of Addison, Prior, and Gay—but on Shakespeare himself he had more to say, approving the very look of the statue as Shakespearian in execution:

> Here too sweet *Shakespeare*, Fancy's fav'rite child,
> The marble emulates thy power to please;
> With graceful attitude, and aspect mild,
> Expressing native dignity and ease.

By striking down even Shakespeare, that 'ruthless monster' Death, Heber suggests, shows himself to be the worst of all things, an implacable critic:

> Nor thy unrivalled magic's potent charm,
> Nor tender stories of ill-fated love;
> Nor scenes of horror could his rage disarm,
> Or the insensate spectre's pity move.[52]

Poetry, then, is no solution to mortality: 'Vain are all notes, how high soe'er they rise, | All numbers vain, however smooth they flow'. Instead, Heber's Westminster is a place that will eventually be levelled with the dust. On a 'day of gladness', its 'trophied pillars' will vanish, and virtuous spirits will rise to heaven, which will offer its 'applause' to those who merit reward. Literature is no replacement for true religion.

Similar considerations inform Thomas Maurice's *Westminster-Abbey: An Elegiac Poem*, published in 1784, and fully charged with the spirit of what would much later come to be known as 'Bardolatry' (as is discussed in the penultimate chapter of this book). Here, Addison is ignored, while Chaucer, Spenser, Milton, Dryden, and a couple more receive their due measures of praise. Shakespeare receives most of all. Initially, however, when Maurice's dutiful tour of the Abbey brings him to 'that sequestered spot | Where Britain's Bards my tearful homage claim', the sight of so many literary graves appals him:

> Was that pale mass informed with heav'nly fire,
> Genius and wit, is this your destined end?
> Favoured of Phoebus, break thy useless lyre,
> Thy steps already to the grave descend.[53]

Even the 'loftiest fancy' may not ward off the 'unerring dart' of Death—yet Maurice consoles himself with the thought that for these writers, there are 'sublimer trophies': 'their own immortal works survive, | Nor can oblivion's rage those works deface'.[54] Drawing attention back to the 'works', Maurice mentions four plays in as many lines, as means of illustrating what he calls Shakespeare's 'collective' achievement—a 'might' that, in his view, overshadows both the ancients and the moderns:

> Whether we hear thy artful Hamlet rave,
> Or frantic Lear his tale of horror tell,
> With Ariel mount, or tempt the yawning cave
> Where hags of darkness chant the muttered spell.
> Oh! SHAKESPEARE, great in thy collective might,
> Beyond each ancient's loftiest name renowned;
> Who shall pursue thee in thy daring flight?
> Who trace those steps that spurn creation's bound?[55]

In *An Accurate though Compendious Encomium on the Most Illustrious Persons, Whose Monuments are Erected in Westminster-Abbey* (1749), meanwhile, Shakespeare's statue has become 'pensive'; it is a living, thinking re-embodiment of the writer, that 'breathes in *Parian* stone' The poet—an anonymous gentleman of Balliol College, Oxford, who writes his 'heroic poem' in parallel Latin and English texts—gives

*Othello* as an example of the true insight that this 'famed *Bard*' has into the passions, imaginatively restaging the play:

> View the grim *Moor*! by love, to fury wrought;
> Plunged in the whirlpool of perplexing thought.
> Meteorous, his fiery eyeballs roll!
> While passions shake the basis of his soul....[56]

Going beyond the model of discrete praise for one poet after another, however, this vision of Poets' Corner also has Shakespeare's 'lofty strain' improve Dryden's writing for the stage by relieving him of the burden of writing tragedy in heroic couplets—'Unclogged with tuneful rhyme's depressing chain'—and instead, via *Antony and Cleopatra*, leading him to write *All for Love*:

> How *Antony*! how *Cleopatra* moves
> Each breast!...
> See fond excess prevail at glory's cost,
> Beauty triumphant, and a *world well lost*.[57]

*The Rambles of Mr. Frankly* likewise pays tribute to Shakespeare's power to move:

With what sad delight did we all stop to take a view of the pleasing figure, the elegant attitude of our highly venerated Bard. So well wrought the sculpture, so serious our attention, we almost imagined we saw him move. 'Thou wert the honour, as well as pride of Nature,' said I – 'and such thou wilt ever remain. This monument, if not equal to thy desert, does credit to those by whom it was designed—The ashes of Shakespeare will preserve it, and bid defiance to the hand of Time.'[58]

Turning to view the monument to Nicholas Rowe, Julia remarks, 'I cannot read that inscription without tears...Shakespeare and Rowe!—What an exalted pair!'—only for Mr. Frankly to confess himself 'wounded' that she should cry at the thought of these pathetic playwrights. 'Why should we be sad and gloomy, because surrounded by the dead?...it is a consolation...that death and the grave will not triumph for ever.' This was clearly the right thing to say. Julia thanks Mr. Frankly, 'smiling through her tears'.[59]

More such responses to the statues of Shakespeare and his 'neighbours' in Poets' Corner accrue during the latter half of the eighteenth century. Although the language of such poems rarely moves beyond what had long been the conventional phrases of praise ('sweet *Shakespeare*, Fancy's fav'rite child'), it also seems to speak of a newly confident belief in Shakespeare's genius, completely shrugging off the notion that he ought to be measured against neoclassical standards of correctness. Instead, Shakespeare may be 'Beyond each ancient's loftiest name renowned'; he may have an improving effect on Dryden, who certainly did know the rules, as well as on the statue itself, which in its supposedly lifelike dignity 'emulates thy power to please'. And by a nice irony, 'D. M.', the author of *Ancient Rome and Modern Britain Compared. A Dialogue in Westminster Abbey* (1793), imagines Pope himself cowering as he tries to guess the identity of an approaching literary ghost in the Abbey: ''Tis Shakespeare else, with all a poet's rage, | Come to reproach me for his injured page.' (A footnote describes Pope's edition of Shakespeare as 'the worst of his works'; the ghost turns out to be that of the Roman poet Horace.)[60] Shakespeare in this way earns his place in this illustrious national necropolis, among 'the royal, illustrious, great, and celebrated dead' (in the words of Mr. Frankly, quoted as an epigraph to this chapter), and vindicates, in unanticipated ways, the campaigning work of Burlington, Pope, those ladies of quality, and any others who, in 1741, had given both theatregoers and play-readers a focal point for acts of quasi-worship.

Living writers, however, were not always so delighted by Poets' Corner. 'Busts are placed of the dead', explained one satirist, 'by those who suffered them to starve when alive':

Poets here have a marble existence, as the only being that envy and ingratitude can suffer them to enjoy.... The world will not acknowledge a poet in any dress but his shroud. Thus, they honour the dead, to degrade the living. It is common with this people to say one minute, '*We have no poets now*,' and the next, to write elegies, rear tombs, and transcribe inscriptions from the works which they had the instant before been decrying.[61]

Such satire recalls the part of Eliza Haywood's *Female Spectator* that is not quoted when we refer to the benign activities of the Shakespeare Ladies Club: 'it is a melancholy reflection to a poet, that he must be *dead* before he can arrive at the end of his ambition....'[62] In this sense, the statue in the Abbey is an indication of what kind of writer Shakespeare became after 1741—one who had arrived at the 'end of his ambition'—

lending him a dignity and a persona in the public eye where before, it seems, there had been none. The product, in part, of a theatrical campaign, the monumental Shakespeare would respond by providing the theatre with an iconic image of vernacular poetic genius. It was a newfound status that Garrick would soon turn to personal advantage.

### 'Very laudable'

In the meantime, in early March 1741, Goodman's Fields found itself staging *The Fatal Curiosity* by Lillo ('founded on fact, which happened in the year 1618, and is recorded in the Annals of James I') and *Harlequin Student; or, The Fall of Pantomime. With the Restoration of the Drama*, 'The whole to conclude with a representation of SHAKESPEARE'S MONUMENT, *as lately erected* at Westminster Abbey, with a full complement of deities and muses to bless the scene: Jupiter, Mars, Mercury, Cupid, Minerva, Melpomene, Thalia, and Ganymede. Thanks to the Licensing Act, however, this immortal tribute had to be presented in the guise of a 'CONCERT of vocal and instrumental MUSIC'. And at Drury Lane, *The Merchant of Venice* had just reached its ninth performance of the season.[63]

Macklin's Shylock seems to have been the right performance at the right moment—an attempt to give back to Shakespeare's play some of its terrible power, just as, beyond the theatre, the statue in Poets' Corner offered a correlative figure for that seriousness.

Many years after the event, Macklin gave an account of the first night of his revival to William Cooke that is a classic of its kind: an anecdote of personal triumph on the stage, calculated to capture the excitement of not only reinterpreting Shylock but, as he saw it, having his convictions about what Shakespeare intended by the part vindicated by the audience's response. On 14 February, Macklin recollected, the 'two front rows of the pit, as usual, were full of the critics', and, as he looked 'through the slit of the curtain', he was pleased to see them: 'I wished, in such a cause, to be tried by a *special jury*.' His fellow actors remained unconvinced by Macklin's intentions for the role, specifically his carefully researched costume:

When I made my appearance in the green-room, dressed for the part, with my red hat on my head, my picqued beard, loose black gown, &c. and with a confidence which I never before assumed, the performers all stared at one another, and evidently with a stare of disappointment.[64]

As the moment of truth came nearer, Macklin confessed, 'my heart began to beat a little'—but his initial reception from the audience, 'one of the loudest thunders of applause I ever before experienced', could not have been more favourable. And he was only getting started, the opening scenes being 'rather tame and level'. He was saving himself for the third act:

> At this period I threw out all my fire; and, as the contrasted passions of joy for the Merchant's losses, and grief for the elopement of Jessica, open a fine field for an actor's powers, I had the good fortune to please beyond my warmest expectations—The whole house was in an uproar of applause—and I was obliged to pause between the speeches, to give it vent, so as to be heard.

Finally, in the trial scene, Macklin 'wound up the fullness of my reputation: here I was well listened to; and here I made such a silent yet forcible impression on my audience, that I retired from this great attempt most perfectly satisfied'. When he received the applause of the audience (which holds up the performance), his fellow players, and the 'nobility and critics' (who come to the green room at the end), Macklin basked in the moment.[65] Fêted at once, he received a further mark of approbation a few days later, when the same Frederick, Prince of Wales who visited Stowe, and his family, attended a performance, and chose the occasion to bring their daughter, the Lady Augusta, this being 'the first time of her honouring any theatre with her presence'; more royals were to follow on 9 March.[66]

When Macklin took his benefit on 7 April, the production was on its seventeenth night (according to contemporary newspaper advertisements; Cooke's *Memoirs* nudges it up to the nineteenth night), and he played to an 'overflowing audience': 'Lord Bolingbroke made him a present of twenty guineas'.[67] Bolingbroke had, in the meantime, hosted a rendezvous in Battersea at which Pope had complimented Macklin 'very highly' on his performance, and asked him why he had adopted that red hat for the part:

> ...and he answered, because he had read that Jews in Italy, particularly in Venice, wore hats of that colour. 'And pray, Mr. Macklin,' said Pope, 'do players in general take such pains?' I do not know, Sir that they do; but as

I had staked my reputation on the character, I was determined to spare no trouble in getting at the best information.' Pope nodded, and said, 'it was very laudable.'[68]

The story of Macklin's Shylock belies the groundswell of interest in Shakespeare in the years running up to 1741. At the same time, it anticipates the future triumphs of other actors in Shakespearian roles in its presentation of truth to nature as an act of cultural recovery—of wearing the 'authentic' costume, say, or rediscovering the correct way to play a particular character. And in the meeting it inspired between the editor and the actor, at the family seat of an earl, here was also a foretaste of what Macklin's sometime friend David Garrick would go on to achieve.

# *Garrick*

*The following verses, dropped in Mr.* GARRICK's *Temple of Shakespeare, at Hampton, are said to have been written by a gentleman, whose poetical productions have been very deservedly admired.*

WHILE here to SHAKESPEARE *Garrick* pays
His tributary thanks and praise,
Invokes the animated stone,
To make the poet's mind his own;
That he each character may trace
With humour, dignity, and grace,
And mark, unerring mark, to men,
The rich creation of his pen.
   Preferred the prayer—the marble god,
Methinks I see assenting nod;
And pointing to his laurelled brow.
Cry—'Half this wreath to you I owe.
Lost to the stage, and lost to fame,
Murdered my scenes, scarce known my name,
Sunk in oblivion and disgrace
Among the common scribbling race,
Unnoticed long thy Shakespeare lay,
To Dullness and to time a prey;
But lo! I rise, I breathe, I live
In you, my representative!
Again the hero's breast I fire,
Again the tender sigh inspire,
Each side, again, with laughter shake,
And teach the villain's heart to quake;

All this, my son, again I do,
I,—no, my son—'tis I and you.'
    Whilst thus the grateful statue speaks,
A blush o'erspreads the suppliant's cheeks:
'What, half thy wreath? Wit's mighty chief!
O grant! (he cries) one single leaf!
That far o'erpays his humble merit,
Who's but the organ of thy spirit.'
    *Phoebus* the gen'rous contest heard,
When thus the God addressed the bard:
'Here! take this laurel from my brow;
On him your mortal wreath bestow;
Each matchless, each the palm shall bear;
In heav'n, the bard; on earth, the play'r.'[1]

Up to this point, this book has traced certain parallel developments in Shakespearian culture during the first half of the eighteenth century—the creation of rival editions of his works shaped by conflicting ideological forces, untidily reflected in the waxing and waning popularity of Shakespeare's plays in performance. One latent theme here is the interaction between how those plays were staged, how they were edited, how their author was perceived in the 'public sphere'. A play, Steele wrote in the preface to *The Conscious Lovers* (1722), is 'to be seen'; 'the greatest effect of a play in reading is to excite the reader to go see it'.[2] If that hierarchy of reading and theatre-going was true of old English plays as well as new ones (such as Steele's influential sentimental comedy), then by the mid-1730s, Shakespeare was in a good position, with the cheap reissues of Jacob Tonson, Jr and Robert Walker potentially widening the audience for his plays in performance. The entrance of David Garrick on this mixed scene in 1741 invites us to take stock of these imbricated activities and their combined contributions to the process of Shakespeare's absorption into the broad stream of English culture. This is because Garrick—traditionally celebrated principally as a great actor—also stands at a point where these forces intersect. And this, it seems to me, plays as much of a significant role as his performances on stage, if not a determining role, in shaping the reception of Shakespeare for the rest of the century.

## The Seven Ages of Garrick

*Epigram.*—1761.
Says Garrick, amongst other sociable chat,
'What could *I* without Shakespeare do? pray tell me that.'
    'Twas replied —
'Great connections you have with each other, 'tis true:
But, *now*—what can Shakespeare do, sir, without you?'[3]

There are relatively few performers whose lives could be commemorated with a monument along the lines of George Winchester Stone, Jr and George M. Kahrl's 'critical biography' of David Garrick, which follows an alternative, cross-patterned structure. It divides Garrick's life into seven 'ages'—The Apprentice, The Manager, The Dramatist, The Producer, The Private Man, The Actor, The Close—but these are not chronologically discrete phases, of course, apart from the first and the last. More remarkably, Stone and Kahrl can divide Garrick's activities into sections such as 'David Garrick, Esquire' (on his relationship with five of his closest friends, including William Hogarth), 'The Literary World of Scholarship' (since Garrick was a bibliophile who supported literary scholars and made his library available to them, and would eventually present his superb collection of old English plays to the British Museum), 'Garrick's Own Plays' ('Garrick's itch for writing satisfied itself with a piece every year save six from 1740 until he retired in 1776'),[4] 'Garrick's Adaptations of Older Plays', 'Garrick Abroad: An Heir to the Classical Traditions', 'Garrick's Theatrical Innovations' (such as keeping the audience off the stage and, by importing new lighting effects, creating an 'Artificial Day' in the theatre),[5] 'Garrick the Occasional Poet', 'Garrick's Friendships with Women of Distinction', 'Patron of the Arts', and finally—lest we forget—'Garrick's Great Comic Roles' and 'Garrick's Great Tragic Roles'.

More conventionally, the year 1741 is usually given as the point at which general histories of the English theatre or studies of Shakespeare in performance introduce this essential figure in their story. Near the beginning of the season after Macklin had made his mark as Shylock at Drury Lane, Garrick made his London debut in the title role of *Richard III* (in Colley Cibber's adaptation of Shakespeare). He had come to London a few years earlier with his friend Samuel Johnson, who had been his schoolmaster at the short-lived school Johnson established at Edial Hall, outside Lichfield; both would become dominant cultural figures over the coming decades.

With that first season, Garrick at once earned a shining reputation for the ingenuity and energy of his stage interpretations of a great variety of parts—he could not only play the villainous Richard III, but the foolish fond old man King Lear, the plain foolish Abel Drugger in *The Alchemist* by Jonson, the libertine Lothario in *The Fair Penitent* by Rowe. Also greatly admired were his portrayals of Hamlet, Benedict in *Much Ado about Nothing*, Sir John Brute in *The Provoked Wife*, and Bayes in *The Rehearsal*, and he would play almost 100 different characters in total between 1741 and 1776.[6] Like Macklin, he appears to have won the approval of the older generation, with both Alexander Pope and (more reluctantly) Cibber approving his early performances at Henry Giffard's theatre in Goodman's Fields. Successful seasons in Dublin, Drury Lane, and Covent Garden, combined with a good head for business, meant that by 1747, he was in a position to go into partnership with James Lacy as joint managers of Drury Lane. The opening of the house for their first season in charge gave Garrick an opportunity to declare his artistic allegiance, in the words of a prologue written by Johnson, probably in collaboration with Garrick:

> When Learning's triumph o'er her barb'rous foes
> First reared the stage, immortal Shakespeare rose;
> Each change of many-coloured life he drew,
> Exhausted worlds, and then imagined new:
> Existence saw him spurn her bounded reign,
> And panting Time toiled after him in vain:
> His pow'rful strokes presiding truth impressed,
> And unresisted passion stormed the breast.

The prologue then devotes another eight lines to considering Jonson's 'studious patience, and laborious art'; then more on the 'Wits of *Charles*' for whom 'intrigue was plot, obscenity was wit' (and 'as they felt, they writ'), the decline of tragedy, 'crushed by rules' so that 'Nature fled', and the rise of pantomime, before finally challenging the audience to 'prompt no more the follies you decry', and threatened with a grim future of more and more empty-headed, Harlequin-led spectaculars: 'who the coming changes can presage, | And mark the future periods of the stage? | ... Perhaps, where *Lear* has raved, and *Hamlet* died, | On flying cars new sorcerers may ride.'[7]

The play that night was to be *The Merchant of Venice*, with Macklin as Shylock. Many more Shakespearian performances were to follow. Yet it was one of those dreaded 'follies', a pantomime, that became the most performed piece of all at Garrick's Drury Lane, and, what is more, possibly as a result of a Shakespearian 'battle': in the autumn of 1750, Covent Garden and Drury Lane staged simultaneous productions of *Romeo and Juliet*, which both ran for consecutive nights for close to a fortnight. Inspired perhaps by the experience of giving a certain speech so often, Henry Woodward, Mercutio to Garrick's Romeo, wrote a pantomime for Christmas called *Queen Mab*; it was to be performed on forty-five nights in its first season alone.

Garrick's own dramatic writings, usually afterpieces or other (very) light entertainments, tend to drop the name of Shakespeare or quote the lines most liable to be recognized by the audience frequently. It was Garrick who made the pantomime a traditional Christmas fixture in the calendar, despite getting Woodward into serious trouble by inserting some satire on Covent Garden into *Harlequin Ranger* in 1752, and when Woodward left Drury Lane a few years later, Garrick wrote his own (anti-)pantomime, *Harlequin's Invasion*, in which the star of the show is not Harlequin himself, who unconventionally is a speaking part on this occasion, but Shakespeare. At the climax of the show, 'the Bard' rises through the trap door as Harlequin sinks, having failed to conquer Mount Parnassus. A rousing patriotic scene has 'many of Shakespeare's characters enter' during a chorus that runs 'Come away, come away, come away. | His genius calls and you must obey'. 'Thrice happy th'nation that Shakespeare has charmed', Garrick enthuses, while renewing the challenge to the audience of that prologue on the opening of Drury Lane eleven years earlier:

> Ye Britons may fancy ne'er lead you astray,
> Nor e'er through your senses your reason betray.
> By your love to the Bard may your wisdom be known,
> Nor injure his fame to the loss of your own....[8]

In fact, this was part of a sustained campaign on Garrick's part to play on and naturalize the audience's familiarity with Shakespeare. The opera-loving Mrs Riot in his skit *Lethe* decries the taste for 'your Shakespeares and your Johnsons [sic]', while unwittingly alluding to *Othello* with her outcry of distaste for this antiquated stuff: 'Oh, you goats and vandals!'[9] The farce *Miss in Her Teens* pays tribute to *Twelfth Night* by restaging a duel between two highly unwilling duellists. The prologue to *The Male-Coquette* compares those 'slaves to fashion' who stay up all night gambling, 'Whose minds eternal vigils keep; | Who, like Macbeth, have murdered sleep', and whose vices will appear to them in this satire like 'Banquo's ghost', causing them to cry out 'Hence, horrid farce!'[10]

Such allusions nurtured the idea of an association between Garrick, Shakespeare, and Drury Lane by means other than performances of Shakespeare's plays. This is not quite what Paul Whitehead means in his 'Verses, dropped in Mr. GARRICK's Temple of Shakespeare, at Hampton' by the line 'In heav'n, the bard; on earth, the play'r', but it does provide a context for them—and for further non-theatrical modes of endorsing or celebrating Shakespeare.

Like the conventional claims of various Shakespeare editors to have outdone one another and finally rescued Shakespeare's plays from textual corruption, the 1747 prologue indicates that Garrick's much-praised versatility as an actor was also a necessary quality to the eighteenth-century theatre manager. A whole theatrical evening might involve a combination of the following elements: a previously unperformed, topically weighted prologue; the main piece, being a new or old play of five acts (and if an old play, such as Shakespeare's, one that has to be trimmed to public taste as closely as possible); new songs or new dances, possibly as interludes between acts; a new epilogue; an afterpiece, usually a two- or three-act farce; more singing and dancing; an announcement, to close, of coming attractions. It was not mere lip service that made Garrick and Johnson put themselves in the audience's hands when it came to determining the repertoire at Drury Lane—the audience could be loudly responsive, both as individuals and collectively, and disaffection could mean disaster. Theatre historians rightly point out that in his revivals of Shakespeare, Garrick often made more alterations than he advertised (while at the same time, often going further than his contemporaries in restoring passages from the folios or quartos to the inherited texts for the stage), but it ought to be remembered that Garrick, for much of the ensuing thirty years, was highly successful in judging what the audience would take and what they wouldn't.

While his staging of *The Chinese Ballet* in 1755, choreographed by the Swiss Jean Georges Noverre with dancers from France, has sometimes been cited as Garrick's most serious misjudgement as manager, as xenophobia led to rioting in the theatre, there was also his attempt to abolish the old practice of admitting people for half-price after the third act of the main piece in the spring of 1763. That, too, led to rioting; and Garrick and his wife Eva Maria at that point decided to take a long holiday, embarking on a tour of the Continent. Shakespeare went with him: fêted in Paris by the *salonnières*, he apparently performed the dagger scene from *Macbeth* for audiences who could not understand English, and explained how he had learned how to play Lear in his madness by visiting Bedlam. But he would not perform in England again until 1765.

Age and illness combined to make those performances rarer occurrences during the final decade of Garrick's career, and a substantial number of those appearances were in a walk-on part in *The Jubilee* (as will be seen in the following chapter), an after-effect of the Jubilee in Shakespeare's honour that Garrick held at Stratford-upon-Avon in 1769. By then, however, the connection between Garrick and Shakespeare had long been virtually proverbial. 'Sacred to Shakespeare was this spot designed', he had said of Drury Lane at the opening of the 1750–1 season, in a prologue to *The Merchant of Venice* again, 'To pierce the heart and humanize the mind'.[11]

Shakespeare was indeed the cornerstone of Garrick's success. The first and last performances in tragic roles Garrick gave on the London stage were as Richard III; Shakespeare, he proclaimed in Stratford-upon-Avon, during the celebrations he organized there in Shakespeare's honour in 1769, was a 'demi-god', or even 'The god of our idolatry!'[12] Of the 129 'original and engraved portraits in stage characters' listed for Garrick in the *Biographical Dictionary*, forty-nine represent him in Shakespearian roles (including one plate that depicts him as King Lear, Macbeth, Richard III, and Hamlet).[13] At times, the 'connexion' between them, as the epigram from 1761 has it, could even seem to be more in Shakespeare's favour than his: 'What could

*I* without Shakespeare do? pray tell me that.' 'But, *now*—what can Shakespeare do, sir, without you?' The first role he played in the season after his marriage, in 1749, was 'Benedick *the Married Man*', and it amused him that it was already rumoured that he would play the part, as an in-joke between him and 1,000 theatregoers.[14] Edward Moore had already made the connection between the Shakespearian character and the 'private' life of the Shakespearian actor in 'An Ode to Mr. Garrick upon the Talk of the Town about his intended Marriage' by opening it with an epigraph from *Much Ado about Nothing*: 'When I said I would die a bachelor, I did not think I should live till I were married' (2.3.230–2).

Benedict would go on to be the Shakespearian role he played most often—albeit sometimes without speaking a single word. Out of the ninety-six roles Garrick played between 1741 and 1776, that is, eighteen were in plays by Shakespeare; and out of the twelve roles he played eighty times or more, five are Shakespearian, with only one other dramatist represented more than once in that dozen: Ben Jonson.[15] It is an impressive tally, but at the top of that list of Garrick's roles is Benedict—not the Benedict he played in *Much Ado about Nothing* itself (which he did play 113 times), but the Benedict of the pageant in *The Jubilee*. This was a walk-on part that he 'played' 153 times in all, amid a procession of other characters from Shakespeare (an extension of the same idea in *Harlequin's Invasion*), from 1769 onwards. Although the Shakespeare Jubilee had been financially disastrous, Garrick had quickly recouped his losses the following season, by staging at Drury Lane a comic version of the pageant originally intended for the streets of Stratford—its popularity meant that he ended up making a cameo appearance as a non-speaking Benedict in the final decade of his career more often than he played the role proper over three decades.

### Commentary and alteration

As for Garrick's acting: the critics struggled to find an adequate language to describe it, and in much of the theatre criticism of the time, there are problems of impartiality, both in his favour and against him. But the intensity of adulation for Garrick goes beyond puffery. 'The noun most frequently used by contemporaries to describe Garrick's comic performances is *vivacity*', write his biographers, George Winchester Stone, Jr, and George M. Kahrl, 'a suggestive term, but worn thin by repetition'.[16] In tragedy, meanwhile, a 'recurring word' is '*new* or *novel*', registering 'the surprise felt at Garrick's fresh ways of communicating insights into characters often familiar'. 'Words save for *inimitable* often failed the critics.'[17] But whatever else it was, it was exactly right for Garrick's contemporaries. A poem, by Thomas Davies, has Garrick tell Nature herself that Shakespeare 'paints stronger and better than you'; 'Not a word in his volumes I ever could see', Nature replies, 'But what from my records he stole'.[18] Francis Gentleman effusively praises Garrick as 'the best illustrator of, and the best *living comment* on, SHAKESPEARE, that ever has appeared, or possibly ever will grace the British stage', saying that this was 'merely echoing the public voice'.[19] And in the similarly flattering homage paid by the literary scholar George Steevens, the power of Garrick's acting was such that it could replace critical commentary altogether:

I am contented with the spirit of the author you first taught me to admire, and when I found you could do so much for him, I was naturally curious to know the value of the materials he had supplied you with; and often when I have taken the pen in my hand to try to illustrate a passage, I have thrown it down again with discontent when I remembered how able you were to clear the difficulty by a single look, or particular modulation of the voice, which a long and laboured paraphrase was insufficient to explain half so well.[20]

Although his versatility had its limits—his Othello, for instance, was not regarded as one of his 'capital' parts—this aspect of Garrick's acting is crucial to his performances of Shakespeare's plays. That he could illuminate a text in performance with unexpected touches and character-inspired physicality is the necessary counterpart to the alterations he made to the plays—a dying speech for *Macbeth*, for instance, or the removal of rhymes and puns from *Romeo and Juliet*. These stage 'readings' of the plays were more 'inspired readjustment' than 'living commentary'. But their impact is undeniable. When he was still in his twenties, Garrick's rendition of Lear's curse on his daughters, Macklin told his biographer, 'seemed to electrify the audience with horror', while the reconciliation with Cordelia reduced them to tears.[21] These moments were obvious opportunities to create bravura effects, but Garrick could find ways of enlivening even the dullest, non-Shakespearian text. Arthur Murphy, in his biography of Garrick published in 1801, and vividly recalling an incident from the 1750s, went so far as to say that in one play, a rather stiff tragedy called *Virginia* by Samuel Crisp, the actor 'crowned' the performance in the way he spoke just two words, far excelling the promise of the script itself, during a Roman trial scene:

Garrick, representing *Virginius*, stood on the opposite side of the scene, next to the stage-door, with his arms folded across his breast, his eyes riveted to the ground, like a mute and lifeless statue. Being told at length that the tyrant is willing to hear him, he continued for some time in the same attitude, his countenance expressing a variety of passions, and the spectators fixed in ardent gaze. By slow degrees he raised his head; he paused; he turned round in the slowest manner, till his eyes fixed on *Claudius*; he remained silent, and after looking eagerly at the impostor, he uttered in a low tone of voice, that spoke the fullness of a broken heart, '*Thou traitor!*' The whole audience was electrified; they felt the impression, and a thunder of applause testified their delight.[22]

By the time Murphy wrote his biography of Garrick, however, theatre criticism and an interest in communicating the minutiae of individual performances had become well-established habits; much of the published praise of Garrick from his own lifetime, and of his contemporaries, tends to be generalized, praising attributes such as the quality of voice, elegance of gesture, etc. (whereas the marvellously detailed descriptions of Garrick in performance by George Christian Lichtenberg were not published in full in English until 1938).[23] As noted in the previous chapter, Macklin outlived all his peers to inspire a couple of biographies around the end of the eighteenth century. One of the most striking of Garrick anecdotes, has him saying a line in *Macbeth*, 'There's blood upon thy face', so compellingly that his addressee, one of the murderers, forgot to reply ''Tis Banquo's then', and exclaiming in horror instead: 'Is there, by God?'[24] But its source appears to be the unreliable memoirs of John Taylor, *Records of My Life* (1832), and while it seems too good to be untrue (minor roles were often taken by less experienced actors, and Sarah Siddons testified to being overawed by Garrick in a similar way in *Richard III*), theatre historians and biographers have been accordingly coy about identifying their source when they repeat the story.

More difficult to miss is the hostile vein of criticism in which Garrick is figured as a disturbingly Harlequin-like figure. For the bombastic Theophilus Cibber, the son of Colley, Garrick suffered from an 'over-fondness for extravagant attitudes, frequently affected starts, convulsive twitchings, jerkings of the body, sprawling of the fingers, flapping the breast and pockets:—A set of mechanical motions in constant use,—the caricature of gesture, suggested by pert vivacity' (that word again); he also had a 'pantomimical manner of acting, every word in a sentence' and, in his speech, a 'wilful neglect of harmony, even where the round period of a well-expressed noble sentiment demands a graceful cadence in the delivery'.[25] An army officer called Thomas Morris found him to be guilty of 'pantomime-gesture; and all trick...miserable expedients fit only for a booth in a fair'.[26] These descriptions evince an anxiety about acting and the text, and a suspicion of the non-verbal performance. Deidre Shauna Lynch has also seen here 'traces of neoclassicism's aesthetic canons, which underscored the baseness of particularized representations by associating them with a putatively female enthusiasm for [trivialities]'.[27] To some playgoers, Garrick was not so much elucidating as obscuring the sacred texts of Shakespeare. It would not have surprised them to learn that Garrick did actually play Harlequin early in his acting career, if they had not heard the rumour by then: Garrick had written to his elder brother to reassure him that when a fellow actor was taken ill at Goodman's Fields, he had 'put on the dress & did 2 or three scenes for him', but it had been kept a secret.[28] That the young Garrick could pass for a Harlequin, however, is an indication of qualities that would shortly help to make his name as a Shakespearian actor.

Garrick retired in 1776, and died a few years later, in 1779; he was buried at the foot of the Scheemakers statue of Shakespeare in Westminster Abbey. An ostentatious memorial followed some years later, alluding allegorically to the idea of Garrick as the great interpreter not just of Shakespeare but the other 'English dramatic poets': 'GARRICK is throwing back a veil or curtain, supposed to have obscured the venerable Bards, whose heads appear on medallions in the recess.'[29] This was the monument with an inscription by an actor, Samuel Jackson Pratt, that so irked Charles Lamb.

After his death, Garrick's admirers could reverently say, as Garrick had once said of Shakespeare, and Shakespeare's Hamlet had (more or less) once said of his father, 'We ne'er shall look upon his like again'. It is typical of Garrick's achievement that this motto—the climactic line of his *Ode upon Dedicating a Building and Erecting a Statue, to Shakespeare, at Stratford upon Avon*, emblazoned on tickets for the Jubilee and in the engravings of him delivering that *Ode*—should be an adaptation. Hamlet says of his father, more plainly, without the rise in poetic register of Garrick's 'ne'er', 'I shall not look upon his like again' (1.2.187). Although often seen as a restorer of Shakespeare's plays to the stage in their original form, as already mentioned, Garrick subjects them to the same treatment he would give to any play—cutting them and adding to them in order to suit contemporary taste. Particularly drastic in this respect were his abridgements of *The Winter's Tale* as *Florizel and Perdita* and *The Taming of the Shrew* as *Catharine and Petruchio*—introduced on the same night in January 1756 with a prologue in which Garrick, likening the theatre to a tavern, the poets to vintners, and the actors to waiters, proclaimed: ''Tis my chief wish, my joy, my only plan, | To lose no drop of that immortal man.' Yet the prologue is frank in its acknowledgement that *Florizel and Perdita* is a three-act version of a five-act play; it has simply been 'confined and bottled for your taste'.[30] The double bill did not escape severe criticism at the time, but the stageworthy durability of Garrick's adaptations is itself a comment on his astuteness as Shakespeare's dramaturge: both were still being performed at the end of the eighteenth century.

By contrast, when Garrick and Edward Capell produced a version of *Antony and Cleopatra* 'fitted for the stage by abridging only',[31] it was a significant event—3 January 1759 is the date of the first recorded performance of the play—but a commercial failure, playing only six nights and then never again. It had been splendidly staged, with new costumes and 'fine scenes', but, according to the prompter Richard Cross, it 'did not seem to give the audience any pleasure or draw any applause'.[32] The problem might well have been Garrick's own performance as Antony. He later admitted to Steevens that he had found the role a 'laborious' one'.[33] Steevens replied:

Your Antony and Cleopatra was a splendid performance; but you were out of love with it because it afforded you few opportunities of showing those sharp turns and that coachmanship in which you excel all others.[34]

This particular exchange, in 1775, between the actor and the literary scholar is interesting for other reasons, too: at this late date in his career, Garrick is writing for advice on what neglected Shakespeare play Drury Lane might produce next; *Richard II* is suggested but agreed to be (on Garrick's reading of the most recent edition, Steevens's revision of Samuel Johnson's edition) 'one of the least interesting of his historical plays—it will not do'; Garrick is unaware of Nahum Tate's adaptation of the play, which Steevens mentions;[35] Steevens recommends *Troilus and Cressida*, 'if it were well clipped and doctored', on the basis that '[James] Quin played Thersites once with success; and what has once pleased may please again'.[36] This is not, in other words, the Shakespeare of Garrick's public propaganda but a dramatist of uneven achievements, ripe for improvement—the performing text of *Hamlet*, for example, he revised at least three times[37]—and Steevens seems attuned to the risk-averse conservatism of the stage in his suggestion that Garrick ought to stick to whatever material has been tried and tested. This is not to say that Garrick was insincere in his adoring declarations about Shakespeare—he did, after all, manage to stage twenty-six of Shakespeare's plays in his twenty-nine years as manager of Drury Lane—but his 'commentary' was a theatrical and pragmatic one. Devotee though he was, he could still write a puerile take-off of a scene from *Julius Caesar*, called 'Ragandjaw', starring 'Brutarse' and 'Cassiarse'; it is not seen to merit a place in *The Plays of David Garrick*, appearing instead in a scholarly journal, published around the same time as those much more dignified volumes appeared.[38]

Garrick's theatrical Shakespeare was also informed not only by correspondence and conversation with scholars such as Steevens, Capell, and Johnson, but by his own research. The anecdote usually deployed to illustrate this point, referring to Garrick's announcement in January 1744 that he was going to appear in *Macbeth* as Shakespeare wrote it, hinges on Quin's piqued reaction to the news: 'Don't I play *Macbeth* as Shakespeare wrote it?' Garrick tells him to 'consult the original and not borrow his knowledge of Shakespeare from the altered copies of his plays'.[39] To this story might be added the more formal, indirect piece of testimony, from the prefatory material to Francis Gentleman's *Introduction to Shakespeare's Plays, Containing an Essay on Oratory*, in which Garrick is seen to be supportive of Gentleman's work, but concerned 'lest the prunings, transpositions, or other alterations, which, in his province as a manager he had often found necessary to make, or adopt, with regard to the text, for the convenience of representation, or accommodation to the powers and capacities of his performers...be misconstrued into a critical presumption of offering to the literati a reformed and more correct edition of our author's works'. Instead, Gentleman assures the reader, the work is entirely theatrical rather than textually prescriptive.[40]

Garrick owned numerous old folios and quartos, and, like any good student, made copious notes on the plays. A conversation with friends about the reference to the 'Mobled Queen', Hecuba, in *Hamlet* shows that Garrick kept a 'memorandum book, where I had collected every scrap about Shakespeare'. Regarding this particular phrase, although he had been unable to recollect the details initially, he had been able to consult Warburton, Johnson, and Capell's glosses.[41] Edmond Malone believed that Garrick had studied the plays 'with more assiduity than any of his predecessors', and felt that one reason for the rise in the dramatist's reputation—which had been 'yearly increasing' and was now 'fixed upon a basis, which neither the lapse of time nor the fluctuation of opinion will ever be able to shake'—was Garrick's 'admirable performance of many of his principal characters' and the 'frequent representation of his plays in nearly their original state'.[42] Hence the triumphal note on which Malone ends the 'Historical Account of the Rise and Progress of the English Stage', published in 1790, in his edition of the plays and poems: 1741, the year of Garrick's debut, figures here as theatre's *annus mirabilis*.

## The Garrick myth

The myth of Garrick is a simple but attractive one. It is the story of a young man who, like Shakespeare himself, comes from the provinces to the city with no great advantages except for his potential; his 'natural' style of acting causes a sensation; his restoration of many, previously neglected plays by Shakespeare, whom he venerates, makes him a revolutionary force in English theatre ('Learning's Triumph...'). His geniality, as the epitome of the easy-going eighteenth-century gentleman, is equally legendary (something that Garrick, one of the most frequently painted figures in eighteenth-century art, cultivated: in paintings such as the glorious conversation piece by Johann Zoffany, for example, now in the Garrick Club, depicting the Garricks happily lolling outside the Temple to Shakespeare that stood on the Thames-side lawn of their property in Hampton). Virtue and industry are rewarded—Garrick's place in the pantheon of performers who are more than 'just' performers is assured.

To the palpable annoyance of some modern theatre historians, the myth persists, at least in some respects. Garrick is still seen to be a pioneer, the one outstandingly 'natural' actor (whatever that means) of the eighteenth century, and the true restorer of Shakespeare, as Malone depicts him. It was not Garrick, however, who was principally responsible for bringing about a Shakespeare revival on the London stage. Arthur H. Scouten, taking a statistical approach to the available data for theatrical performances at all London theatres during the first half of the eighteenth century, shows that only a few of Shakespeare's plays had not been staged in London during the decade prior to Garrick's debut—and actually fewer plays by Shakespeare were stock pieces at the end of Garrick's time as manager of Drury Lane than at the beginning, there being twenty-two Shakespeare plays in the repertory in 1747 but only thirteen by 1776.[43] Arthur John Harris argues that it was not Garrick but his fellow manager George Colman who first started to restore Shakespeare's *King Lear* to the stage, in 1768, rather than Garrick, a notion arising only on the suggestion of two nineteenth-century theatre historians, James Boaden and John Genest.[44] And of course, Garrick did not do it alone: Hannah Pritchard played an equally celebrated Lady Macbeth to his Macbeth; Susannah Cibber, Margaret Woffington, Elizabeth Younge, and Ann Barry were all highly praised while at Drury Lane; James Quin, Spranger Barry, and Charles Macklin were all, in different ways, worthy competitors in various Shakespearian roles.

This corrective, anti-Garrick impetus is well founded in a desire to re-examine the Garrick myth. Thanks partly to the publication of an epic compilation of playbills, cast lists, newspaper advertisements, and more, *The London Stage, 1660–1800: A Calendar of Plays, Entertainments and Afterpieces* (1960–8), a day-by-day listing of all known performances, it is possible to look again at how Garrick's Drury Lane fared against Covent Garden, where, for example, it was the production of Macnamara Morgan's adaptation of *The Winter's Tale*, as *The Sheep-Shearing: or, Florizel and Perdita*, that prompted Garrick to write his own version. And despite Garrick's genuine restorations in Shakespeare's plays, his interpolations and abridgements ('clipped and doctored') are often seen—perhaps unfairly—to be risible. His *Romeo and Juliet*, for instance, features a passage of dialogue, following Otway's Romanized adaptation of the play as *The History and Fall of Caius Marius* (1679), in which the lovers are briefly and tantalizingly awake and alive together in the tomb, before Romeo dies of the poison he has already taken. It must have been extremely effective on the stage. His *Antony and Cleopatra*, while advertised as 'fitted for the stage by abridging only', brings forward Enobarbus's famous speech about the 'barge she sat in' into the first scene, and assigns it to a newly invented member of Octavius' party, Thyreus. And meanwhile, he continued to stage Cibber's alteration of *Richard III* and Tate's *King Lear*, despite belated pleas for him to attempt a restored *Lear*—which he declined to do, explaining that it was too late for him to unlearn Tate.

That might sound like a poor excuse, but Garrick attempted no new parts after he came back from the hiatus of the Grand Tour, and was clearly feeling his age: the number of his appearances dropped from 100 in the season before he left the country to 10 on his return. (At his autopsy in 1779, it was discovered that he had been born with only one kidney, which is some explanation for the frequency of his illnesses and increasing difficulties with fatigue.)[45] Late in 1772, he did what he acknowledged to be an 'imprudent' thing by acting in a new alteration of *Hamlet*. 'I had sworn I would not leave the stage till I had rescued that noble play from all the rubbish of the fifth act', he wrote of this alteration a few years later; 'I have brought it forth without the Grave-digger's trick and the fencing-match.'[46] Later critics have, sure enough, despised it. But Vanessa Cunningham makes the intriguing suggestion that he had 'frenchified' *Hamlet* in order to allow him to go on playing a physically demanding part.[47] It was certainly worth doing, consistently bringing in full houses.[48] On his final appearance in the role, on 30 May 1776, tickets that normally sold for a few shillings sold for a guinea each—and they sold out within about two hours.[49]

In the final decade of his career, then, Garrick's appearances on stage were rarer, becoming special occasions in themselves. 'Posterity will never be able to form the slightest idea of his perfections', Garrick's protégé Hannah More wrote. 'The more I see him, the more I wonder and admire.'[50] 'Posterity' loomed over the 'farewell' season in which he gave some of his most popular roles for the last time. Garrick was becoming a part of theatre history.

But in his adherence to the old alterations of Shakespeare, and his acceptance of the necessity of making adjustments to any play he revived, Garrick stands at all but the end of a tradition, at least as far as the major London theatres are concerned, rather than at the beginning. This is not to underplay the novelty of his acting style, but to eschew seeing him purely as a pioneer. In the course of her study of Thomas Betterton and the management of the Lincoln's Inn Fields theatre at the beginning of the eighteenth century, Judith Milhous quotes a contemporary parody of this other great actor-manager turning to a familiar authorial figure, in the hope of weathering difficult times:

*Betterton*...enters his closet, and falls down on his knees, and prays. O Shakespeare, Shakespeare! *What have our sins brought upon us! We have renounced the ways which thou hast taught us, ... let the streams of thy* Helicon *glide along by* Lincolns-Inn-Fields, *and fructify our Soil....* He rose, and rose much comforted: with that he falls to work about his design, opens the volume and picks out two or three of *Shakespeare's* plays.[51]

On this view, Garrick's career, dazzling though his performances on stage might be, looks more like a feat of return or consolidation than a revolution. At the same time, he was modernizing his theatre, clearing spectators off the stage, introducing innovative new lighting effects, and embracing a patriotic culture in which Shakespeare was an important prop, as in the epilogue he wrote for Hannah Pritchard to deliver at the end of her last performance in 1768: 'may the stage...be *English* still. | Merits you have, to other realms unknown; | With all their boastings, *Shakespeare is your own!*'[52]

Forward- or backward-looking, Garrick certainly managed to make Shakespeare *his* own. Would England ever see his like again?

# *Johnson's* Plays, *Garrick's*
# *Jubilee*

In the October of this year [1765] he at length gave to the world his edition of *Shakespeare*, which, if it had no other merit but that of producing his preface, in which the excellencies and defects of that immortal bard are displayed with a masterly hand, the nation would have had no reason to complain. A blind indiscriminate admiration of Shakespeare had exposed the British nation to the ridicule of foreigners. Johnson, by candidly admitting the faults of his poet, had the more credit in bestowing on him deserved and indisputable praise; and doubtless none of all his panegyrists have done him half so much honour. Their praise was, like that of a counsel, upon his own side of the cause: Johnson's was like the grave, well-considered, and impartial opinion of the judge, which falls from his lips with weight, and is received with reverence. What he did as a commentator has no small share of merit, though his researches were not so ample, and his investigations so acute as they might have been, which we now certainly know from the labours of other able and ingenious critics who have followed him. He has enriched his edition with a concise account of each play, and of its characteristic excellence. Many of his notes have illustrated obscurities in the text, and placed passages eminent for beauty in a more conspicuous light; and he has, in general, exhibited such a mode of annotation, as may be beneficial to all subsequent editors.

(James Boswell, *Life of Johnson*)[1]

Great Homer's birth sev'n rival cities claim,
Too mighty such monopoly of fame;

Yet not to birth alone did HOMER owe
His wond'rous worth; what EGYPT could bestow,
With all the schools of GREECE and ASIA joined,
Enlarged th'immense expansion of his mind.
. . .
       But happier STRATFORD, thou
With incontested laurels deck thy brow;
Thy Bard was thine unschooled, and from thee brought
More than all EGYPT, GREECE, or ASIA taught.
Not HOMER's self such matchless honours won;
The Greek has rivals, but thy SHAKESPEARE none.
     (Thomas Seward, 'On SHAKESPEARE's Monument at
                   Stratford upon Avon')[2]

It is difficult to offer anything more than informed guesses about how extensively Shakespeare was read during the eighteenth century: the supply of books in this period is not necessarily a reliable guide to demand. Interest in his works, however, can be put in the context of the general expansion of the reading public. Small by modern standards, England's population grew impressively across the eighteenth century, from about 5.5 million in the late 1720s to 6 million by 1760, and between 7 and 8 million by the end of the century.[3] The economy steadily grew throughout the middle years of the century, with a sharper acceleration beginning around 1780. By 1801, London would be a city of nearly 1 million people, making it the largest in Europe.[4] Literacy among the population as a whole was likewise increasing at a rate that remains a subject of debate among historians, but seems to have varied widely according to regional policies on education: in Scotland, for example, by the end of the century, adult literacy stood at something like 90 per cent of the population; in England, it was only about 65 per cent for men and 50 per cent for women. Edmund Burke put the total reading public at 80,000 people in 1790, a tellingly low estimate coming from this defender of the *ancien régime*.[5] Later historians have pointed out that while many people were still unable to sign their name in the middle of the century, 'cheap editions and digests' were in demand long before that, as were periodicals that emulated the polite tone of *The Spectator*: for instance, the would-be publisher of Johnson's edition of Shakespeare, Edward Cave, was printing 9,000 copies per issue of the *Gentleman's Magazine* within a few years of its creation in 1731. One source claims that circulation peaked at 15,000 copies a month as Walpole fell from power in the winter of 1741. The spread of circulating libraries offered an alternative form of publication, from the 1740s onwards, although Shakespeare is by no means the most conspicuous author in their collections, in which he competed with modern books of travel and history, as well as abundant specimens in a new and popular genre: the novel.[6]

Discovering who exactly was reading what may be tricky, but it is easier to see that the booksellers considered Shakespeare's plays to be an assured part of the business. Don-John Dugas suggests in *Marketing the Bard* that the publication of Nicholas Rowe's edition of Shakespeare's *Works* in 1709 had an immediate impact that exceeded the expectations of its publisher, Jacob Tonson, who printed a new edition almost at once, and another a few years later. This is a reminder that republication may give us some indication of demand for a particular title, more than the initial publication, perhaps. Editions of Shakespeare's *Works* after Rowe, of which there were at least five by the 1750s, would be reissued, revised, enlarged, and broken down so that individual plays could be published separately. Sir Thomas Hanmer's would be reprinted four times before Oxford University Press produced a second edition in 1770. When Samuel Johnson came to edit Shakespeare, he could take as the basis for his own text the fourth edition of Theobald's. When Garrick prepared *Romeo and Juliet* for revival, he worked from Pope or Hanmer.[7] And besides the official revisions for republication, there were offshore operations that imply a growing market for these plays. The Dublin booksellers George Grierson and George Ewing, for example, moved quickly to take advantage of Pope's edition, producing new editions of *The Tempest*, *Hamlet*, and the whole edition in eight volumes within a year of the original's publication. Two equally enterprising booksellers in Dublin, Abraham Bradley and John Smith, 'pirated' Theobald's edition in 1739, printing it as seven duodecimo volumes (the less squashed original had appeared as seven octavo volumes); among the plays they made available individually, *Richard II* appears with 'The end of the fourth volume' left on the last page, and Shakespeare's name omitted from the title page—although it is impossible to say if this was just an oversight, or a sign that they believed their customers would not care who wrote the play. Then again, elaborate promises on the title page suggest otherwise. A Dublin *Macbeth*, for instance, appeared in 1750 as 'Carefully corrected by the best copies: with notes explanatory, &c. and the beauties of the author pointed out according to Mr Pope's edition. To which is prefixed, the argument of the play: and remarks thereon'. Dublin remained, in general, the leading centre for the dubious practice of unauthorized reprints of London publications throughout the century.

Selling plays in print was made more enticing by the presence of live theatre. In London, in the mid-1770s, an admirer of Shakespeare's comedies in performance could buy *The Tempest*, *As You Like It*, or *Much Ado about Nothing* 'as performed at the Theatre Royal, Drury-Lane', with notes from Lewis Theobald's collected edition of 1733, which had reappeared only a couple of years earlier in its ninth edition. By 1790, taking into account both 'legitimate editions' and 'five spurious ones printed in Ireland, one in Scotland, one at Birmingham, and four in London, making in the whole thirty-five impressions', and given the typical print run of 1,000 copies for such works, Edmond Malone reckoned that 'not less than 35,000 copies of our author's works have been dispersed, exclusive of the quartos, single plays, and such as have been altered for the stage'.[8] Include those other categories and the number of copies of plays by Shakespeare in circulation—even on a conservative estimate, and allowing that a print run of 1,000 copies did not necessarily mean 1,000 copies sold—increases vastly.

Along with this widening readership for Shakespeare came an intensification of critical writing about him. Heavily adapted or not, many of the plays had become stock pieces in performance—*Hamlet*, *King Lear*, and *Othello*, among the tragedies, for instance, joined in the 1740s by Garrick's *Macbeth* and *Romeo and Juliet*—while print worked in tandem with performance to consolidate playgoers' familiarity with a piece, enabling them to return to it and become better acquainted with it. Theatrical criticism and literary criticism often intertwine in this period, as readers of Shakespeare sought to demonstrate that their own understanding of a given play exceeded that of the stage. Some collected editions of the plays, however, incorporated a form of criticism more in keeping with play-reading than theatre-going.

The year 1753 saw the publication of the first Scottish edition of Shakespeare, *The Works of Shakespeare. In which the Beauties observed by Pope, Warburton, and Dodd, are pointed out,* which described the author in the 'Scots editors preface' as a 'distinguished character' whose works ought to be in 'great demand...among the learned and polite', while also being appropriate to 'a laudable zeal for promoting home manufactures'. But the title of the Scottish edition also acknowledges that Shakespeare had already been the subject of sustained critical attention, and that the incorporation of the most positive result of this attention—the approval and discovery of Shakespeare's 'beauties'—was part of its appeal, as evidence perhaps of how the 'learned and polite' of England had responded to the plays. The Scots editor (once thought to be the clergyman and man of letters Hugh Blair) can not only adduce the critical observations of three Englishmen to justify this new edition, but could begin by reporting the various comments of Shakespeare's English editors on one another. Warburton and Theobald are here assessing Rowe; Warburton gives his view on Pope and warns against Theobald's 'great acrimony of expression' on the subject of Pope's edition, 'evidently flowing from personal prejudice'. The Scottish editor gives Warburton's views of Theobald and Hanmer without qualification, and uncritically reproduces the Bishop's remarks on his own edition. He then has the compiler of *The Beauties of Shakespeare,* William Dodd, of whom more will be said in the following chapter, state his preference for Theobald over his rivals, condemning Hanmer's editorial procedures as 'unjustifiable' and Warburton's as 'somewhat more generous to us' but leading nonetheless to 'shameful blunders'.[9]

Over the preceding half-century, the wider discourse of literary criticism had created many opportunities for the expression of differences of opinion like these, sometimes furiously petty ones, and these disputes were by no means confined to the editions of his works. As the market for periodicals grew, so did the discussion about Shakespeare, particularly in the theatre. William Popple could argue in 1735, in *The Prompter,* against the current stage interpretation of Polonius as a fool. An anonymous contributor to the *Gentleman's Magazine,* in 1748, compared Shakespeare's morality with Otway's. And of the stage apparitions in *Macbeth,* the year before the Scots edition appeared, Garrick's friend Bonnell Thornton could opine in

*Have at You All, or The Drury Lane Journal* that the 'mealy faces, white shirts, and red rags stuck on in imitation of blood are rather objects of ridicule than terror': 'I would willingly confine all dumb ghosts [the ghost of Hamlet's father being thereby excepted] beneath the trap-doors'.[10]

As early as 1712, meanwhile, John Dennis had suggested that there might be a readership for a work of criticism almost entirely devoted to this one author with *An Essay on the Genius and Writings of Shakespeare: with Some Letters of Criticism to the Spectator*, and sporadically somebody else agreed with him—the anonymous author of *Some Remarks on the Tragedy of Hamlet, Prince of Denmark* (1736), for example, or Samuel Johnson with his *Miscellaneous Observations on the Tragedy of Macbeth* (1745). Warburton's edition of 1747 provoked several vociferous attacks, some of which had greater critical value than the edition itself: *An Enquiry into the Learning of Shakespeare, with Remarks on Several Passages of his Plays* by Peter Whalley, *Critical Observations on Shakespeare* by John Upton, and Thomas Edwards's *Supplement to Mr. Warburton's Edition of Shakespeare* (all 1748, although the last was subsequently enlarged and republished more than once as *The Canons of Criticism*).

Besides bickering over equally spurious emendations, these contributions to a growing body of critical writing found much to value in Shakespeare, but much to condemn as well. The future Master of an Oxford college, Henry Felton, could praise Shakespeare as a 'wonderful genius, a single instance of the force of nature, and the strength of wit' in 1709, as Rowe's edition of the *Works* came out: 'The fire of his fancy breaketh out into his words and sets his readers on a flame. He maketh the blood run cold or warm, and is so admirable a master of the passions that he raises your courage, your pity, and your fear, at his pleasure; but he delighteth most in terror.'[11] John Dennis, writing ten years later, could note that if Shakespeare's 'most celebrated' plays were to be staged '*De novo* without a cabal, without character or prepossession' (implying that his name carried some weight in the theatre by this time, *pace* Robert Hume's argument in 'Before the Bard'), they would be hissed and damned: 'the present spectators of tragedies . . . will endure no modern tragedy in whose principal character love is not the predominant quality.' They would also dislike the 'faults' that Dennis blamed on the taste of Shakespeare's audience, 'perpetual rambles, and his apparent duplicity... or triplicity of action, and the frequent breaking the continuity of the scenes'.[12]

Even much later, in 1745, Eliza Haywood could express surprise at Theophilus Cibber's decision to return to Shakespeare's *Romeo and Juliet*, in preference to the drastic redressing of the tragedy by Otway, *Caius Marius*. The 'admirable author' of the original, she believed, 'had he lived to see the alteration, would have been highly thankful and satisfied with it'. Indeed, with Garrick seeing the same production and deciding that he could restore more of Shakespeare, she thought the rewriting ought to have gone further and disposed of the Nurse, who stuck out as an oddity in Otway's Roman scenes: 'It is, methinks, inconsistent with the character of a Roman Senator and Patrician [i.e., the father of Juliet, who is renamed Lavinia by Otway] to suffer himself to be entertained for half an hour together with such idle chat as would scarcely pass among old women in a nursery.'[13]

Opinions of this variety partly help to explain other rewritings of and borrowings from the plays during this period, from comic efforts like *The Comical Gallant, or The Amours of Sir John Falstaffe* by Dennis (adapted from *The Merry Wives of Windsor*, 1702), William Burnaby's *Love Betrayed* (*Twelfth Night*, 1703), and *A Bickerstaff's Burying* by Susanna Centlivre (*The Tempest*, 1710), to the tragic ones including the unperformed expansion of *Julius Caesar* into two parts by John Sheffield, Duke of Buckingham in 1723, and historical plays such as Colley Cibber's *Papal Tyranny in the Reign of King John* (1745) and the anonymous and unpublished adaptation of *Henry V* as *The Conspiracy Discovered; or, French Policy Defeated* (1746). Comedies seemed especially ripe for alteration: there was good material buried there amid the obscurities in, say, *The Taming of the Shrew*, the Induction of which was adapted twice over in 1716, both times as *The Cobbler of Preston*, with an inflection of patriotism and loyalty suitable to the time of George I's accession to the throne. The lively version by Charles Johnson ends with the Sly character declaring that he will 'from this hour... mix loyalty with my liquor': 'Henceforth I'll never rail against the Crown... But with true Protestants cry, Live King GEORGE'.[14]

And there are further signs of healthy irreverence in the efficient recycling of two plays to make one novelty, as in Charles Johnson's

*Love in a Forest* (again, a topical comedy, with elements from *As You Like It, A Midsummer Night's Dream, Love's Labour's Lost*, and more),[15] and James Miller's synthesis of *Much Ado about Nothing* and Molière's *Princesse d'Elide* to create *The Universal Nothing* (1737). Apparently, early audiences did not mind this adaptive subgenre, the 'hybrid' play—Cibber's *Richard III* might be said to fall into this category, and the method perhaps seems more understandable in the case of chronicle plays—but hardly any that I know of survived into the repertory of the later eighteenth century.

These theatrical responses to Shakespeare imply critical positions not unlike those of Haywood, Dennis, and others. They attest to the enduring interest in certain plays, adapted or not (*Othello* and *The Taming of the Shrew*, to take two contrasting examples), and a turn to others in search of novelty—as would seem to be the case with not only Theobald's *Double Falsehood*, putatively based on a play outside the published canon, but with the 'hint' Matthew Draper took from *The London Prodigal*, dubiously attributed to Shakespeare, a couple of years later, and turned into *The Spend-Thrift*. Shakespeare, for critics and dramatists alike, showed his age in his vulgarities and other faults, which necessitated alteration, at the same time as he remained Felton's 'single instance of the force of nature, and the strength of wit'. The 1760s elicited contrasting developments out of these responses to Shakespeare, in the form of Samuel Johnson's edition of *The Plays of William Shakespeare* and the 'Jubilee' celebrations of Shakespeare in his place of birth, Stratford-upon-Avon in Warwickshire, devised by Johnson's former pupil David Garrick—the first Shakespeare 'festival'.

## The Jubilee: an uncritical interlude

Sometimes seen as an amusingly inexact response to Shakespeare—a festival in his name during which none of his plays were acted, as if Stratford, a town without a permanent theatre at the time, was a fit place to produce anything like the extravagant effects demanded by a Drury Lane audience—the Jubilee festivities of September 1769 came about because Francis Wheler, the Warwickshire borough's Steward of the Court of Records, thought Garrick might be persuaded to donate a statue or picture of Shakespeare, as well as one of himself, for the new town hall. In return, he was to receive the freedom of Stratford, symbolically delivered in a box made of wood from Shakespeare's own mulberry tree. Garrick liked that idea, but went one further, possibly on the suggestion of George Alexander Steevens,[16] and announced his plans for a celebration of Shakespeare in Stratford on the stage at Drury Lane in June 1769. The initial scheme had already been announced in the *St James's Chronicle*:

> . . . a jubilee in honour and to the memory of Shakespeare will be appointed at Stratford the beginning of September next, to be kept up every seventh year. . . . At the first jubilee, a large handsome edifice, lately erected in Stratford by subscription, will be named Shakespeare's Hall, and dedicated to his memory.[17]

This detail often goes missing from concise accounts of the Jubilee, although it is not clear how serious the idea of a repeat performance every seven years was intended or taken to be—or when it was actually dropped. As it turned out, the Jubilee was, notoriously, a wash-out: September has never been the most trustworthy of months for outdoor festivities in Britain. There was meant to be a procession of Shakespearian characters, involving over 200 actors, through the streets of Stratford, but Garrick's partner James Lacy refused to permit the costumes from the theatre to be spattered with mud and rain; Garrick postponed it one day, and cancelled it the next. The roof of the 'hastily completed' rotunda leaked while Garrick recited his new 'Ode to Shakespeare'; although that went down very well, apparently the mock-attack on Shakespeare then performed by Thomas King slightly misfired. 'We were enthusiastic admirers of Shakespeare', recalled one guest, James Boswell, who had turned up in full Corsican dress to promote his new book about his most recent island adventures, 'We had not time to think of cavilling critics'. At night, the fireworks ('Diamond pieces of stars and fountains, porcupine's quills, tourbillons, pyramids of Chinese fires') damply refused to ignite. Finally, for that second of the Jubilee's three days at least, the masquerade went ahead—in the rotunda that was by that point surrounded by a completely flooded meadow. Reports of other major and minor disasters gleefully made their way back to London, fulfilling the prophecies of failure that had already filled the newspapers over the summer.[18] Garrick's financial losses have been put at £2,000.

The story is incomplete, however, without the chapter in which the irrepressible 'Steward' of the Jubilee recovers superbly from disaster: although Garrick's rival manager, George Colman, was first to stage a successful comedy inspired by the Jubilee at the start of the following season, *Man and Wife; or, The Shakespeare Jubilee* in October 1769, his effort was soon eclipsed by Garrick's afterpiece *The Jubilee*. With eighty-eight performances in that season alone, it was one of the sensations of the century, with almost sixty more performances still to come before Garrick retired.

Garrick therefore made a good return on everything he had invested in the Jubilee—not just his own money, but the stories of local ignorance and opportunism ('Toothpick cases, needle cases, punch ladles, tobacco stoppers, inkstands, nutmeg graters, and all sorts of boxes made out of the famous mulberry tree...') and the songs he had written for the occasion. The pageant of Shakespeare's characters could go ahead. He sends himself up with a reference to an inn where all the rooms have been renamed temporarily after the plays, and he is found in *Much Ado about Nothing*, 'the Steward with his mulberry box upon his breast, speaking his fine Ode to music'.[19] In other words, Garrick's Jubilee and Garrick's *Jubilee* had the makings of a metropolitan hit all along. Songs, digs at provincial types, and a vicarious dose of Shakespeare were promising ingredients for a London audience.

As for the trip to Stratford itself, Jean Benedetti has put it succinctly: 'Garrick turned the whole of Stratford into a theatre.'[20] But if Stratford was a theatre, what was the play? In another age, Garrick's biographer Ian McIntyre might be right to call this a 'curious festival—at which not a single work of Shakespeare's was performed', but the absence of any actual dramatic pieces was not a significant cause for criticism at the time. Instead, the Jubilee confirms Shakespeare's status as the national poet by gesturing (as well as it can, despite the rain) towards the emblematic essentials of the 'Complete Plays'. No performance is needed; that work has already been done at Drury Lane, hence Boswell's response to King, whose foppish part was to criticize Shakespeare for disturbing the passionless ennui of the truly civilized.

And meanwhile, the Duke of Dorset (High Steward of the borough), the Duke of Manchester, Lord and Lady Pembroke, Lord and

Lady Spencer... the names alone of a few of the grandees who made the pilgrimage to Stratford—along with the theatrical luminaries Garrick, Colman, Macklin, Kitty Clive, the politician Charles James Fox, the Bluestockings Catherine Macaulay and Elizabeth Carter, possibly the Poet Laureate, William Whitehead, but definitely not Samuel Johnson—attest to its fashionable and prestigious aspect. The horse race on 8 September was appropriately won by a man who said he knew 'very little about the plays of Master Shakespeare' when Garrick presented him with the Jubilee Sweepstakes Cup, engraved with Shakespeare's arms.[21]

In other words, despite the obvious unifying theme of the first Shakespeare festival in Stratford (it was Garrick's only attempt to organize one there, but others did follow, in fact, starting the following year), its significance perhaps lies in the sheer frivolity of the occasion, the terms of easy entertainment in which Shakespeare was to be presented. While others argued over Shakespeare's beauties and faults, and edited the plays, it is a mark of Shakespeare's absorption into the culture of the period that such an event could go ahead among people who had only the vaguest idea about who Shakespeare was. Londoners knew of a Jubilee as an 'entertainment in one of the public gardens':

The pretext of a jubilee might be some military victory, but Apollo or Peace would do if nothing more timely presented itself. The name brought with it an aura of masks, dancing, a temple to something or other exploding in fireworks at the climax of the evening, noise and jostle, crowds overly gay if not actually rowdy.[22]

Just as the Jubilee at Stratford had lacked a play by Shakespeare, Horace Walpole noted that the Jubilee masquerade held at Ranelagh Gardens in 1749 'in the Venetian manner' had 'nothing Venetian in it'.[23] One had taken place the year before Garrick's Jubilee in honour of the King of Denmark's visit. These themes were excuses for pleasure-seeking, socializing, dressing up—but it could be tellingly taken for granted that people sometimes had only the vaguest idea about what the theme meant. Their attention was elsewhere. For Terry Castle, who mentions both the Venetian and the 'Shakespeare' Jubilees in *Masquerade and Civilization* (1986), beyond the outbursts of hedonism that these events could involve, the masquerade functions as a 'meditation on cultural classification and the organizing dialectical schema of eighteenth-century life'; they are 'in the deepest sense a kind of collective meditation on self and other'. They also take place on a grand scale, sometimes involving thousands of people, making them 'part of the imagery of urbanity itself'.[24] Garrick's Stratford Jubilee has to be considered as a part of this continuum of these apparently popular and idiosyncratic events. Michael Dobson rightly calls it the 'culmination of Shakespeare's canonization', in that it embodies a paradox:

By the 1760s Shakespeare is so firmly established as the morally uplifting master of English letters that his reputation no longer seems to depend on his specific achievements as a dramatist: a ubiquitous presence in British culture, his fame is so synonymous with the highest claims of contemporary nationalism that simply to be British is to inherit him, without needing to read or see his actual plays at all.[25]

### Johnson and Shakespeare

The *Gentleman's Magazine* owed a large measure of its success to the labours of the young Samuel Johnson. Born in the year of Rowe's edition of Shakespeare, Johnson had walked from Lichfield to London with Garrick, in March 1737, and gradually established himself as the most formidable man of letters of the time: a critic, biographer, essayist, poet, and, of course, lexicographer, not forgetting his claim to being a dramatist, with the tragedy *Irene*, and a novelist, with the remarkable *Rasselas* (he had also worked as a parliamentary reporter for the *Gentleman's Magazine*.) And as a lexicographer alone, Johnson demonstrated a profound interest in Shakespeare: after proposing an edition of the plays in 1745, he worked for the best part of a decade on his *Dictionary*, first published in two volumes in 1755, a vastly influential and warmly received work in which Shakespeare's plays are the most frequently quoted source of examples apart from the Bible. Johnson proposed for the second time to edit those plays the following year. The *Dictionary* had already shown that he was deeply familiar with the whole oeuvre. *Coriolanus* gave him an instance of the verb 'To vamp' ('To piece an old thing with some new part') in use: 'You wish | To *vamp* a body with a dangerous physic, |

That's sure of death without.' *1 Henry VI* and *King Lear* gave him two examples of a 'shaking marsh; a bog that trembles under the feet': 'Your hearts I'll stamp out with my horse's heels, | And make a *quagmire* of your mingled brains' and 'Poor Tom! whom the foul fiend hath through ford and whirlpool, o'er bog and *quagmire*'. He even showed on a couple of occasions that he was familiar with a long poem, albeit under the title *Tarquin and Lucrece*: 'Who fears a sentence, or an old man's saw, | Shall by a painted *cloth* be kept in awe.'[26] Beyond the implicit claim here for Shakespeare's status as an English classic to put alongside some of Johnson's other major sources (Addison, Dryden, Milton, and Swift), here is a hint of the emphasis that Johnson's edition of Shakespeare would place on the overdue task of elucidating Shakespeare's sometimes obsolete language and obscure sentiments. He reused certain glosses from the *Dictionary* in his edition of Shakespeare—although the relationship between the *Dictionary* and Johnson's edition of Shakespeare, between the editor and the lexicographer, is a complex one overall, with each informing the other, perhaps, rather than the *Dictionary* serving as a straightforward resource for its own compiler.[27]

The superiority of Johnson's *Plays of William Shakespeare*, when the edition eventually appeared in 1765 (and note the break with the tradition lasting from Rowe to Warburton of giving the collection the elevated title of Shakespeare's *Works*), is more immediately apparent in his elegant response to the welter of pamphlets, alterations, and editions that preceded his own, in the opening pages of his preface. 'Antiquity' in a work of literature, he notes, is a quality sometimes thought to be worth reverence in itself: 'Some seem to admire indiscriminately whatever has been long preserved, without considering that time has sometimes co-operated with chance.' To discriminate critically, however, the 'great contention of criticism', is to 'find the faults of the moderns, and the beauties of the ancients'. The current and enduring conversation (or contention) between critics is a necessary one:

The reverence due to writings that have long subsisted arises therefore not from any credulous confidence in the superior wisdom of past ages, or gloomy persuasion of the degeneracy of mankind, but is the consequence of acknow ledged and indubitable positions, that what has been longest known has been most considered, and what is most considered is best understood.[28]

Affirming the value of Shakespeare, then, has a double significance for Johnson, as it affirms the value of criticism in turn: Shakespeare has 'gained and kept the favour of his countrymen'.[29] And although Johnson does not indulge in the kinds of typographical devices employed by Pope and the Scots edition to extend that process of discrimination to the texts of the play in his edition, he makes it plain that, for him at least, general acclaim does not mean that Shakespeare is infallible. His plots are 'loosely formed' and he has 'no regard to distinction of time or place'. As a narrator, he could be guilty of 'a disproportionate pomp of diction and a wearisome train of circumlocution'. A pun (or 'quibble') is, famously, his 'fatal Cleopatra', for which he would willingly sacrifice 'reason, propriety and truth'.[30] But the undisciplined inventiveness that unites these failings is at its most offensive when Johnson considers Shakespeare's lack of interest in providing what every *good* story needs—a moral:

He...is so much more careful to please than to instruct, that he seems to write without any moral purpose. From his writings indeed a system of social duty may be selected, for he that thinks reasonably must think morally; but his precepts and axioms drop casually from him; he makes no just distribution of good or evil, nor is always careful to show in the virtuous a disapprobation of the wicked; he carries his persons indifferently through right and wrong, and at the close dismisses them without further care, and leaves their examples to operate by chance. This fault the barbarity of his age cannot extenuate; for it is always a writer's duty to make the world better, and justice is a virtue independent on time or place.[31]

These absolute terms of engagement are characteristic of Johnson's general critical practice, and apply equally to what he sees as one of Shakespeare's great strengths:

Nothing can please many, and please long, but just representations of general nature. Particular manners can be known to few, and therefore few only can judge how nearly they are copied. The irregular combinations of fanciful invention may delight a-while, by the novelty of which the common satiety of life sends us all in quest; but the pleasures of sudden wonder are soon exhausted, and the mind can only repose on the stability of truth.

*Shakespeare* is above all writers, at least above all modern writers, the poet of nature; the poet that holds up to his readers a faithful mirror of manners and of life. His characters are not modified by the customs of particular places, unpractised by the rest of the world; by the peculiarities of studies or professions, which can operate but upon small numbers; or by the accidents of transient fashions or temporary opinions: they are the genuine progeny of common humanity, such as the world will always supply, and observation will always find. His persons act and speak by the influence of those general passions and principles by which all minds are agitated, and the whole system of life is continued in motion. In the writings of other poets a character is too often an individual; in those of *Shakespeare* it is commonly a species.[32]

In his admiration for Shakespeare's genius for characterization, then, although Johnson himself is careful to consider all aspects of the drama, he points a way forward for literary criticism, anticipating a phenomenon noted by Brian Vickers: the growth during the final third of the eighteenth century of 'character criticism', an interest in the individual characters freed from the constraints of neoclassical criteria.[33] Those puns and loosely formed plots do not deter him from saying that 'nothing is essential to the fable, but unity of action'—although he is also careful to speak respectfully of the 'dramatick rules' even as he discards them.[34] In their place, he finds that Shakespeare's excellence lies in his disobedience to unnatural notions of what is proper or necessary to a play:

Other dramatists can only gain attention by hyperbolical or aggravated characters, by fabulous and unexampled excellence or depravity, as the writers of barbarous romances invigorated the reader by a giant and a dwarf... *Shakespeare* has no heroes; his scenes are occupied only by men, who act and speak as the reader thinks that he should himself have spoken or acted on the same occasion: Even where the agency is supernatural the dialogue is level with life.... His story requires Romans or kings, but he thinks only on men. He knew that *Rome*, like every other city, had men of all dispositions; and wanting a buffoon, he went into the senate-house for that which the senate-house would certainly have afforded him.[35]

Unfortunately for British and European theatre, neoclassicism had not yet had its day—far from it—but away from the stage, *readers* of Shakespeare were coming around to this way of thinking. It was not long after the publication of Johnson's edition, for example, that Thomas Whately wrote his *Remarks on Some of the Characters of Shakespeare*, although that work would not be published until 1785; further examples include the *Essays on Shakespeare's Dramatic Characters* published by William Richardson (1774, 1783–4, and 1788–9), and

Maurice Morgann's engaging *Essay on the Dramatic Character of Sir John Falstaff* (1777), in which he argued that the fat knight was no coward, and prompted a fine response from Richard Stack in 1788 ('These are strange arts by which Shakespeare has drawn our liking toward so offensive an object [as Falstaff] . . . in the gay wit we forget the contemptible coward').[36] This is not to say that there were not neoclassical elements to this new phase of thinking about Shakespeare's characters—questions of consistency and moral purpose still counted for a great deal—but the concentration of later critics on, say, Hamlet's 'unity of a divided mind' depend on the same appreciation of Shakespeare as the psychologically adept creator of characters who is praised in Johnson's preface.[37] It cannot be entirely a coincidence that Shakespeare's characters were precisely what Garrick set out to celebrate with his procession through Stratford-upon-Avon in 1769, incongruous though the comparison may seem.

The critical enthusiasm for an aspect of Shakespeare's dramaturgy that Johnson sees as unaffected by the 'accidents of transient fashions or temporary opinions' reflects something of the universalizing proclivities of 'Dictionary' Johnson himself. Likewise, while looking down in the conventional way on Shakespeare's audience, Johnson gives a good pragmatic reason for Shakespeare to take his plots from the 'most popular' novels of his day: 'his audience could not have followed him through the intricacies of the drama, had they not held the thread of the story in their hands'.[38] But it also informs his sense of how Shakespeare should be read (not seen on the stage), as urged in one of the most celebrated passages of eighteenth-century critical prose:

Notes are often necessary, but they are necessary evils. Let him, that is yet unacquainted with the powers of Shakespeare, and who desires to feel the highest pleasure that the drama can give, read every play from the first scene to the last, with utter negligence of all his commentators. When his fancy is once on the wing, let it not stoop at correction or explanation. When his attention is strongly engaged, let it disdain alike to turn aside to the name of *Theobald* and of *Pope*. Let him read on through brightness and obscurity, through integrity and corruption; let him preserve his comprehension of the dialogue and his interest in the fable. And when the pleasures of novelty have ceased, let him attempt exactness, and read the commentators.

Particular passages are cleared by notes, but the general effect of the work is weakened. The mind is refrigerated by interruption; the thoughts are diverted from the principal subject; the reader is weary, he suspects not why; and at last throws away the book, which he has too diligently studied.[39]

This is delightful advice coming from a critic who was sometimes himself associated with indolence (not least over this edition of Shakespeare) but whose diligence also produced prodigious wonders.

On the other hand, Johnson claims to retain all of Pope's notes, 'that no fragment of so great a writer may be lost'[40]—suggesting an ambiguity in Johnson's mind about his readers. They are to ignore the notes as best they can, first time round at least—the plays are to be read with as little mediation as possible—at the same time as the accrued wisdom of past commentators must be respected, too, and must play its part in Johnson's edition. 'It is to be lamented, that such a writer should want a commentary; that his language should become obsolete, or his sentiments obscure', Johnson writes,[41] and his anxiety over the threat the passage of time poses to the comprehensibility of Shakespeare's language leads him to supply his own notes, too, that show a distinctly lexicographical tendency, glossing words and phrases, as well as arbitrating between rival readings, or sometimes offering a markedly personal response.

In this spirit, Johnson remarks of 'love's visible soul'—namely, Helen in *Troilus and Cressida*—that the 'visible' is Hanmer's. Other editions have the opposite reading: '*invisible*, which perhaps may be right'.[42] 'This wrongs you' in *The Merry Wives of Windsor* is worthy of a threefold gloss ('This is below your character, unworthy of your understanding, injurious to your honour') and a parallel from *The Taming of the Shrew* ('You wrong me much, indeed you wrong yourself ').[43] The 'fashion of the time' in *The Two Gentlemen of Verona* is glossed as the 'modes of courtship, the acts by which men recommended themselves to ladies'.[44] And Johnson's piety stands aghast at the horror of what Hamlet suggests he wants to do to Claudius, when he has the chance to kill him while he seems to be at his prayers ('Now might I do it pat'):

This speech, in which *Hamlet*, represented as a virtuous character, is not content with taking blood for blood, but contrives damnation for the man that he would punish, is too horrible to be read or to be uttered.[45]

Many more such examples might be given of Johnson's efforts to redeem Shakespeare's obscurities for contemporary readers. The main point, however, is made by Boswell's summing-up from his *Life of Johnson*, quoted at the beginning of this chapter: it was by 'candidly admitting the faults of his poet' that Johnson 'had the more credit in bestowing on him deserved and indisputable praise'. This was decidedly not the Jubilee route to making of Shakespeare the national poet. Johnson was prepared to say that *Twelfth Night* was 'elegant and easy' in its 'graver' scenes and 'exquisitely humorous' in others, but that the marriage of Olivia and Sebastian 'wants credibility, and fails to produce the proper instruction required in the drama, as it exhibits no just picture of life'.[46] Some plays inspired no final comment at all. The *Henry VI* plays 'have not sufficient variety of action, for the incidents are too often of the same kind; yet many of the characters are well discriminated'.[47] And *King Lear* inspires a long final note, including the confidence from Johnson that 'I was many years ago so shocked by *Cordelia*'s death, that I know not whether I ever endured to read again the last scenes of the play till I undertook to revise them as an editor'.[48] In a rare direct reference to the contemporary stage, Johnson noted Tate's version of the play and the audience's preference, like his own, for *Lear* with a happy ending.

The late 1760s were remarkable, then, for producing, in the Jubilee, an event that brashly deified Shakespeare the author at the same time as his texts were coming under intense scrutiny from Johnson, the most influential critic of the age—for offering praise that was, in Boswell's words, 'like that of a counsel, upon his own side of the cause' and criticism 'like the grave, well-considered, and impartial opinion of the judge'. More was to follow. The year after Johnson's edition appeared, George Steevens, who had given Johnson almost fifty notes, published *Twenty of the Plays of Shakespeare, Being the whole Number printed in Quarto During his Life-Time, or before the Restoration* in four volumes, the first eighteenth-century attempt to reclaim the quartos and, even more boldly, *Shake-speares Sonnets*, as they were called in 1609, and *A Louers Complaint*. Edward Capell's edition in ten small octavo volumes, *Mr William Shakespeare his Comedies, Histories, and Tragedies*, appeared in 1767 (albeit without the volumes of notes and variants that remained incomplete at Capell's death in 1781). And the year before Garrick's Jubilee took place, Johnson's edition of Shakespeare was reprinted without alterations.

A few years later, however, in 1773, it reappeared, considerably reworked by Steevens, with contributions from, among others, Johnson himself (it has been misleadingly supposed that he 'took little part in the actual revision', and his name was just on the title page for commercial reasons).[49] This was a significant advance on the first edition. The first time round, Johnson had not achieved everything that he or others had wished for; in his *Proposals for Printing, by Subscription, the Dramatick Works of William Shakespeare*, for instance, he had optimistically suggested that in order to prepare his edition he would 'read the books which the author read'.[50] Nonetheless, with his inimitable critical authority, and his efficient reproduction of the dialogue between commentators, Johnson had succeeded in initiating a new phase in the editing of Shakespeare's plays—an achievement consolidated by the edition of 1773. The 'variorum' format he had adopted became the basis for the further editions and commentaries of later eighteenth-century scholars such as Richard Farmer, Edmond Malone, Isaac Reed, and George Steevens.

Farmer, the author of an *Essay on the Learning of Shakespeare* (1767), contributed 247 notes to the Johnson-Steevens edition of 1773, published in an appendix to the tenth volume, and contributed to the *Supplement to the Edition of Shakespeare's Plays Published in 1778* published by Malone in 1780, to Reed's edition based on that of Johnson and Steevens in 1785, and to Steevens's edition again of 1793. Steevens alone wrote thousands of notes for several editions, while the unsung George Tollet suggested fifteen notes for the 1773 edition, more than 400 notes to Steevens for the 1778 edition, and another three in the *Supplement*.[51] Others, such as Thomas Warton, contributed on a lesser scale.

The generous medievalist and editor of Chaucer, Thomas Tyrwhitt, made some useful criticisms of Johnson's edition in his *Observations and Conjectures upon Some Passages of Shakespeare* (1766), not least in his suggestion that Johnson could have 'spared' himself from having to write 'a long note...with some conjectures' on a single word in *Cymbeline*, if only he had looked at the Second Folio: 'Collating is certainly dull work; but I doubt whether, upon the whole, an editor would not find it the shortest and easiest, as well as the surest, method of discharging his duty.'[52] The note was duly replaced with a less tortuous gloss by Steevens in 1773, and Tyrwhitt went on to assist Steevens, Reed, and Malone, in turn. He provided the *Supplement* of 1780, for instance, with a long note, a formidable essay in itself, in which he refuted virtually everything Warburton has to say about chivalric romance—'I should humbly advise the next editor of Shakespeare to omit it'—to Malone's obvious delight, as he wryly suggested that Warburton's long note on this subject could now never be omitted because Tyrwhitt's 'judicious observations' had given it 'a value it certainly had not before'.[53]

The spirit of co-operation between these learned commentators sometimes gave way to ugly disputes (involving the pugnacious Joseph Ritson, say, or the unreliable John Monck Mason), of which the footnoted bouts of parallel readings, best guesses, theories about textual corruption are the innocent-seeming textual remnants. And these disagreements could have monstrous results. By the early 1800s, Reed was overseeing a variorum edition—fundamentally based on the work of Johnson and Steevens, but now extending to twenty one volumes—with successive editors' prefaces and advertisements taking up the whole of the first volume, and the play texts beginning in the fourth volume, and proceeding at a basic rate of about two plays per volume. Although these ultimate productions of the post-Johnson era show that much work was done in this period that was of lasting value and interest, they also include plenty of speculative creativity and notes hopelessly answering notes. Here is Johnson himself suggesting that a rhyme is 'intended' at one point in *Romeo and Juliet*, when the lovers are dead and the watchmen come on their investigation, which he proceeds to 'restore' (the italics emphasize his points of departure from the received text):

> Raise up the Montagues. Some others, *go*.
> We see the ground whereon these woes do lie,
> But the true ground of all *this* piteous *woe*
> We cannot without circumstance descry.

Steevens remarks: 'It was often thought sufficient, in the time of Shakespeare, for the second and fourth lines in a stanza, to rhyme with each other.' Then he adds, uneasy in the presence of a pun: 'It were to be wished that an apology as sufficient could be offered for this Watchman's quibble between *ground*, the earth, and *ground*, the fundamental cause.'[54] Exchanges of this nature seldom reveal more about Shakespeare than they do about the attitudes of his annotators.

Sometimes, in addition, they simply meet a phrase that is beyond them. When Parolles starts lying for his life in *All's Well That Ends Well*, the disguised Bertram says: 'A pox on him! he's a cat still.' 'That is, throw him how you will', Johnson explains, 'he lights upon his legs.' Steevens begs to differ: 'Bertram has no such meaning. In a speech or two before, he declares his aversion a cat, and now only continues in the same opinion . . . .' 'I am still of my former opinion', says Johnson. 'The speech was applied by King James to [Sir Edward] Coke, with respect to his subtilties of law. . . .' Finally, Malone adds, concluding a long paragraph: 'There cannot, therefore, I think be any doubt that Dr Johnson's interpretation'—and here he repeats Johnson's reading, in case the reader has lost track or interest by this point—'is founded on a misapprehension'.[55]

Reed humbly thought he ought to retain all of this—that is what a variorum edition does, after all. But it is a curious legacy, given its origins in an edition that originally advised the reader to 'attempt exactness, and read the commentators' only when 'the pleasures of novelty have ceased'.

As suggested at the beginning of this chapter, it is unclear exactly how many readers Shakespeare had at any given point during the eighteenth century; the same goes for estimating how many took Johnson's advice. In any case, with the *Donaldson* v. *Beckett* ruling of 1774, the Tonson monopoly on Shakespeare was terminated—and since this was a case that actually related to the illicit publication of *The Seasons by James Thomson*, it might be thought of as a significant instance of the eighteenth century's 'influence' on Shakespeare. Shakespeare was now completely in the public domain. As it happens, the ruling coincided with the publication of John Bell's edition of the plays as they were acted at Covent Garden and Drury Lane, which would remain in print until the wend of the century. *Bell's Edition of Shakespeare's Plays*, in the words of one commentator, represented 'what playgoers had been seeing on stage, and it was what they wanted to read'.[56] The business of making and selling books was thoroughly imbricated with the business of adapting and performing plays.

# *As Shakespeare Says*

We clearly find genius within the words of Shakespeare's texts, hence our horror at these attempts [by Restoration and eighteenth-century dramatists] to rewrite or remove his words. Equally clearly, the playwrights and critics of the Restoration and eighteenth century, while they revered the poet, did not revere his language *per se*. In the intervening two hundred and fifty years, attitudes toward Shakespeare and his text have been inverted. This shift is not simply an attempt to canonize an author...but an attempt to canonize words, a crucial distinction. Shakespeare as author also becomes Shakespeare as document.

(Jean I. Marsden, *The Re-Imagined Text*)[1]

For Samuel Johnson, Shakespeare's plays, despite their faults, were full of 'practical axioms and domestic wisdom', as well as brilliantly lifelike characters, drawn from nature. But to go about collecting from these plays a 'system of civil and economical prudence' by extracting 'particular passages' would be to miss the point: 'his real power is shown...by the progress of his fable, and the tenor of his dialogue; and he that tries to recommend him by select quotations, will succeed like the pedant in *Hierocles*, who, when he offered his house to sale, carried a brick in his pocket as a specimen'.[2]

Although couched in typically general terms, Johnson's ruling here applies very well to a contemporary phenomenon: *The Beauties of Shakespeare: Regularly selected from each Play* by the 'Macaroni Parson', William Dodd. Here was a selection of 'particular passages' that promised to offer Shakespeare purified—to give the reader the best of Shakespeare, concisely, and thus to transform him from a writer of drama (where his 'real power' lay) into a sagacious, apothegmatic guide to human nature. It was also a publication that prioritized Shakespeare's words over everything else—whereas Johnson, while keeping the total effect of the drama in mind, would probably have said that Shakespeare's unique achievement lay in his creation of characters drawn from nature.

Initially published in two volumes in 1752, Dodd's anthology took exactly the approach that Johnson rejected, systematically aggregating passages from the plays, and giving them titles that fixed their meaning and removed them from their dramatic context to give them a universal application or character-specific context: 'Danger', 'Honour', 'The blessings of a low station', 'Calpurnia to Caesar, on the prodigies seen the night before his death', 'England, invincible, if unanimous'. Dialogue is not excluded but would not appear here to be essential to the beauty of Shakespeare's writing; Dodd provides an index for readers in a hurry to find an apt quotation to illustrate 'Rhymers, ridiculed' or 'Royalty, the miseries of', and frequent footnotes that show the care he took to consult a variety of recent editions, as well as, notably, Theobald's supposed adaptation based on Shakespeare, *Double Falsehood*. Dodd also suggests emendations and glosses of his own, and glances at the subject of theatrical improvements on Shakespeare when he gives 'Romeo's last speech over Juliet, in the vault', beginning 'O, my love, my wife!' There is also the ghost of an acknowledgement here that these 'beauties' lose their force without the 'progress of fable':

I have given the reader this last speech of *Romeo*, rather to let him into the plot, and convince him of the merit of the alterations made in it, than for any singular beauty of its own; *Romeo*'s surviving till *Juliet* awakens, is certainly productive of great beauties, particularly in the acting.[3]

It is also *Romeo and Juliet* that leads Dodd to pay homage to the power of the stage, and say that 'no comment' is needed when the play is seen performed by 'some of the best and most judicious actors that ever appeared on any stage'.[4] But *The Beauties of Shakespeare* had an enduring appeal of its own: a revised edition appeared in 1757 and a third posthumously in 1780; it was certainly still in print late in the nineteenth century, although Edwin Eliott Willoughby, in an essay that tells the extraordinary story of how the once-fashionable preacher Dodd's later attempts to raise the funds to publish an edition in full led him to the gallows in 1777, claims that it was still in print in 1935. Either way, Willoughby is probably right to claim that this anthology is 'the piece of Shakespeariana in publication for the longest period of time'.[5]

Dodd's immediate influence is palpable in an edition of Shakespeare published the following year, *The Works of Shakespeare. In which the Beauties observed by Pope, Warburton, and Dodd, are pointed out*, showing that Pope's conception of the edition as a repository for critical judgements rather than just the author's corrected texts still had its adherents. The writer and sometime actress Elizabeth Griffith followed up with *The Morality of Shakespeare's Drama Illustrated* (dedicated, incidentally, to Garrick, who had produced her most successful play, *The School for Rakes*, in 1769), in which she confessed that hers was not an entirely original project, but it needed doing just the same:

Our author's poetical beauties have been already selected, though they needed it not, as they are undoubtedly so striking as scarcely to require the being particularly pointed out to any reader capable of conceiving or relishing them; but a single line, sometimes a word, in many instances throughout his Works, may convey a hint, or impress a sentiment upon the heart, if properly marked, which might possibly be overlooked, while curiosity is attending to the fable, or the imagination transported with the splendour of diction, or sublimity of images.[6]

This was not, in other words, about just any 'single line' or 'word', but the 'sentiment' that they might embody. The dramatic context does not vanish here, but is approved according to ethical rather than aesthetic principles (assuming, of course, that the two can be separated). *Richard III* accordingly inspires Griffith to write:

Every representation, either of a scene or season of peace, is peculiarly soothing to the human mind. . . . But when it is contrasted with the opposite condition of tumult and war, the delight rises infinitely higher. There are many such descriptions as this in Shakespeare; and as the imbuing the mind with such contemplations, must certainly have a moral tendency in it, I am glad to transcribe every passage of the kind I meet with in him.[7]

By contrast, Griffith could find little to say about what she treated as Shakespeare's first plays, *The Tempest* and *A Midsummer Night's*

*Dream* ('his youthful imagination must naturally be thought to have been more sportive and exuberant, than his riper judgment might have permitted indulgence of '),[8] as was conventionally if uncertainly thought. She approves of Helena's observation that 'Our remedies oft in ourselves do lie', in *All's Well That Ends Well*, on the grounds that the speech contains 'some excellent well-spirited reflections here thrown out, to encourage men in the exertion of all their active faculties towards the advancement of their fortunes'. She can barely bring herself to quote Lear's curse on his daughters at all, they are 'so very horrid and shocking to humanity'.[9] And the importance of getting the words exactly right is reflected in the presence of footnotes that provide glosses and record the variant readings. Like Dodd, Warburton, and other commentators, Griffith might feel 'tempted' to alter the text for clarity's sake—as in the case of Julius Caesar's suspicious attitude to a lean and hungry intellectual, 'Yet if my name were liable to fear, | I do not know the man I should avoid, | So soon as that spare Cassius', which leads instead to a self-reassuring piece of literary criticism on the single word 'name':

I was tempted to change this word to *mind*, as being more intelligible; but I recollected that Shakespeare meant to make Caesar affect to speak of his name, as his person—He says afterwards, in the same speech, For always I am Caesar; and throughout in the same style.[10]

*Julius Caesar* similarly inspires Griffith to vent her spleen against Ben Jonson for daring to quote a line incorrectly, purely, as she sees it, out of 'envious malice', and going on to apologise to the reader for diverging from the texts themselves: 'there is a proper moral in defending the Author of this great code of Ethics, from any aspersion thrown out against his sense, meaning, or character'.[11] *The Morality of Shakespeare's Drama Illustrated* is therefore of interest for its steps in the direction of what Alfred Harbage would later call the myth of Shakespeare's authorial infallibility.[12] Even when she does not quote the lines in question—that curse in *King Lear*, for example—she is ready with an explanation for it. 'Shakespeare, I am convinced, supplied them merely in order to raise an abhorrence in his audience, against two of the greatest crimes in the black list of deadly sins, namely, ingratitude and undutifulness....'[13]

Griffith also seems to take a wary interest in Shakespeare's female characters. She notes of the Princess and her ladies in *Love's Labour Lost* (sic) that they seem to talk 'very philosophically' about love, but then adds what she believes they ought to have said about it: 'Sense is always a match for sense, and can be overreached by folly only...'tis natural to humour those fondlings, whom 'tis thought vain to reason with'.[14] Of Hermione's 'noble spirit of parental sentiment' on trial for adultery in *The Winter's Tale*, she approves and pays the lines beginning 'Behold me | A fellow of the royal bed' a high compliment: 'The beautiful sentiment expressed in the last lines...must draw tears of pity from virtuous mothers, and should [draw] those of another kind from vicious ones, puts me in mind of a parallel passage in Scripture.'[15] 'There is a very proper hint given here to women, not to deviate from the prescribed rules and decorums of their sex', she writes of some dialogue between Rosalind and Celia in *As You Like It*.[16] It is an intriguing extension of the work of the Shakespeare Ladies Club in the 1730s.

An anthology on these lines really did suggest a 'system of civil and economical prudence' drawn from 'particular passages'. Beyond the anthologies and the collected editions of Shakespeare, however, the idea of fragmenting Shakespeare's works, not necessarily derived directly from Dodd or Griffith, but in parallel to them, was fast catching on. Johnson, in his *Proposals for Printing, by Subscription, the Dramatic Works of William Shakespeare* of 1756, had ruled out the idea of a Pope-like imposition of taste on the text of his putative edition of Shakespeare ('The editor, though he may less delight his own vanity, will probably please his reader more, by supposing him equally able with himself to judge of beauties and faults, which require no previous acquisition of remote knowledge').[17] In other contexts, nonetheless, the second half of the eighteenth century was free to deploy those same renowned beauties as it pleased: separated from their 'parent' plays and adopted many times over, as epigraphs for novels, and allusions in stage-plays, poems, and periodicals.

On stage, snippets of Shakespeare serve as an obvious source of knowing humour, sometimes simply as in-jokes: towards the end of Arthur Murphy's afterpiece *The Way To Keep Him* (first performed in the spring of 1760 at Drury Lane, and successful enough to be expanded into a main piece the following year), an imposture is exposed: the erring husband Mr Lovemore, living up to his name, finds himself trapped between his wife and the widow, Mrs Bellmour, he has been secretly wooing in the guise of Lord Etheridge. It is an awkward moment; 'Aye, now my turn is come', Lovemore says in an aside, as he resigns himself to his fate.[18] Step forward Sir Brilliant Fashion, a man who 'does everything fashionably' and 'talks so lively' that he is 'never at a loss', to mock him: 'By all that's whimsical, an odd sort of adventure this—my Lord [*Advances to him.*], my Lord— my Lord Etheridge, as the man says in the play, "Your Lordship's right welcome back to Denmark".'[19]

'As the man says in the play'—the man in question being Osric and the play *Hamlet*, as many members of the audience would have known—is a brilliantly casual way to introduce Sir Brilliant's gratuit- ous moment of wit, and a compliment to the understanding of those cognoscenti who might recognize it as a theatrical allusion, since the part of Lovemore was created by David Garrick, famed for his performances as Hamlet. (And the actor who played Sir Brilliant, John 'Gentleman' Palmer, would in turn play Osric to Garrick's Hamlet later in the season; perhaps Palmer took the chance to practise his entrance in *The Way To Keep Him*, since the line about Denmark is Osric's first, albeit spoken here for the purpose of mocking a pretend lord rather than greeting too ostentatiously a real prince.) Such allusions separated the insiders from those whose knowledge of the theatre was a little hazier, such as Mrs Lovemore's waiting-woman, Muslin, who, much earlier in *The Way To Keep Him*, manages to confuse *Catharine and Petruchio*, Garrick's adaptation of *The Taming of the Shrew*, with the name of a character from *Romeo and Juliet* (while also confusing 'chattels', another word here for 'goods', with 'cattles'):

Ma'am, was you ever at the play of Catherine and Mercutio? The vile man calls his wife his goods, and his cattles, and his household stuff.—There you may see, Ma'am, what a husband is....[20]

There seems to be a subtler use of some of the same ideas in Goldsmith's comedy *She Stoops To Conquer* (1773), which has two young gentlemen from London arrive at a country inn in the first act, only to be told that they are lost. 'We wanted no ghost to tell us that', replies one of them, Marlow, taking his cue from *Hamlet*; the quotation seems to mean nothing to the countrymen.[21] But if the ghost of Old Hamlet cuts a rather more regal figure than Tony Lumpkin, they share a dramatic role in their respective plays, feeding the protagonist dangerous information, suggesting they take a course that will lead them into peril. Likewise, faced with an imminent encounter with the enemy—namely, Marlow, the husband chosen for her—Kate Hardcastle exclaims: 'Would it were bed time and all were well.'[22] The reference is ominous but comic, too, aligning her with Falstaff, of all people, in *1 Henry IV* before the Battle of Shrewsbury. And Shakespeare seems to have been generally on Goldsmith's mind, given that the finally accepted epilogue he wrote for the play is a pastiche of the Seven Ages of Man speech from *As You Like It*, and that there seems to be a hint of Milton's well-known lines about Shakespeare warbling his woodnotes wild in Mrs Hardcastle's remonstrations with her son: 'No, Tony, you then go to the alehouse or the kennel. I'm never to be delighted with your agreeable, wild notes, unfeeling monster!'[23] All that is needed is a mulberry tree, which duly shows up in the fifth act, to persuade the reader, if not the audience, that such incidental details are consistent with Goldsmith's general hopes for the play as a rejection of false delicacy and sentimental elements in English drama, and a return to the 'laughing comedy' of earlier English playwrights—not only Shakespeare but Farquhar, too, whose work is also invoked in the play.

Out of such celebrations of the theatrical, quotable Shakespeare come such plays as Isaac Jackman's *All the World's a Stage* (1777) and John O'Keeffe's *Wild Oats* (1791), in which theatricality plays an even more explicit, dominant part in proceedings. Jackman's farce, first performed at Drury Lane as a benefit, went down well enough to become a stock piece, and follows Garrick's *Jubilee* and Goldsmith's *She Stoops* in confirming the comic value—for London audiences—of rustic ignorance and lack of refinement, and is set in Shrewsbury in a house where theatricality is turning the place upside down: Diggery 'nearly smothered that silly hussy, Tippet, in the oven a few days ago', after saying he would 'break open the door of it with the kitchen poker, and that would be playing *Romo*'.[24] Othello frames the play as the hero is introduced quoting it at will, then assuring the helpless paterfamilias: 'Fear not my government.' The heroine reports on a private rehearsal of the scene in which 'the blackamoor smothers his wife', only her acting partner had 'blacked all his face with soot and goose dripping'; this little scene is only discovered because: 'When Cymon kissed me in bed, he blacked my left cheek so abominably, that when I came down to breakfast in the morning, the family were all frightened out of their wits. Mrs. Bridget bid me go to the glass; and when I looked at myself—lord, lord, how I did laugh! I told them the whole story. And do you know, that I am locked into my room every night since.'[25]

Of a similar order are certain allusions to Shakespeare in eighteenth-century fiction. There are celebrated depictions of theatrical scenes in Henry Fielding's *Tom Jones* (1749; when Partridge is marvellously taken in explicitly by Garrick's Hamlet, feeling the fear that he feigns on seeing the ghost) and Frances Burney's *Camilla* (1796; 'The actors were of the lowest strolling kind.... Othello, therefore, was equipped as king Richard the third, save that instead of a regal front he had a black wig'),[26] but the adoption and attribution to Shakespeare even of two-word phrases is not difficult to find elsewhere (as in, for example, the 'impatient thoughts' of the twitchy Lord Grondale in Robert Bage's *Hermsprong*, 1796, ostentatiously tagged 'as Shakespeare says' by Miss Fluart).[27]

After the pioneering work of Robert Gale Noyes in *The Thespian Mirror: Shakespeare in the Eighteenth-Century Novel* (1953), perhaps Kate Rumbold's attentive reading of varying mid-eighteenth century appropriations of Shakespeare in the novel is the most useful as a guide to the basic issues.[28] Rumbold draws a distinction, for example, between the 'visibility of overt quotations' that are 'rarely innocuous', and 'hidden allusions that require more detective work'. In particular, Rumbold finds, 'a tang of the theater' attends quotations from Shakespeare's plays, complicating our response to them and their apparently polite discourse. That complexity may be found in everything from *Clarissa* (1748), with Lovelace's heavy doses of self-dramatization, or *Tristram Shandy* (1759–67), in which Dr Slop enters '*unwiped, unappointed, unannealed*, with all his stains and botches on him', in a parody of Hamlet's ghost, 'motionless and speechless',[29] to the polite convention deployed by Fanny Hill, the narrator and heroine of John Cleland's *Memoirs of a Woman of Pleasure* (1748–9), who takes Romeo's description of the 'womb of death', the tomb of the Capulets where

Juliet lies (he thinks) dead, as 'Gorged with the dearest morsel of the earth', and transforms it into a kind of theatrical obscenity.

It may be no coincidence that Cleland had been finishing his notorious book in the Fleet prison, and would not be released until after it was published, at the same time as Garrick was preparing his version of *Romeo and Juliet* (which retained the 'dearest morsel' line) for its first performance at Drury Lane on 29 November 1748. The first volume of *Memoirs of a Woman of Pleasure* had been announced only eight days earlier in the *General Advertiser*. Although it seems possible, if not likely, that a version of the novel had been in circulation since the 1730s,[30] it is possible that Cleland added his reference to *Romeo and Juliet* in the autumn of 1748, in response to the play's sudden topicality.

In the history of the eighteenth-century novel, then, Shakespeare plays a significant supporting role, one that, for certain novelists at least, depends crucially on his status as a dramatist. When a dubious but amusing piece of work such as *The Life and Extraordinary History of the Chevalier John Taylor* (1761) tells the reader that 'The Doctor stares like Hamlet', it is clear that this is a stage-Hamlet the author has in mind.[31] And it is the performed (not read) *Hamlet* that also haunts Tobias Smollett's picaresque novel *The Life and Adventures of Sir Launcelot Greaves* (serialized in the *British Magazine*, 1760–1, and published in book form in 1762). Although presented principally as a variation on a theme of Cervantes, in its use of a chivalrously 'mad' protagonist as a vehicle for social satire, *Launcelot Greaves* alludes several times to specific theatrical moments from Shakespeare. Indeed, the novel seems to stage dramatic entrances repeatedly, from Sir Launcelot's first entrance, carrying his squire, Timothy Crabshaw, over his shoulder, into the Black Lion Inn—which is 'perhaps a rough remembrance of Orlando's pietà-like entrance with old Adam in *As You Like It*'—'armed cap-a-pie', like the ghost of Hamlet's father.[32] 'Hey day! What precious mummery is this?' responds one of the onlookers. 'What, are we to have the farce of Hamlet's ghost?'[33]

In good epic fashion, however, Smollett has here begun his narrative *in medias res*. Sir Launcelot gets to make another first entrance when his godson Tom Clarke recounts the story of his earlier 'first appearance' before an audience of several hundred people, including rival factions in local politics: 'there was just such a humming and clapping of hands as you may have heard when the celebrated Garrick comes upon the stage in King Lear, or King Richard, or any other top character.... While he spoke, all was hushed in admiration and attention—you could have almost heard a feather drop to the ground.' The speech concluded, there is 'such a burst of applause as seemed to rend the very sky'.[34] Such a comparison comes naturally to Tom, it seems. He is soon revealed to be quite familiar with the London stage. Sir Launcelot emerges from a night in a chapel that is supposedly haunted by the ghost of his 'lunatic' great uncle, who had killed himself there, and dons the armour of his great-grandfather, 'a great warrior, who lost his life in the service of his king'. As above, there is a crowd outside to meet him, only this time they run off in terror, tripping up both Timothy and Tom as they go. The squire receives a 'thwack' from the knight's lance for his pains; for Tom's part:

I freely own I was not altogether unmoved at seeing such a figure come stalking out of a church in the grey of the morning; for it recalled to my remembrance the idea of the ghost in Hamlet, which I had seen acted at Drury-lane, when I made my first trip to London; and I had not yet got rid of the impression.

In other words, it is not only Sir Launcelot who is under the influence of art. Live theatre exercises a quixotic power over Tom, just as epic and romance do over others. The recollection of Sir Launcelot's emergence at daybreak has the kind of extreme physical effect on Tom that Hamlet's encounter with the ghost completely fails to have on Partridge in *Tom Jones*: 'his eyes began to stare, and his teeth to chatter'. At least one of his auditors at the Black Lion, Dolly, immediately catches the same mood, 'growing pale, and hitching her joint stool nearer the chimney'.[35]

Later in the century, a more lurid transformation of the end of *Romeo and Juliet* than Cleland's occurs in *The Monk* (1796) by Matthew Lewis: at one point, the teenage Antonia, an unwilling Juliet, drinks an opiate and comes round at night to find that she is trapped in a tomb with Ambrosio, her would-be Romeo, at her side. Lewis's grotesque rewriting of the scene seems to draw specifically on the Garrick stage version of the play, in which the lovers are briefly alive in the tomb at the same time. Antonia wakes to see 'three putrid half-corrupted Bodies' beside her. 'A lively red, the fore-runner of returning animation, had already spread itself over her cheek', just as Romeo observes in the play: 'beauty's ensign yet | Is crimson in thy lips and in thy cheeks' (5.4.59–60). But *The Monk* travesties the scene: like Juliet in the Garrick version of the play, Antonia comes round and is confused by her surroundings, and does not at first know the man who embraces her: 'Where am I?...why am I here?' (*Romeo and Juliet* in the Garrick version: 'Where am I? Defend me, powers!... Why do you force me so? I'll ne'er consent. | ... | I'll not wed Paris: Romeo is my husband', 5.4.73, 86, 88).

Unlike Juliet, however, Antonia is transfixed and terrified by the place itself—'Here are nothing but graves, and tombs, and skeletons!'—and by the lustful eagerness of Ambrosio himself. Romeo makes a crucial distinction between the tomb and the lovers' salvation ('Rise, rise, my Juliet, | And from this cave of death, this house of horror, | Quick let me snatch thee to thy Romeo's arms...', 5.4.76–7), while Ambrosio collapses them into a ghoulish singularity, as he kisses her and she struggles: 'Why these terrors, Antonia?...What fear you from me, from one who adores you? What matters it where you are? This sepulchre seems to me love's bower; this gloom is the friendly night of mystery, which he spreads over our delights!' The final horror is that Ambrosio rapes Antonia, and later, whereas Juliet stabs herself, Lewis has Ambrosio stab her as she attempts to escape—so the end of *Romeo and Juliet* is replayed once more as her true love, Lorenzo, arrives just too late to do anything but watch her die. To cap it all, because Lewis has not yet gone far enough, Ambrosio finds out later that Antonia was his sister, thus further wrenching the fabric of the play out of shape.[36]

Not all Gothic fiction is so extreme in its adaptation of Shakespearian material and its use of allusion to heighten the drama of a scene. Ann Radcliffe, for example, treats Shakespeare as a source of melodramatic epigraphs, as Lewis does (each volume of *The Monk* begins with an epigraph taken from Shakespeare), and the slight adaptations or emendations she makes can be very much of their time. From Garrick's *Macbeth*, and Johnson's anonymously published essay on the same play, she derives her reading of two lines for an epigraph in *The Romance of the Forest* (1791): 'My way of life | Is fall'n into the sear, the yellow leaf ' (5.3.22–3) is rendered here as 'My *May of life* . . .'. (Garrick had kept the emendation in his performance text, despite Johnson changing his mind about it.)[37] In the same novel, Radcliffe's heroine Adeline becomes a reader of English literature in the French mountains:

> She frequently took a volume of Shakespeare or Milton, and, having gained some wild eminence, would seat herself beneath the pines, whose low murmurs soothed her heart, and conspired with the vision of the poet to lull her to forgetfulness of grief.[38]

The scenery even inspires Adeline to attempt to write a poem of the 'higher kind' herself, recite sonnets (though not Shakespeare's), and sing her own compositions inspired by 'that rich effusion of Shakespeare's genius', *A Midsummer Night's Dream*.[39]

Other Gothic novels continue and develop this pattern of prose fiction inspired by stage sensation. There is *The Castle of Otranto: A Gothic Story* (1764) by Horace Walpole, with yet more ghostly interviews ('Speak quickly, said Matilda; the morning dawns apace', with its impatient echo of the opening of *A Midsummer Night's Dream*: 'Now, fair Hippolyta, our nuptial hour | Draws on apace', 1.1.1–2).[40] There is *The Old English Baron: A Gothic Story* (1777), in which Clara Reeve likens the task of imitating Walpole's seminal contribution to the genre, without destroying the Gothic essence of the thing, to imitating Shakespeare ('the unities may be preserved, while the spirit is evaporated').[41] And with *The Midnight Bell, A German Tale* (1798), Francis Lathom produced what is apparently the first instance of a novel's title being taken from a line by Shakespeare. Here is evidence of the movement to 'canonize words' recognized by Jean Marsden as the accompaniment to the movement to canonize the author; and it was not just a passage full of beautiful lines that made moral sense to an anthologist, but a phrase that brought with it a desirable aura of antiquity and mystery. While the epigraph on *The Midnight Bell*'s title page is actually from *Othello*—'A round unvarnish'd tale', it promises (1.3.90)—for the title itself, Lathom chooses a few ominous words, from *King John*, a play that was more popular in the 1790s than it would be in later years: 'If the midnight bell | Did with his iron tongue and brazen mouth | Sound on into the drowsy race of night . . . I would into thy bosom pour my thoughts' (3.3.37–9, 53). In the novel, the majority of the epigraphs come from Shakespeare, in fact, from the full range of histories, comedies, and tragedies. And Lathom's use of *King John* meant that the phrase would appear in Jane Austen's *Northanger Abbey* (revised around 1800, but not published until almost twenty years later) as one of the six 'horrid' Gothic novels named by Catherine Morland and Eleanor Tilney in Bath.

This brief survey can only suggest a few ways in which Shakespeare's texts were being reconstructed and anthologized during the second half of the eighteenth century, at the same time as they were also being quoted in new contexts in fragments. Beyond books and plays, his words were becoming well established in other media—in the musical settings of Thomas Arne, Samuel Webbe, and Richard Stevens,[42] in the satirical prints of James Gillray, in the paintings of William Hogarth, Francis Hayman, Nathaniel Dance, Angelica Kauffmann, Henry Fuseli, to name only a few. By the 1760s, Michael Dobson points out in *The Making of the National Poet*, readers were spoilt for choice: there were 'dictionaries of Shakespearean quotations, essays on Shakespeare, biographies of Shakespeare, poems on Shakespeare, even a Shakespearean novel (*Memoirs of the Shakespeare's-Head in Covent Garden. By the Ghost of Shakespeare*, published anonymously, in two volumes, in 1755)'.[43] In the coming decades, not only readers, but theatregoers, art-lovers and musicians would not have to look too hard to find hints of Shakespeariana, in other forms, too.

# Shakespeare Abroad

*Abroad*...2. Out of the house.
                        Welcome, Sir,
This cell's my court; here have I few attendants,
And subjects none *abroad.*    *Shakespeare's Tempest.*
Lady — walked a whole hour *abroad*, without dying after it; at
least in the time I staid; though she seemed to be fainting, and
had convulsive motions several times in her head. *Pope's Letters.*

    (Samuel Johnson, *A Dictionary of the English Language*)[1]

Sir *Wil.*  Where gets he Books to read? And of what Kind?
  Tho' some give Light, some blindly lead the Blind.
*Sym.*   Whene'er he drives our Sheep to *Edinburgh* Port,
  He buys some Books of History, Sangs or Sport;
  Nor does he want of them a Rowth at Will,
  And carries ay a Pouchfu' to the Hill:
  About ane *Shakespeare*, and a famous *Ben*,
  He aften speaks, and ca's them best of Men:
  How sweetly *Hawthrenden* and *Stirling* sing,
  And ane ca'd *Cowley*, loyal to his King,
  He kens fou well, and gars their Verses ring.
  I sometimes thought he made o'er great a Frase,
  About fine Poems, Histories and Plays.
  When I reprov'd him anes,—a Book he brings,
  With this, quoth he, on Braes I crack with Kings.

    (Allan Ramsay, *The Gentle Shepherd; A Scots pastoral comedy*)[2]

'Abroad', for Johnson as for Pope as for Shakespeare, did not necessarily mean being out of a country; it could simply mean being

outdoors. For Shakespeare to be 'abroad' could be as simple a matter as taking a book up a hill, as Allan Ramsay's gentle shepherd does, to radically liberating effect—'a Book he brings, | With this, quoth he, on Braes I crack with Kings'. (Despite Presbyterian hostility, incidentally, Edinburgh had seen performances of *Macbeth* and *The Jew of Venice* around 1715; Ramsay himself was involved in running the Edinburgh Players, who toured both north and south of the Scottish capital, before being shut down by the Licensing Act of 1737.) Modern readers, pastoral or not, can take the mobility of Shakespeare for granted: in the twenty-first century, his works are a global phenomenon, as represented by the diverse riches of the World Shakespeare Festival in 2012, with its Brazilian and Mexican spins on the history plays, its Tunisian *Macbeth*, its Welsh *Coriolanus*, and *A Midsummer Night's Dream* in Russian. The study of this 'global Shakespeare', or even 'global Shakespeares', has become a new way to think about his works, to think about the worlds that they contain.

But were things so different in 1786, when the Russian Empress Catherine the Great adapted *The Merry Wives of Windsor* as *This 'Tis To Have Linen and Buck-Baskets*, as a means of satirizing the Russian taste for all things French? Or when, later in the same year, she attempted to write serious dramas in a Shakespearian historical mode, pointedly rejecting neoclassical conventions for chronicle plays based on Russian history?

'What differentiates us from the Restoration is that while we feel free to alter Shakespeare's context, we do not change his text.'[3] This kind of alteration, as identified by Jean I. Marsden, is partly what the previous chapter was about—the presence of what were often Shakespeare's words quoted exactly in anthologies and novels, of the fragmented texts in new contexts. Geography, religion, language, and politics determine the boundaries for some variations on the same theme: what happens when there is no option but to change every word of a text in order to make it comprehensible? Or when the writer's nationality is seen to be a vital part of his identity?

In the modern sense of the word, 'abroad' is somewhere where it was relatively difficult to find Shakespeare (the name, the plays in performance, and the playbooks) before the eighteenth century. But some were keen to export him. In the early 1700s, the 'learned and ingenious' William King could wish that this was not the case:

'Tis Pity, that the finest of our *English* Poets, especially the Divine *Shakespeare*, had not communicated their Beauties to the World, so as to be understood in Latin, whereby Foreigners have sustained so great a Loss to this Day; when all of them were inexcusable, but the most Inimitable *Shakespeare*. I am so far from being envious, and desirous to keep those *Treasures* to ourselves, that I could wish all our most Excellent Poets translated into Latin, that are not so already.[4]

Instead of this scholarly solution to the problem, the world had another idea. Shakespeare was to be translated just as required, with local variations, not into a lingua franca but other vernacular tongues—French, German, Italian, Russian, and others. By the time Catherine the Great went through her phase of intense interest in Shakespeare, for example, some of his plays could be read in French, German, and Russian translation.[5] The beginnings of that international recognition desired by King were not uniform but decidedly haphazard.

## France et al.

The French response, for example, was conditioned by its ambivalent relationship with England. In the years immediately before the publication of his edition of Shakespeare, Nicholas Rowe had played a supporting role in negotiations that led to the Union between England and Scotland of 1707—a moment that saw the creation of 'Great Britain', an 'invented nation', in the words of the historian Linda Colley, 'superimposed, if only for a while, onto much older alignments and loyalties'. And this realignment of these adjacent kingdoms took place under conditions imposed by their relation to Continental Europe, and one noisy neighbour in particular—France:

It was an invention forged above all by war. Time and time again, war with France brought Britons, whether they hailed from Wales or Scotland or England, into confrontation with an obviously hostile Other and encouraged them to define themselves collectively against it. They defined themselves as Protestants struggling for survival against the world's foremost Catholic power. They defined themselves against the French as they imagined them to be, superstitious, militarist, decadent and unfree. And, increasingly, as the wars went on, they defined themselves in contrast to the colonial peoples they conquered, peoples who were manifestly alien in terms of culture, religion and colour.[6]

These circumstances, mixing belligerence with self-definition against a common foe, could only enhance the appeal of Shakespeare as a native or 'natural' writer whose dramas routinely disobey all those 'unfree' rules that were seen to constitute the core of the French neoclassical aesthetic. And anti-French sentiment best explains recurrent bursts of popularity for *Henry V*. Aaron Hill had reworked it in 1723, introducing some much-desired femininity into the play with a breeches role; the 1746 abridgement of Hill's version, called *The Conspiracy Defeated*, had topical appeal, in the aftermath of the Jacobite Rebellion the previous year, in its depiction of 'French Policy Defeated' and disloyal noblemen exposed and punished. Between these two versions came the first revival of the original in over a century, at Covent Garden in 1738, by request of the Shakespeare Ladies Club. The play became an annual fixture during the Seven Years War of 1756 to 1763, with the playbills promising the spectacle of 'the Conquest of the French at Agincourt', and again in the early years of the French Revolution, when John Philip Kemble played the role of Henry sixteen times at Drury Lane between 1789 and 1792.[7]

Yet French culture remained crucial to the new Britons, despite their suspicion of French manners and morals, and speaking French remained a crucial accomplishment of gentility. The reading of French literature in general 'shaped British criticism and aesthetics': 'A survey of more than 200 eighteenth-century British libraries has shown that eight out of ten contained works by Voltaire.'[8] In turn, however, Voltaire, one of the greatest writers of the period, would become renowned as the great enemy of Shakespeare. He had spent a couple of years in London in the middle of the 1720s, and seen *Othello*, *Hamlet*, and *Julius Caesar*. They did not wholly impress him. Shakespeare, he argues in his *Lettres philosophiques* (1734), might have 'un génie de force...de naturel & sublime' (a powerful genius, natural and sublime), but he lacked 'bon gout' (good taste) and 'la moindre connoissance des règles' (the least sense of the rules).[9] And he went on criticize *Othello* for its indecorum (Othello strangling Desdemona on stage) and *Hamlet* for its gravediggers, before offering a much-flattened 'To be or not to be' as an example of one of Shakespeare's beauties:

Demeure; il fau choisir, & passer à l'instant
De la vie à la mort, ou de l'être au néant.
Dieux cruels![10]

This was, Voltaire warned, no substitute for the original: 'quand vous voyez une traduction, que vous ne voyez qu'une foible estampe d'un beau Tableau' (when you see a translation, you see only a poor print of a beautiful painting).[11] That he really did see beauty in the plays he had studied closely is clear. Indeed, in one of his most popular tragedies, *Zaïre* (1732), he emulated the jealousy and the pathos of *Othello* (as *Zara*, the play was immensely popular in England, and the early translation was at some point revised by Garrick to come closer to the spirit of Voltaire's original).[12] And he can sound jealous himself of Shakespeare's arrant disregard for the rules:

A poet, I am accustomed to say, is a free man who subjugates language to his genius; a Frenchman is a slave to rhyme, forced on occasion to devote four verses to the expression of a thought which an Englishman can capture in a single line. An Englishman says what he pleases, a Frenchman only what he can contrive: one runs over a huge course, the other walks in fetters along a slippery and narrow path.[13]

But Voltaire believed that French poetry required these restraints, and he strongly resisted the movement in France towards approving Shakespeare's barbaric plays, as the first French translations appeared from Pierre Antoine de La Place, taking up half of the eight volumes of his *Théâtre Anglois* (1745–9), albeit for the most part as plot summaries. La Place also provocatively claimed that Aristotle, if he had seen Shakespeare's plays, would have torn up the rules and started again. Soon Voltaire's fellow *philosophes* were likewise learning to admire what he could not, giving him considerable attention in both *Le Nouveau Dictionnaire historique* (1756) and the *Encyclopédie*: 'this Shakespeare was a terrible mortal', Diderot wrote, 'a colossus who was gothic, but between whose legs we would all pass without our head even touching his testicles'.[14]

Voltaire responded with his *Appel à toutes les nations de l'Europe* (1761), in which he once again condemned the plays' crudeness and likened them to sorcery. English pilgrims to his estate at Ferney could find him still ready to do battle with a writer he continued to admire but regarded as fundamentally a barbarian. 'I'll tell you why we admire Shakespeare', James Boswell tried to tell him in 1764. Voltaire cut in: 'Because you have no taste.'[15] He praised and condemned Shakespeare again that same year, in his *Commentaries on Corneille*. Eventually, he had d'Alembert, Diderot's fellow editor of the *Encyclopédie*, read out a letter before the Académie française, on 25 August 1776, once more reiterating his stock views on the subject—a gesture worthy of King Canute.

By the 1770s, the party in favour of Shakespeare in France was strong. Garrick had been in France before Boswell and made a great impression on the same intellectuals Voltaire was trying to dissuade from embracing the Shakespearian dramatic ethos. Hester Thrale noted the presence of busts of Milton, Shakespeare, Pope, and Dryden in the Parisian drawing room of Madame du Boccage, the translator of *Paradise Lost*.[16] Sébastien Mercier published the approving *Du Théâtre, ou Nouvel Essai sur l'Art dramatique* in 1773, and Pierre Le Tourneur's prose translations of Shakespeare began to appear in 1776, adorned with the King and Queen at the head of the list of subscribers. When the Académie heard out Voltaire's letter on Shakespeare and the threat he posed to French good taste, Elizabeth Montagu was present in order to hear this 'most blackguard abusive invective';[17] her highly regarded reply to him, *An Essay on the Writings and Genius of Shakespear* (1769), promptly appeared in French translation.

On the Paris stage, meanwhile, the pioneering Shakespearian dramatist was the man who inherited Voltaire's seat in the Académie, Jean-François Ducis, whose translations are far from being the irregular dramas of his predecessor's nightmares. Between 1769, when his *Hamlet* appeared, and 1792, when his *Othello* appeared, Ducis was responsible for a total of five French translations of tragedies by Shakespeare—the others beside *Hamlet* and *Othello* being *Romeo and Juliet* (1772), *King Lear* (as *Le Roi Lear* in 1783), *Macbeth* (1790)—plus one history play, *King John* (as *Jean Sans-Terre, ou La Mort d'Arthur* in 1791). Since Ducis could not read or speak English, he used the partial translations of La Place, who had gone some way towards 'frenchifying' Shakespeare by merely translating the major scenes in his chosen plays, linked by narrative passages in prose. Ducis went further. He rewrote the plots, replaced blank verse with the six-beat alexandrine couplets, and renamed the characters; he tried to reduce the size of the casts to manageable, neoclassical proportions, although he was also willing to add where he felt something was missing: Macbeth and his wife 'Frédegonde', for example, gain a son. 'Je vois avec plaisir', his father says, 'son aimable innocence'[18]—only for the dynastic violence and bloody paranoia of Shakespeare to be replaced with the climactic self-destruction of a family.

Ducis's *Hamlet* was first performed in the same year as Garrick's Jubilee, and pre-empts some of the changes in Garrick's own, equally radical reworking of the play. It goes further by raising Ophelia to virtually the same rank as the prince, and reducing the ghost of Hamlet's father to a presence in his mind only. If the emphasis was the 'drame de famille' and the fragility of Hamlet himself, the tragedy is still 'naturalized' for a French audience. By contrast, on the first performance of *Othello*, at the Comédie Française in November 1792, not long after France had, like the Venice of the play, become a republic, the audience's horrified response to the death of the inno-cent heroine showed that he had not gone far enough to meet their expectations. Ducis was forced to provide an alternative ending, a 'dénouement heureux', in which disaster is averted just as he stands over not Desdemona but 'Hédelmone', with his dagger drawn (this Othello chooses to stab her rather than smother her), and with 'tout prêt à l'en frapper'.[19] Voltaire had been right to warn of Shakespeare's brutal indifference to poetic justice.

This *Othello* also emerged at a moment when France and England had diverged politically. The French Revolution of 1789 had already resulted in the slaughter of thousands; and the Republic, declared on 22 September 1792, would baptize itself with the blood of tens of thousands more. Joseph Talma, the celebrated actor who played Ducis's Othello, was under suspicion of being 'insufficiently patriotic and pro-revolutionary',[20] and the enthusiasm for republicanism of Ducis himself waned as he witnessed the chaos and the violence it had engendered. In the event, he and Talma would both survive this bloody period, as would their *Othello*—over the first half of the nineteenth century, it appeared another seventy times at the Comédie Française[21]—yet they lived in fear of a very different outcome throughout that first year of the republic. While the Girondins were on trial for treason in October 1793, Ducis sent a copy of the play to the head of the National Convention: 'Reçevez, mon illustre con-citoyen, le *sans-culotte* Othello. ...' Under suspicion at the time,

Talma played the role during that trial, and again on the last day of the month, when the Girondins were guillotined.[22]

Ducis was a Shakespeare worshipper in the mould of Betterton and Garrick before him, on the other side of the Channel. 'He celebrated each year what he called the *fête de Saint-Guillaume* (Shakespeare's birthday) by placing a wreath on the bust of the English poet that adorned his study, and he kept on his worktable an engraving of Garrick in the role of Hamlet.' Changes to the plays (as far as he knew them) he apparently made reluctantly.[23] In altering Shakespeare so drastically, however, he opened the way to alterations of his alterations across Europe. There were two unsuccessful attempts to bring the Ducis *Hamlet* to Spain, for instance: an anonymous, apparently unperformed translation; and *Hamlet, rey de Dinamarca*, in 'assonanced hendecasyllables' by the Madrid farceur Ramón de la Cruz, staged in 1772 for only five nights, and not published until 1900.[24] It was not until 1798 that Leandro Fernández de Moratín published a more faithful prose translation of the play from the English rather than the French version, with a short Life of the author, and, despite his Voltaire-inspired disapproval of Shakespeare, managed to confine his criticisms to his notes. Although it was subsequently 'reprinted, imitated, and even plagiarized on numerous occasions throughout the nineteenth and twentieth centuries',[25] however, Moratín's *Hamlet* was never staged. The neoclassical considerations that led Garrick to adapt the same play so radically towards the end of his career apparently remained influential still, at the end of the eighteenth century, on Continental attitudes to the staging of Shakespeare's plays. It was *Otelo; ó, el Moro de Venecia*—a translation of Ducis's *Othello* by Teodoro La Calle—that proved to be the first successful adaptation of Shakespeare for the Spanish stage, when it appeared in Madrid in 1802. Like Montagu listening to Voltaire's letter at the Académie, the English took note and remained unimpressed. 'We fancy few English readers, who have enjoyed this sublime production of their favourite poet in their vernacular tongue', remarked *The Monthly Magazine*, 'would be satisfied with this translation of a translation.'[26]

The last quarter of the century, meanwhile, saw translations of Ducis's *Hamlet* into Italian, Russian, and possibly Polish.[27] His *King Lear* and *Othello* also appeared in Russian in the early nineteenth century. (A non-Ducis translation, of *Julius Caesar*, was banned in

Russia in the wake of the French Revolution.) It was by not one but two or three degrees of separation that Shakespeare was reaching a wider audience.

## Germany and America

It was not the same for everywhere beyond Great Britain. Knowledge of Shakespeare certainly preceded Voltaire's sojourn in London, albeit seldom proceeding from the same spirit of intense admiration that moved Ducis.[28] In Germany, there were versions of *Hamlet* (1710), *Julius Caesar* (1741, the first complete translation of one of Shakespeare's plays), *Romeo and Juliet* (1761), and *The Tempest* (1762), in print or performance, before Christoph Martin Wieland began publishing his translation of twenty-one of the plays into prose (1762–6), to be followed by the complete translation of all the plays (again in prose) by Johann Eschenburg (1775–7), and the seminal work of A. W. Schlegel, Ludwig Tieck, and Dorothea Tieck (1797–1833). At Biberach, Hamburg, Vienna, Prague, and Mannheim, theatrical productions of the plays became increasingly common: Schlegel's *Hamlet* appeared in Berlin in 1799; followed the next year by Schiller's *Macbeth* at Weimar.[29] The German explosion of interest in Shakespeare, which would have a profound impact on the study of Shakespeare universally, from the 1800s onwards, contrasts starkly with the disagreements of Voltaire et al., and is epitomized in Karl Philipp Moritz's autobiographical novel *Anton Reiser* (1785–90), in which the young protagonist borrows a copy of Shakespeare, whose *Romeo and Juliet* he has seen at the theatre: 'what a new world now suddenly opened up for his powers of thought and feeling!'

> Here was everything he had hitherto thought, read, and felt, and much more besides.—He read *Macbeth*, *Hamlet*, *Lear*, and felt his spirits irresistibly drawn upwards—every hour of his life in which he read Shakespeare became inestimably precious.—At every step he now lived, thought, and dreamed Shakespeare....[30]

For their evening entertainment, Anton and his friend Philipp begin reading Shakespeare in Wieland's translation, and their '*Shakespearean Nights*', with 'coffee at midnight' become the means by which, despite Anton's melancholy, 'his imagination took a loftier flight':

Thanks to Shakespeare he was guided through the world of human passions—
the narrow circle of his idealistic existence had been extended—he no longer
led such a solitary, insignificant life, lost amid the crowd—for he had shared in
the feelings felt by thousands of others when reading Shakespeare....[31]

Thus inspired, Anton's own writings take on a Hamlet-like air: 'How
sad is man's existence—and we make this trifling existence unbearable
for one another, instead of relieving one another's burdens by familiar
sociability in this wilderness of life....How dreary, how sad are all
things here around me!—And I must wander about, forsaken and
solitary—no prop, no guide!'[32]

In other words, here was a decidedly anti-neoclassical response to
Shakespeare and to life—it is through Shakespeare that Anton com-
munes, he feels, with 'thousands of others', and tries to make sense of
things. For Moritz and his contemporaries, Shakespeare lent himself
perfectly to current concerns. Johann Gottfried Herder, taking his
cue from Friedrich Nicolai and Heinrich von Gerstenberg, recognized as much in his essay on Shakespeare in *Von deutscher Art und
Kunst* (1773, 'On German Character and Art'). Here he salutes Shakespeare as 'Sophocles' brother precisely where he seems so dissimi-
lar, only to be inwardly wholly like *him*'. Shakespeare is true to the
world of his time, Herder argues, and cannot be bound by the rigid
conventions of another era; the same goes for Sophocles. Both are
great in different ways because they wrote and excelled in different
ages. In other words, paradoxically, this is a historical and a national-
ist view of how to create universal drama. For Herder, the unities of
time and space are 'insubstantial', 'mere shadows', next to '*action*...
the working of the soul', and to attempt to reduce a play by Shakespeare to something else is to miss the point:

Examine whichever play you wish, dear reader, whether *Lear* or the *Richards*,
*Julius Caesar* or the *Henrys*, even the supernatural plays and the divertisse-
ments, especially *Romeo and Juliet*, that sweet drama of love, a romance even
in every detail of time and place and dream and poetry—examine the drama
you have chosen and try to subtract something from its nature, to exchange it,
or even to simplify it for the French stage—a living world in all the authenticity of its truth transformed into this wooden skeleton—a fair exchange, a
fine transformation that would be! Deprive this flower of its soil, its sap and
vital force, and plant it in the air; deprive this person of place, time,

individuality—and you have robbed him of breath and soul, leaving him nothing more than a simulacrum of a living being.[33]

The essence of a Romantic response to Shakespeare emerges out of Herder's exuberant argument—and in rejecting the false deities of French neoclassicism (Racine, Corneille, Voltaire . . . ) and entering the 'living world' of the alternative, he is proposing an alternative course for German culture. With the translations of Schlegel and the Tiecks (father and daughter), Shakespeare became a kind of honorary German classic, and the beneficiary of one of the great translation projects of the age. 'Truly great poetry does indeed transcend its historicity', as the essay's modern translator and editor, Gregory Moore, explains, 'But it can do so only if it is constantly reinterpreted, reinvented, reinvigorated. . . . Just as Shakespeare built on what went before him, so we must build on Shakespeare'.[34] And it is, furthermore, the eighteenth-century creation of the cult of genius that enables Herder to identify Shakespeare as a kind of second Creator, a God of the imagination: in Moore's account, it is the poet Edward Young's *Conjectures on Original Composition* (1759, translated into German the following year) that gives Herder and his contemporaries the concept of this kind of literary genius, untroubled by the rules that bound a Ducis or a Voltaire. Shakespeare's power is of a different order: 'An *Original* may be said to be of a *vegetable* nature; it rises spontaneously from the vital root of Genius; it *grows*, it is not *made*'.[35] For the Germany of Herder and Moritz, Schiller and Goethe, Shakespeare showed the way to their own cultural awakening.

Bearing these intoxicating notions in mind, however, it might be suggested that an equally grand 'creation' of Shakespeare's was simultaneously happening on the other side of the Atlantic Ocean.

The constant trade between Great Britain and its colonial territories in North America carried with it a certain number of books: there are sightings of the Fourth Folio and Rowe's 1709 edition in the records of Virginian plantations in the early 1800s, while the Library Company of Philadelphia obtained their copy of Hanmer's 1744 edition on the advice of Benjamin Franklin. In their compact history of Shakespeare in America, Virginia Mason and Alden T. Vaughan can point to three Presidents of the United States—John Adams, his son John

Quincy Adams, and Thomas Jefferson—who all, through British imports, became deeply acquainted with his works, although Jefferson's father Peter also owned a copy that stayed in the family.[36] In 1771, only three years after Capell's edition appeared, Jefferson can be found suggesting that his friend Robert Skipwith buy a copy.[37] He himself owned the same edition, and annotated it in a scholarly way, with a copy of Thomas Percy's *Reliques of Ancient English Poetry* to hand, in which he found verbal parallels; later, he added to his collection Capell's *Notes and Various Readings to Shakespeare*, *A Concordance to Shakespeare* by Andrew Becket, and Dodd's *Beauties of Shakespeare*. In London, he saw the great Sarah Siddons as Lady Macbeth and Portia, and in 1789, the year of his return from Paris to America, he was 'trying to obtain an accurate portrait of Shakespeare to hang at Monticello' (his home in Charlottesville, Virginia).[38] He was also still prepared to buy a new edition of Shakespeare in middle age, collecting the complete run of John Bell's edition on fine paper, published between 1785 and 1788, as well as the annotations.[39] The first American edition of Shakespeare, meanwhile, would not appear until 1795, and the title page still describes it as being 'Corrected from the Latest and Best London Editions'.

There is evidence of American theatrical activity in the eighteenth century, too. Although it lags somewhat behind the surviving records of imported books, partly because of a strong religious prejudice against theatricality and the permanent establishment of the theatre business in American towns and cities, what appears to be the first recorded performance of a play by Shakespeare on American soil, of *Romeo and Juliet* in New York in 1730, notably precedes the better-known London revivals of that play by Theophilus Cibber and Garrick by many years. The crucial point, however, is that while colonial Americans depended to a large extent on the mother country for their cultural life, they kept up with the British in adopting Shakespeare as *their* national poet, making his plays the most performed of all over the second half of the century, and drawing him, so the argument goes, into the mental lives of at least two of the new country's Founding Fathers, Adams and Jefferson. Famously, on a pilgrimage to Stratford-upon-Avon in 1786, they found the English standard of reverence for the sacred Bard not up to their own.

And while it is obvious that the American Revolution, culminating in the final victory at Yorktown in 1781 and the Treaty of Paris in 1783, constitutes a break with the colonial past, the dip in Shakespeare's popularity was soon shrugged off; Shakespeare was too useful to be discarded along with the monarchy and the unequal relationship between American subjects and the British. Adams, as the Vaughans point out, used *Macbeth* to 'criticize England's maltreatment of its colonial progeny', and *Coriolanus* to 'illustrate the perils of internecine politics'.[40] It is possible that Shakespeare is indeed 'woven into the very fabric of America', as Barbara A. Mowat has suggested—even the Constitution itself.[41] For the leading playwright of the Jacobean King's Men, the eighteenth century could hardly have brought about a more radical change of context, even if the words on the page remained, in theory, the same.

# Unreal 'Shakspeare'

Friend Marle,
I never longed for thy company more than last night: we were all very merrye at the Globe, when Ned Alleyn did not scruple to affyrme pleasantely to thy friend Will, that he had stolen his speeche about the qualityes of an actor's excellencye, in Hamlet hys tragedye, from conversations manyfold whych had passed between them, and opinyons given by Alleyn touchinge the subject. Shakespeare did not take this talke in good sorte; but Jonson put an end to the strife, wittylie remarking, This affaire needeth no contentione; you stole it from Ned, no doubt; do not marvel; have you not seen him act tymes out of number?

G. PEEL[1]

Did it belatedly occur to the author of *Biographia Literaria* (1777), the polymathic physician Dr John Berkenhout, that this letter, in which the Elizabethan poet and dramatist George Peele writes to his friend and fellow writer Christopher Marlowe with news of a jovial gathering, was actually a forgery? In his book, Berkenhout merely writes, 'Whence I copied this letter, I do not recollect; but I remember that at the time of transcribing it, I had no doubt of its authenticity'. In fact, it is its *inauthenticity* that is in no doubt whatsoever, and it has been ascribed to George Steevens, dubbed the 'Puck of Commentators' by William Gifford for some of his more mischievous scholarly interventions.

All the basic stereotypes of 'ye olde English' spelling are here: adding the letter 'e' to a few words, changing 'i' to 'y', adopting a loosely Elizabethan idiom ('This affaire needeth no contention'), and dropping the names we might know, providing us with a glimpse of these literary eminences, conveniently gathered together for us, in one easy view. In this sense, it is too good to be true—which was perhaps its most appealing quality, in that it seeks to satisfy a certain intense curiosity about the man and the theatrical milieu to which he belonged that was, in large measure, a creation of the cultural conditions of the eighteenth century. It later came to be known by a belated rival play-wright's coinage: George Bernard Shaw called it 'Bardolatry'.

For Bernard Shaw, writing in 1901, in the preface to his *Three Plays for Puritans*, 'Bardolatry' is a term of abuse. He offers it as a counter-blast to those 'Shakespear [sic] fanciers who, ever since his own time, have delighted in his plays just as they might have delighted in a particular breed of pigeons if they had never learnt to read', and praised instead with those 'genuine critics, from Ben Jonson to Mr Frank Harris' who 'have always kept as far on this side of idolatry as I'. Between Shakespeare-worship and the wholesale adaptation of Shakespeare—those 'disgraceful farces, melodramas, and stage pageants which actor-managers, from Garrick and Cibber to our own contemporaries, have hacked out of his plays as peasants have hacked huts out of the Coliseum'—he argues there is a connection. The 'mutilators of Shakespear...never could be persuaded that Shakespear knew his business better than they', yet they 'have ever been the most fanatical of his worshippers':

The late [American playwright] Augustin Daly thought no price too extrava-gant for an addition to his collection of Shakespear relics; but in arranging Shakespear's plays for the stage he proceeded on the assumption that Shakespear was a botcher and he an artist.... It was the age of gross ignorance of Shakespear and incapacity for his works that produced the indiscriminate eulogies with which we are familiar. It was the revival of genuine criticism of those works that coincided with the movement for giving genuine instead of spurious and silly representations of his plays. So much for Bardolatry![2]

In its conflation of 'the Bard' with 'idolatry', however, Shaw's coinage might also be seen as an ironic extension of eighteenth-century discourse about Shakespeare, while his little joke of adapting a dismissive cry from Colley Cibber's *Richard III* ('Off with his head. So much for Buckingham!') in order to bid good riddance to the egregious era of those 'disgraceful farces' hacked out of greater plays, only confirms the rhetorical effectiveness of one of the great Shakespeare adaptations. The Coliseum trope, likewise, recalls similar architectural imagery in the prefaces of Pope ('one may look upon his works . . . as upon an ancient majestic piece of Gothick Architecture') and Theobald ('The Attempt to write upon SHAKESPEARE is like going into a large, a spacious, and a splendid Dome thro' the Conveyance of a narrow and obscure Entry').[3] Shaw has thoroughly absorbed the language of Bardolatry.

Later critics, furthermore, have taken up Shaw's paradoxical insight that it is the more uncritical writer-worship that produces the grandest, the most 'indiscriminate' of eulogies—while the 'honest' Shakespearian, reading by the light of 'genuine criticism', must be ready to find and admit faults. 'Paradoxical as it may seem', Lucyle Hook wrote in 1953, 'it is possible that the preservation of Shakespeare even in garbled form during the Restoration period made certain his present reputation' (and it ought to be acknowledged that Hook in turn anticipates Michael Dobson's better-known and more fully developed argument in *The Making of the National Poet*):

> Specifically why this is true is to be found, not in contemporary seventeenth-century critical accounts, but in theatrical ephemerae: Davenant, 'god-son' and youthful idolator of the regular visitor to the inn at Oxford, transmitted his love and respect for Shakespeare to Thomas Betterton, the ideal repository for theatrical lore and practice; and we do not have to wait for Garrick to see Shakespeare idolized . . . . Shakespeare became the lodestar to which the aspiring writers of tragedy turned, but since morals and modes and even language had changed, it was necessary for playwrights to interpret Shakespeare according to the lights of actors and audience.[4]

Looking back to the Restoration period, and the Shakespeare-worship of Davenant and Betterton, Hook saw that Bardolatry *avant la lettre* certainly existed among some people in the theatre business; and the wider developments of the 1730s, the monument in Westminster Abbey erected in 1741, testify to an expansion of the cult, even before Garrick took it to new extremes with the Jubilee celebrations in Stratford-upon-Avon and his string of restorations and alterations of Shakespeare's plays, guided by a canny sense of the popular demands of morals, modes, and language. While this cult supported and drew strength from an intensification of critical and scholarly activity relating to Shakespeare's works, it was to have strange, unintended consequences before the century was out. Had John Berkenhout lived beyond 1791, he might have fallen for a similar trick to the one that has left its Puckish impression on *Biographia Literaria*, carried out on a much larger scale—one that more extravagantly demonstrates the errors of judgement that Bardolatry could induce.

### The texts after the Tonsons

Both Jacob Tonson the Elder and his nephew Jacob Tonson the Younger had died in the 1730s, the business being carried on after that, until the late 1760s, by the nephew's sons (yet another Jacob and the less involved Richard). Again, a family firm, the Rivingtons, took over the rights to publish trade editions of Shakespeare, for £1,200; by contrast, half the rights to Ben Jonson were sold off for a mere £60.[5] The final Tonson publications are among their most significant for the study of Shakespeare. This was the time of George Steevens's *Twenty of the Plays of Shakespeare, being the whole number printed in quarto during his life-time, or before the Restoration*, as well as *Mr William Shakespeare his Comedies, Histories, and Tragedies*, edited by Edward Capell. Both editions recognized that the earliest known texts of Shakespeare were not to be disregarded as mere piracies or inaccurate versions foisted on an ignorant public. Steevens, despite his misgivings, was prepared to reintroduce readers to the original text of *Shakespeare's Sonnets* and *A Lover's Complaint*, as published in 1609, instead of the adulterated Benson version of 1640, while it was probably the eccentric Capell who went furthest in recognizing the earliest quartos as potentially superior in authority to the received versions. 'The quarto's [sic] went through many impressions', he wrote in the introduction to *Mr William Shakespeare his Comedies, Histories, and Tragedies* (the title page goes on to emphasize the significance of those quarto editions): 'in each play, the last is generally taken from the impression next before it, and so onward to the first...And this further is to be observ'd of them: that, generally speaking, the more distant they are from the original, the more they abound in faults; 'till, in the end, the corruptions of the last copies become so excessive, as to make them of hardly any worth'.[6] The same could be said of the seventeenth-century folio compilations of Shakespeare's plays.

Unfortunately, Capell's edition appeared under unhelpful circumstances—the notes being published separately, many years after the appearance of the texts themselves—and, as was so often the case, his practice has not been found to be consistent with the radical principles advanced in his introduction.[7] Later commentators, however, have argued that this does not justify the contemporary neglect of his work. For Simon Jarvis, if there was indeed a 'sudden break between pre-enlightened and enlightened practices of textual criticism', it occurred with Capell rather than earlier, with Lewis Theobald, or later, with the work of the Irish scholar and lawyer Edmond Malone, and especially *The Plays and Poems of William Shakspeare* (sic), published in ten volumes in 1790. At the beginning of *Shakespeare Verbatim*, Margreta de Grazia observes that Malone's edition 'came out during a time of conceptual and political upheaval'—that he gave a copy of his book to his friend Edmund Burke, who in return gave him a copy of his *Reflections on the Revolution in France*. While Malone's innovations 'render...obsolete' the general tendencies of previous editors, and posit an authentic 'Then' cut off from the textually polluted 'Now', Burke wrote of the French Revolution as a shattering of the old order, granting the individual, egregiously 'cut off from past dispensations and dependencies' in his view, 'new powers of self-determination'.[8] This is a forceful and compelling reading of the situation. But as Jarvis notes, the idea of such a break is itself problematic: 'new theoretical practices do not spring fully formed from the mind of the innovator'; 'earlier practices' leave their mark on 'newer methods'. It is tempting to suppose that Malone's 1790 edition, for example, coincided closely enough with the moment of a clean political break from the past in France, the Revolution of 1789; but in both cases, the past would not go quietly.[9]

In the final decades of the eighteenth century, new editions of Shakespeare proliferated, attended by sometimes combative responses, in the form of book reviews and pamphlets. There were the innovative editions of individual plays by Charles Jennens (better known to musicologists as Handel's librettist) produced over consecutive years in the early 1770s, including an edition of *King Lear* anonymously and dismissively reviewed by Steevens in December 1770. There was the great sequence of revised versions of Samuel Johnson's edition that involved—among others, who contributed notes—Steevens, Edmond Malone, and Isaac Reed, and endured into the 1790s. There were the further essays and commentaries of John Monck Mason, Thomas Tyrwhitt, Joseph Ritson, Walter Whiter et al. As the figure of Shakespeare the author grew in cultural authority, knowing precisely what he wrote became vital—as did knowing more about him as a person, either through both his writings (if possible) or through documentary evidence (which was proving frustratingly difficult to locate).

With regard to both life and works, the aim could be presented as a noble one: to become better acquainted with genius. Had Shakespeare, for example, any hand in the group of plays not published as his until the second impression of the Third Folio appeared in 1664? His first eighteenth-century editor, Nicholas Rowe, had simply included them all: *Pericles Prince of Tyre*, *The London Prodigal*, *The History of Thomas Lord Cromwell*, *Sir John Oldcastle Lord Cobham*, *The Puritan Widow*, *A Yorkshire Tragedy*, and *The Tragedy of Locrine*. Many of Rowe's successors had varied in opinion on the matter without paying it anything in the way of systematic attention. By contrast, in his seminal edition of 1790, the formidable Malone rejected them all, with the ambiguous exception of *Pericles* ('The most corrupt of Shakespeare's other dramas, compared with *Pericles*, is purity itself '),[10] but cast doubt on other plays, too. 'On what principle the editors of the first complete edition of our poet's plays admitted this into their volume, cannot now be ascertained', Malone wrote of *Titus Andronicus*, relegating it to the final volume of his 1790 edition. 'The most probable reason that can be assigned, is, that he wrote a few lines in it, or gave some assistance to the author, in revising it, or in some way aided him in bringing it forward on the stage.'[11] In his 'dissertation' on the *Henry VI* plays, he argued that they were not '*originally* and *entirely*' Shakespeare's, but were originally the work of 'some ancient dramatist'.[12]

In his decades-long devotion to the task of editing Shakespeare and uncovering the 'real' Shakespeare (down to the name, which he insisted was spelt 'Shakspeare'), from this 'Attempt' and the

*Supplement* to the Johnson-Steevens edition of 1778 (published in 1780, it contained the apocryphal plays, long poems, and the Sonnets), to the posthumously published variorum edition of *The Plays and Poems of William Shakspeare* (published in 1821 in twenty-one volumes), Malone might be said to be himself symptomatic of the Shakespeare cult, at the same time as the object of his studies was to reach back beyond the received impression of Shakespeare of the eighteenth century (of Rowe's Life, for instance, which Malone rejected almost entirely, regretting that it had been written at all) to the correct original. And although, as mentioned, his 1790 edition might not have been as revolutionary in practice as is sometimes suggested, its reputation was high enough at the time to earn its editor not only respect but envy, from Steevens, and spite, from the cantankerous Ritson.

In Steevens's case, the rivalry was both a methodological and a personal matter, as the older man bristled at the younger, whose work seemed so arrogantly to sweep aside his own. Ritson might have felt the same way, but he formulated his attacks as not only expressions of critical indignation but a defence of English culture from a hostile takeover. Malone, he writes anonymously in a collection of corrections to the 1790 edition, *Cursory Criticisms on the Edition of Shakspeare Published by Edmond Malone*, is 'ignorant of the English language', and is both wrong and impudent in his attempts to correct Johnson: 'such is the absurd consequence of an Irish editor attempting the illustration of an English author'. Malone 'makes an uncommon fuss with his pretensions of adhering to the old copy', but Ritson spots him veering from it and not explaining why he does so—'not . . . the only instance he has given us of his want of truth, fidelity, candour, and consistency'. Of 'the Fool and Death' mentioned in *Pericles* (3.2.1332), Malone remarks that these were characters in the old morality plays. Ritson challenges him to produce a single instance of this, and adds: 'If he can not, what are we to think of the morality of Mr Malone?'[13]

Such heavy-weather invective against Malone as an unauthorized and incapable editor of Shakespeare conveys some sense of how much it now mattered to some to perfect Shakespeare's texts, and claim authority over this ultimate cultural authority. The substance of his criticisms on Malone's textual choices and textual commentary derives from his rejection of Malone's editorial principles. For Ritson, the Second Folio of 1632 carries superior authority to those earlier texts preferred by Malone. Despite his hysterical language, at the heart of the matter is a reaction against the radical return to the earliest texts that Malone's 1790 edition proposes and in some measure carries out. Malone saw this, and astutely replied not in kind, trading insult for insult, but by publishing *A Letter to the Rev. Richard Famer*, dated 23 April, Shakespeare's supposed and conveniently patriotic birthday. Here Malone accepts an insultingly tiny number of Ritson's proposed verbal changes, and suavely rebuts the charges against him, without personal animus, keeping up the pretence that he does not know who the author of *Cursory Criticisms* was. He is also sure to call his accuser a 'monopolizer' who would deny anybody else the right to write about Shakespeare, and to denigrate the Second Folio for its 'capricious innovations'. Historically defined 'authority' he regards as separate from the poetically correct manner of emendation that both he and Ritson practised—freeing him to take a reading from a later edition of Shakespeare on critical grounds, but not slavishly follow its every emendation on grounds of authenticity.[14]

## The Ireland forgeries

The spat with Ritson may also be set against Malone's role as the whistle-blower in another affair from the 1790s: the most infamous Shakespeare forgeries of all, perpetrated by the young William Henry Ireland in the final decade of the eighteenth century. The story has become celebrated as an extraordinary and colourful episode in the history of literary forgery and the cultural life of late eighteenth-century England.

The eighteenth century had a flair for fraudulence, especially of the literary variety. Putting aside the Cock Lane Ghost, the South Sea Bubble, the supposed Formosan George Psalmanazar, and the time Oliver Goldsmith was directed to a private house and tricked into believing it was an inn (a source of inspiration for *She Stoops To Conquer*, he later claimed), there are still some infamous wonders of imposition left over—such as the fifteenth-century monk 'Thomas Rowley' (really the teenage-prodigy-poet Thomas Chatterton) and the third-century bard 'Ossian' (really James Macpherson, the 'translator' of Ossian's epic poem *Fingal*). There is also the 'Shakespeare' of

*Double Falsehood*—and a 'Shakespeare' invented at the end of the century, the author of *Vortigern, An Historical Tragedy*, of which more below, and the loving husband of 'Anna Hatherrewaye', to whom he once wrote in the following terms:

As thou haste alwaye founde mee toe mye Worde moste trewe soe thou shalt see I have stryctlye kepte mye promise I praye you perfume thys mye poore Locke withe balmye Eysses sorre thenne indeede shall Kynges themselves bowe ande paye homage toe itte I doe assure assure thee no rude hande hathe knottedde itte thye Willys alone hathe done the worke....[15]

And so on. This secret and much-sought-after 'Shakspeare' had been discovered in a chest full of old papers at a secret location somewhere in London. The owner of the chest was a gentleman who preferred to live retired from the world, but was prepared, fortunately, to let another William, the young William Henry Ireland, go rummaging through the chest every now and then, and take whatever traces of the Immortal Bard he found there back to his father, the Shakespeare-mad Samuel.

Samuel Ireland had already suffered a dose of disappointment when he had gone to Stratford with his son in search of his idol's undiscovered literary remains in the summer of 1793. They had rushed to Clopton House, a mile outside town, on the tip-off that they would possibly find some of Shakespeare's papers there. 'By God, I wish you had arrived a little sooner!' Samuel was told (presumably he made an irresistible target for teasing): 'Why, it isn't a fortnight since I destroyed several basketsful of letters and papers, in order to clear a small chamber for some young partridges which I wish to bring up alive! And as to Shakspeare, why there were many bundles with his name wrote upon them. Why, it was in this very fire-place I made a roaring bonfire of them....'[16]

Now, anxious to impress, his son brought him, cautiously at first, scraps of revelation. His first forgery was a deed purporting to be signed by four people, one of whom was 'William Shakspeare'. Old parchment was available, and ink that could be mixed to look faint with age. A conveyancer's apprentice, William Henry had the opportunity to practise his hand (or rather, both hands, left and right, for different signatories). The wording was copied. The Bardolatrous Samuel Ireland, the perfect victim for such a hoax, was delighted.

That was in 1794. Things got out of hand over the next two years, as William Henry was called on to produce more and more documents from his entirely fictitious source, that very private gentleman. And Samuel Ireland was far from being alone in falling willingly into the trap. As the fame of his discoveries grew, and Norfolk Street off the Strand (the street no longer exists, but it was not far from Drury Lane) became the new temple for anyone Bardolatrous enough to want to see these relics for themselves, including the actress Dorothy Jordan, the antiquarian George Chalmers, the theatre historian James Boaden, and Samuel Johnson's biographer James Boswell, who reportedly fell on his knees before the holy paper relics of the Bard. To satisfy demand for intimations of genius, Ireland found himself attempting increasingly ambitious ideas. Eventually, he produced enough material for Samuel, a self-taught draughtsman and engraver with a line in 'Picturesque Views', to announce the publication of a volume of facsimiles, *Miscellaneous Papers and Legal Instruments under the Hand and Seal of William Shakspeare*. For the handsome price of 4 guineas, believers in the Shakespeare papers could eavesdrop on the Earl of Southampton thanking the poet for his 'kynde Letterre' ('butte Whye dearest Freynd talke soe muche offe gratitude mye offere was double the Somme butte you woulde accepte butte the halfe...'), Queen Elizabeth thanking him for his 'prettye Verses' ('wee doe Complemente thee onne theyre great excellence'), and Shakespeare himself quashing once and for all those rumours about his religion with a written 'Profession of Faith' ('O Lorde... O cherishe usse like the sweete Chickenne thatte under the covert offe herre spreadynge Wings Receyves herre lyttle Broode ande hoveringe oerre themme keeps themme harmlesse and in safetye...').[17]

*Miscellaneous Papers* attracted some 122 subscribers, including the former Governor-General of India Warren Hastings, the venerable actor Charles Macklin, the politician and owner of Drury Lane theatre Richard Brinsley Sheridan, and the artist Thomas Lawrence. After many more pages of similarly spelt and anachronistically conceived discoveries, they would have come across a masterpiece as nobody had seen it before: the original manuscript of *King Lear*. Here, Shakespeare's spelling remains atrocious (the newspapers learned to mock it, seemingly not caring if it was genuine or not), but his taste shows some signs of improvement. It satisfied some readers, for example, to see the foolings of the Fool exposed as the interpolations of the actors. An excerpt from *Hamlet*—or rather 'Hamblette'—follows, and a new deed of trust addressed to 'John Hemynge', dated 23 February 1611, five years before Shakespeare actually died, that finally mentioned some plays. These include 'Mye Tempest' and 'mye altered Playe of Titus Andronicus', but 'allso mye otherr Playe neverr yett Impryntedd called Kyng Vorrtygerme...'.[18]

William Henry had already delivered on the promise of that deed, and had been putting fragments of *Vortigern* (or *Vortigern and Rowena*) into his father's hand since early 1795. Samuel, in turn, took the play to Richard Brinsley Sheridan, with whom generous terms were eventually agreed. Sheridan's deputy, the dignified leading actor John Philip Kemble thought the play bad enough to be premiered on April Fool's Day (the Irelands objected, and it was moved back to 2 April), and advised his sister, the even more dignified and idolized Sarah Siddons, to have no part in it. Sheridan, in desperate need of money but in no position to judge the play's authenticity, hoped for a long-running success. But inconveniently, amid suspicions about the Irelands and much increasingly partisan discussion in the newspapers, Malone had exposed the folly of the whole business with *An Inquiry into the Authenticity of Certain Miscellaneous Papers...Attributed to Shakespeare*, an extensive commentary that showed up William's ignorance of Elizabethan spelling ('shyllynges' for 'shillings' and so on), poetry, and history. Chalmers and a few others sought to defend the Irelands, but the damage was irreparable: a few days after the publication of Malone's findings, *Vortigern* appeared at Drury Lane. It was laughed off stage, and William Henry soon found himself writing out his confession, *An Authentic Account of the Shaksperian Manuscripts*, in an attempt to clear his father's name.

The audience's responses on the night of the premiere demonstrated that Kemble had been right to be concerned, although it seems possible that he egged them on (the reports are contradictory on this point), eventually giving up the effort to play his own part straight. Even if he had put his all into it, however, it is doubtful that the play could have made a great reputation for itself. Both in its too conspicuous borrowings from other Shakespeare plays and its lack of dramatic momentum, *Vortigern* proved to be a botched job because, as far as Ireland understood it, Shakespearian verse was as easy to emulate as his archaic spelling was to recreate:

> *Vor.* ...here's a secret, and a stinging thorn,
> That wounds my troubled nerves, O! conscience! conscience!
> When thou didst cry, I strove to stop thy mouth,
> By boldly thrusting on thee dire ambition,
> Then I did think myself indeed a god!
> But I was sore deceived, for as I passed,
> And traversed in proud triumph the basse-court
> There I saw death clad in most hideous colours,
> A sight it was that did appal my soul,
> Yea, curdled thick this mass of blood within me.
> Full fifty breathless bodies struck my sight,
> And some with gaping mouths did seem to mock me,
> Whilst others smiling in cold death itself,
> Scoffingly bad me look on that, which soon
> Would wrench from off my brow this sacred crown,
> And make me too a subject like themselves;
> Subject! to whom? To thee, O sovereign death!
> Who hast for thy domain this world immense;
> Churchyards and charnel-houses are thy haunts,
> And hospitals thy sumptuous palaces,
> And when thou would'st be merry, thou dost choose
> The gaudy chamber of a dying king.
> O! then thou dost ope wide thy hideous jaws,
> And with rude laughter, and fantastic tricks,
> Thou clap'st thy rattling fingers to thy sides;
> And when this solemn mockery is ended,
> With icy hand thou tak'st him by the feet,
> And upward so, till thou dost reach the heart,
> And wrap him in the cloak of lasting night.
> *Bar.* Let not, my lord! Your thoughts sink you thus low....[19]

Neither father nor son, present on the night, could recover their reputations after that, and the reputations of those 'believers' in the Norfolk Street discoveries suffered, too. But William Henry did get something right: as Tom Lockwood puts it, what he accurately reproduced was not so much text as context: those three words are 'of a textual culture that is set within, and serves as an earnest of, a wider culture'.[20] In other words, crude though the forgeries might appear in retrospect, they were effective for a while because they perfectly fitted the image of the author licensed by the Shakespeare cult of the time. Ritson, it is worth noting, sensed their inauthenticity but did not have the materials to expose them at his disposal, as Malone did (with superior wealth, in fact, it was he, not Ritson, who became a monopolizer of cultural authority through the building of a unique private library of primary documents and books). The eighteenth-century ideal of Shakespeare presented him as a good man and a good husband, pious (meaning Protestant), and dignified (that word being used again to emphasize the connection between this image and that of Siddons and Kemble as great actors not in comedy but tragedy, lending them gravitas and moral seriousness). William Henry's 'discoveries'—the letter to his wife, the 'Profession of Faith', and the rest—conformed to that image, and it was this fatally anachronistic accuracy that made it so easy for Malone, with his radical sense of the disjunction between the received and the original Shakespeare, to expose them as fictions.

One further irony, then, is that Malone himself infected the serious study of Shakespeare with a more invidious fallacy. His earliest achievement in this area, as already noted, was a well-received 'Attempt' to put Shakespeare's plays into chronological order—an attempt that could draw on both external and internal evidence in a process of mutually supporting deductions that succeeded in overturning some long-held misapprehensions, such as *The Tempest* being an early work because it appears at the beginning of the First Folio. Similarly, he had done readers a great service by restoring the Sonnets to a place in Shakespeare's oeuvre, relating them to the plays and trying to place, again, their order of composition. Eventually, however, as Malone also strove to write the definitive biography of Shakespeare, this familiarity with the Sonnets led him into seeing behind their compressed first-person narratives, puns on the author's name, and seeming allusions to contemporary events, a commentary on the author's own life: these poems were a form of autobiography. It is with Malone's work that 'the question of Shakespeare's "personal" involvement in these poems had been raised irrepressibly'.[21] This is the intellectual path, as James Shapiro describes it in *Contested Will: Who Wrote Shakespeare?*, that led directly to the nineteenth and twentieth centuries' fantasies of the 'real' author of these great works being a great man, such as Francis Bacon or the Earl of Oxford, or even a great woman such as Elizabeth I, rather than a commoner.[22]

It is arguable that Malone's dangerous assumptions about the clues to the life to be found in the works can be connected to other eighteenth-century tendencies connected specifically to theatrical culture. Felicity Nussbaum has suggested how the theatre in this period 'challenged the boundary between public and private, between the virtual and the real'; actresses in particular could both suffer and profit from what she calls 'public intimacy'—a conflation of their public and (supposed) private identities.[23] Performers who impressed the public in particular roles were liable to become indelibly associated with those roles—as Mary Robinson became inseparable in the public eye from the role of Perdita in *The Winter's Tale*, for instance, once a celebrity in another category, the Prince of Wales, became her rumoured Florizel.[24] Theatre critics could take it as read that only a woman who was in love could possibly play Shakespeare's Juliet. Such habits of mind ultimately tend to diminish the status of imaginative acts. In their place, they offer a flattering delusion of an intimate connection between the great performer and her audience, or the literary genius and his admirers. From this error springs the unreal biographical construct of 'Shakspeare' from his plays and poems—an unfortunate distraction from the otherwise diligent and perceptive work of Malone and company, over the last three decades of the eighteenth century.

# Shakespeare for Some Time

By the end of the century, Shakespeare had become one of the basic conditions of cultural and intellectual life in the British Isles, and parts of Western Europe and Northern America, and to break off here is to interrupt a history in which extraordinary things are about to take place: the lectures and essays of Samuel Taylor Coleridge, Charles Lamb, and William Hazlitt (as well as the *Tales from Shakespeare* of Charles and Mary Lamb); Ludwig and Dorothea Tieck's continuation of the great German translation of Shakespeare by A. W. Schlegel; Edmond Malone's final, monumental edition of Shakespeare in twenty-one volumes, completed by James Boswell the Younger; the brief, bright career of Master Betty and the more enduring achievements of William Charles Macready and Edmund Kean. This diverse flowering grew from seeds sown well before the 1800s. 'Shakespeare *and* the eighteenth century', I would suggest, occupies a crucial position in that afterlife not only because of the age's outstanding theatrical interpretations or its most celebrated critical contributions to Shakespeare studies, but because of less conspicuous engagements with his works—the unobtrusive allusions in literature particularly in the late eighteenth century, the reworking of his plays as moral fables for schoolchildren, anticipating the Lambs' *Tales from Shakespeare* (1807)—and the 'failures', too—the critical dead ends, the forgotten performers, the alternative histories. Considering literary developments in their historical contexts means trying to understand and imagine a time when Samuel Johnson, say, could have given up the idea of editing Shakespeare's plays, the Sonnets barely mattered at all, and William Dodd thought it more important to go to France to consult the illustrators for his own (never-to-be-completed) edition of Shakespeare than to put his annotations into order for publication.

Taking note of these other developments provides us with an alternative to a straightforward, linear view of Shakespeare's 'rise' to cultural pre-eminence. It is striking, for example, that as late as 1747 a character called Captain Fluellen could appear in a farce (*The Widow's Wish* by Henry Ward, apparently performed in York) without acknowledgement that it was Shakespeare's or, for that matter, Charles Molloy's: Ward had in fact based his work on *The Half-Pay Officers* (1720), in which Molloy had openly drawn on *Henry V*. We ought to be cautious, then, about putting too early a date on the spread of a general familiarity with Shakespeare's characters, in the case of one play at least. The implication of Ward's borrowing is that mentioning Shakespeare's name in the printed version of the play would have been neither a commercial advantage nor a point of critical necessity.

At the same time, the persistence of a quasi-Newtonian basis for approving of Shakespeare as the poet of 'nature'—a usefully catch-all term, encompassing scientific understanding as much as it did religious beliefs—may be discerned in works of criticism that circulated widely and in marginal works alike. John Berkenhout, that authority on subjects such as botany, natural history, and gout (and also the victim of that Ireland-like forged letter, mentioned in the previous chapter), could liken 'Shakespeare's seven ages' to 'Sir Isaac Newton's seven prismatic tincts', and try to go one better than Sir Thomas Hanmer does (showing how readers engaged with Hanmer, the 'Oxford editor', decades after the first publication of his edition), by suggesting that in *The Winter's Tale* Polixenes ought to rule Illyria rather than the inland Bohemia or—Hanmer's suggestion—'Bithynia'. In terms that are both patriotic and consistent with the 'Newtonian' basis for judging works of the imagination, as discussed in Chapter 3, Berkenhout draws the line at accepting palpable 'absurdities':

Now it is very improbable that Antigonus, who embarked from Sicily for no other purpose than to expose the infant, should make a long voyage, through the Archipelago to the Black Sea. But Illyria bordered on the Adriatic, at a moderate distance from Sicily. These geographical truths are indispensably necessary in every representation, though fabulous. The majority of an English audience may bear an embarkation from Verona; but what would an Italian say, who might be present at the representation? Would he not naturally whisper to his companion—'This great Shakespeare of the English, was an ignorant blockhead.' I have as sincere a veneration for the memory of Shakespeare, and feel his beauties as exquisitely as any of his most enthusiastic commentators; but no veneration for authentic absurdities should prevent me from obliterating his palpable mistakes.[1]

Obliteration and veneration need not be incompatible, then—quite the opposite, for the works of a writer less worthy of praise would not be worthy of such empirically minded interventions. Shakespeare is so good at delineating human nature that it is unbearable, to a mind such as Berkenhout's, to have to put up with basic geographical errors.

Many more examples might be cited of Shakespeare adapted to a specific set of circumstances, in the visual arts, in performance, or in print. The edition of *Macbeth* published in York in 1799, purportedly edited by a puppeteer and his company of wooden commentators. The lecture series on Shakespeare given by William Kendrick in 1774, anticipating those of Coleridge and Hazlitt in their emphasis on Shakespeare's characters and his morality (but only given after the cancellation of his lucrative contract to edit Shakespeare). The poem 'Scots Wha Hae' by Robert Burns that smoothly incorporates *Julius Caesar* into stanzas about the Battle of Bannockburn.[2] The 'Midnight, & Poetic Pageant' organized in honour of the 'great Wizard Painter' Henry Fuseli in the summer of 1783, drawing on the aspects of Shakespeare that had informed Fuseli's own work (the chief instigator of the pageant, appeared to Fuseli 'Armèd at all points in compleat steel' like the ghost of Hamlet's father).[3] Publications such as *Six Old Plays*, justified purely on account of their relation to Shakespeare's oeuvre, or Theophilus Miller's edition of *Othello*, published at Halle in 1794, to accompany his lectures, the only publication in a proposed series for educational purposes. The careers of actors such as John Henderson, George Frederick Cooke, Mary 'Perdita' Robinson, or Sarah Siddons, who played Rosalind in *As You Like It* when conspicuously pregnant, made the role of Lady Macbeth her own (as well as the equally challenging roles of Volumnia in *Coriolanus* and Queen Katherine in *Henry VIII*), and whose final new role was Hermione in *The Winter's Tale* in 1801.[4] Perhaps the most telling of all adaptations is traced in a note by Catherine Bates, published in *Shakespeare Quarterly*, 'Pope's Influence on Shakespeare?'. Here she suggests that one of the overlooked inspirations for *The Rape of the Lock* lies in *Henry V*, in the scene before Harfleur, when Shakespeare's king, among other things, threatens violence specifically against the locks of the town's daughters. Pope's popular poem in turn might have influenced an emendation by Nicholas Rowe of a line in the same scene—and Rowe's reading, with unconsciously 'witty circularity', was to reappear in Pope's own edition of Shakespeare. 'Shakespeare's text is sometimes no more than a tissue of overlapping interpretations and readings', Bates remarks.[5] Though speculative, her own reading may stand for the way in which later generations look back to Shakespeare through eighteenth-century eyes, without necessarily realizing they are doing so. The poet of nature was a product of a media age, in which newspapers carried reports across the country of the latest theatrical sensations, and a more scholarly dialogue could be continued not only within the British Isles but across the Continent.

But as I have sought to demonstrate in this account of the eighteenth-century engagement with Shakespeare, the possibilities of the age are endless, sometimes contradictory, and often most interesting or telling when one kind of activity merges or interacts with another—in the work of editors who are also playgoers, writers trying to impress their patrons, actors who were also 'commentators' on the plays they performed. To repeat a suggestion from the introduction, the study of the eighteenth-century Shakespeare can also serve as a means of reconsidering some of our own assumptions about studying, celebrating, and restaging his works. There are unexpected points of continuity between this period and our own, as well as moments that seem to represent history at its most irreducibly alien. Shakespeare can help us to see it all.

# Chronology of selected eighteenth-century editions of Shakespeare, critical studies, theatrical productions, and related events

This chronology is intended as a guide to the publication of books, the production of plays in the professional theatre, and other Shakespeare-related incidents in the eighteenth century. It should not be regarded as a comprehensive account of the period's engagement with Shakespeare—significant periodical essays, for example, are excluded, and only a sample of the many publications relating to the Ireland controversy are included. It is instead meant to offer a complement to the general argument of this book, illustrating the ebb and flow of interest in Shakespeare over these hundred years, and some of the simultaneous developments in different areas: *Vortigern* as part of Drury Lane's run of Shakespeare productions under John Philip Kemble; the sporadic emergence of Shakespeare in translation across Europe, set against current developments in England.

Short titles for books and plays are given unless there has seemed to be a reason to give a fuller version—to distinguish between works with similar titles, say, or to convey some sense of a book's contents. Alternatively, I have supplied further details from the *English Short Title Catalogue*, the *Oxford Dictionary of National Biography*, and Brian Vickers, ed., *Shakespeare: The Critical Heritage* (London: Routledge & Kegan Paul, 1974–1981).

1700

*Theatre*: Colley Cibber, *The Tragical History of Richard III* ('December 1699 has also been suggested', Vickers, 2, 101); Charles Gildon, *Measure for Measure, or Beauty the Best Advocate*; Thomas Betterton, *King Henry IV, with the Humours of Sir John Falstaff* (adapted from *1 Henry IV*).

1701

*Theatre*: George Granville, *The Jew of Venice* (adapted from *The Merchant of Venice*)

**1702**

*Theatre*: John Dennis, *The Comical Gallant, or The Amours of Sir John Falstaff* (adapted from *The Merry Wives of Windsor*).

**1703**

*Theatre*: William Burnaby, *Love Betrayed; or, The Agreable Disappointment* (adapted from *Twelfth Night*).

**1708**

*Publications*: John Downes, *Roscius Anglicanus, or an Historical Review of the Stage from 1660 to 1706*.

**1709**

*Publications*: Nicholas Rowe, ed., *The Works of Mr. William Shakespeare*, 6 vols.

**1710**

*Theatre*: Susanna Centlivre, *A Bickerstaff's Burying; or, Work for the Upholders* (adapted partly from *The Tempest*; revived in 1715 as *The Custom of the Country*).

*Publications*: Gildon, *The Works of Mr. William Shakespeare, Volume the Seventh* and *The Life of Mr. Thomas Betterton*.

**1711**

*Publications*: *A Collection of the Best English Plays*, 10 vols. (editor unknown; includes *Julius Caesar*, *Macbeth*, *Hamlet*, and *Othello*).

**1712**

*Publications*: Dennis, *An Essay upon the Genius and Writings of Shakespeare: with Some Letters of Criticism to the Spectator*.

**1714**

*Theatre*: Rowe, *The Tragedy of Jane Shore. Written in Imitation of Shakespeare's Style*.

**1715**

*Publications*: Lewis Theobald, *The Cave of Poverty, A Poem. Written in Imitation of Shakespeare*.

**1716**

*Theatre*: Richard Leveridge, *Pyramus and Thisbe: A Comic Masque* (adapted from *A Midsummer Night's Dream*); Christopher Bullock, *The Cobbler of*

*Preston* (adapted from *The Taming of the Shrew*); Charles Johnson, another *The Cobbler of Preston* (also adapted from *The Taming of the Shrew*); William Taverner, *Every Body Mistaken* (adapted from *The Comedy of Errors*).

*Publications*: John Sheffield, *The Tragedy of Julius Caesar, altered* and *The Tragedy of Marcus Brutus* (an unperformed adaptation of *Julius Caesar* in two parts).

## 1717

*Theatre*: Revivals of Thomas Durfey, *The Injured Princess* (adapted from *Cymbeline*) and Edward Ravenscroft's adaptation of *Titus Andronicus*.

## 1719

*Theatre*: Dennis, *The Invader of His Country: or, The Fatal Resentment* (adapted from *Coriolanus*); Theobald, *Richard II*.

## 1720

*Theatre*: Charles Molloy, *The Half-Pay Officers* (adapted from *Henry V*, *Twelfth Night*, and *Love and Honour* by Sir William Davenant).

## 1723

*Theatre*: Charles Johnson, *Love in a Forest* (adapted from *As You Like It*, *A Midsummer Night's Dream* et al.); Aaron Hill, *King Henry V, or, The Conquest of France by the English*; Theophilus Cibber, *Humfrey, Duke of Gloucester* (adapted from *1 Henry VI*) and *An Historical Tragedy of the Civil Wars in the Reign of King Henry VI* (*2 and 3 Henry VI*); Sheffield, *The Tragedy of Julius Caesar* (adapted from *Julius Caesar*).

## 1725

*Publications*: Alexander Pope, ed., *The Works of Shakespeare*, 6 vols.; George Sewell, ed., *The Works of Mr. William Shakespeare. The Seventh Volume*.

## 1726

*Publications*: Theobald, *Shakespeare Restored: Or, a Specimen of the Many Errors, As Well Committed, as Unamended, by Mr. Pope in His Late Edition of This Poet*.

## 1727

*Theatre*: Theobald, *Double Falsehood* (supposedly adapted from a lost play called *Cardenio*).

**1729**

*Publications*: 'Anti-Scriblerus Histrionicus' (John Roberts?), *An Answer to Mr. Pope's Preface to Shakespeare. In a Letter to a Friend. Being a Vindication of the Old Actors who were the Publishers and Performers of that Author's Plays.*

**1731**

*Theatre*: Matthew Draper, *The Spend-Thrift* (adapted from a 'hint' in *The London Prodigal*).

*Publications*: John Hervey, *Iago Displayed* (an attack on Robert Walpole adapted from *Othello*).

*Other Events*: William Kent builds the Temple of British Worthies, including a bust of Shakespeare, for Viscount Cobham, at Stowe.

**1733**

*Publications*: Theobald, ed., *The Works of Shakespeare*, 7 vols.; Robert Walker challenges the Tonson claim to exclusive rights to publish Shakespeare's plays by beginning to publish them separately in cheap editions.

**1735**

*Theatre*: Richard Worsdale, *A Cure for a Scold* (adapted from *The Taming of the Shrew*).

*Art*: William Hogarth, 'A Scene from *The Tempest*'.

**1736**

*Publications*: George Stubbes, *Some Remarks on the Tragedy of Hamlet, Prince of Denmark* (attribution from Vickers, 3, 40; 'sometimes attributed to Sir Thomas Hanmer', according to *ESTC*).

**1737**

*Theatre*: James Miller, *The Universal Nothing* (adapted from *Much Ado about Nothing* and *Princesse d'Elide* by Molière); revival of *King John*.

*Other events*: Licensing Act.

**1738**

*Theatre*: James Carrington ('with the help of Daniel Bellamy', *ESTC*), *The Modern Receipt; or, A Cure for Love* (adapted from *As You Like It*); George Lillo, *Marina* (adapted from *Pericles*).

**1739**

*Publications*: Paolo Rolli translates 'To be or not to be' into Italian.

**1740**

*Theatre*: Hannah Pritchard's 'first major triumph' (*ODNB*) as Rosalind in *As You Like It*, 'Not Acted these Forty Years'.

*Publications*: Colley Cibber, *An Apology for the Life of Mr. Colley Cibber, Comedian*, 2 vols.

*Art*: Hogarth, 'Falstaff Examining His Troops', Francis Hayman, 'The Wrestling Scene from *As You Like It*'.

**1741**

*Theatre*: Charles Macklin plays Shylock in *The Merchant of Venice*; Garrick makes his London debut as Richard III; Samuel Johnson, *Sir John Falstaff in Masquerade* (unpublished farce by the Samuel Johnson from Cheshire).

*Art*: Thomas Bardwell, 'David Garrick as Richard III'.

*Other events*: Monument to Shakespeare installed in Poets' Corner, Westminster Abbey.

**1743**

*Publications*: Sir Thomas Hanmer, ed., *The Works of Shakespeare*, 6 vols., 1743–4; Thomas Cooke, *An Epistle to the Right Honourable the Countess of Shaftesbury, with a prologue and epilogue on Shakespeare and his writings*.

**1744**

*Theatre*: Garrick, *Macbeth*; Theophilus Cibber, *Romeo and Juliet*.

*Publications*: Garrick, *An Essay on Acting*.

**1745**

*Theatre*: Colley Cibber, *Papal Tyranny in the Reign of King John* (adapted from *King John*); J. F. Lampe, *Pyramus and Thisbe* (one-act mock opera based on Leveridge's afterpiece adapted from *A Midsummer Night's Dream*).

*Publications*: Samuel Johnson, *Miscellaneous Observations on the Tragedy of 'Macbeth': With Remarks on Sir T. H.'s Edition of Shakespeare*; Pierre Antoine de La Place, *Le Théâtre Anglois*, 8 vols., 1745–9 (of which the first four volumes are devoted to Shakespeare).

*Art*: Hogarth, 'David Garrick as Richard III'; Hayman, 'The Play Scene from *Hamlet*'.

**1746**

*Theatre*: Anon., *The Conspiracy Discovered; or, French Policy Defeated* (adapted from *Henry V*; unpublished).

**1747**

*Theatre*: Garrick becomes manager of Drury Lane.

*Publications*: William Warburton, ed., *The Works of Shakespeare*, 8 vols.

**1748**

*Theatre*: Garrick, *Romeo and Juliet*; Garrick and Hannah Pritchard play Macbeth and Lady Macbeth together for the first time.

*Publications*: Peter Whalley, *An Enquiry into the Learning of Shakespeare, with Remarks on Several Passages of his Plays*; John Upton, *Critical Observations on Shakespeare*; Thomas Edwards, *A Supplement to Mr Warburton's Edition of Shakespeare* (later retitled *The Canons of Criticism*).

**1749**

*Theatre*: James Thomson, *Coriolanus*.

*Publications*: John Holt, *An attempte to rescue that aunciente, English poet, and play-wrighte, Maister Williaume Shakespere; from the maney errours, faulsely charged on him, by certaine new-fangled wittes* (the second edition of 1750 has a new title: *Remarks on 'The Tempest': or an Attempt To Rescue Shakespeare from the Many Errors Falsely Charged on Him, by His Several Editors*).

**1750**

*Theatre*: Battle of the Romeos, involving simultaneous productions of *Romeo and Juliet* at London's two Theatres Royal.

*Art*: James McArdell (?), 'James Quin as Falstaff '; John Wootton, 'Macbeth and Banquo Meeting the Weird Sisters'.

**1752**

*Publications*: Anon., *Miscellaneous Observations on the Tragedy of Hamlet* (Vickers, 3.452, notes similarities between this pamphlet and John Holt's essay of 1749 ); William Dodd, *The Beauties of Shakespeare*.

**1753**

*Theatre*: John Lee, *Macbeth*.

*Publications*: Charlotte Lennox, *Shakespeare Illustrated: or the Novels and Histories, On which the Plays of Shakespeare are Founded, Collected and Translated from the Original Authors, with Critical Remarks*, 3 vols., 1753–4; Hugh Blair (?), ed., *The Works of Shakespeare. In which the Beauties observed by Pope, Warburton, and Dodd, are pointed out*, 8 vols. (the attribution to Blair is disputed).

*Art*: Benjamin Wilson, 'David Garrick as Romeo and George Anne Bellamy as Juliet in the Tomb Scene from *Romeo and Juliet*'.

**1754**

*Theatre*: Thomas Sheridan, *Coriolanus: or, The Roman Matron* (a conflation of Shakespeare's play and Thomson's); Macnamara Morgan, *The Sheep-Shearing: or, Florizel and Perdita* (adapted from *The Winter's Tale*); Theophilus Cibber, *The Humourists* (based on multiple plays; unpublished).

*Publications*: Zachary Grey, *Critical, Historical and Explanatory Notes on Shakespeare with Emendations of the Text and Metre*, 2 vols.

**1755**

*Theatre*: Garrick, *The Fairies: An Opera*; Francis Gentleman, *Richard II* (unpublished; performed at Bath).

*Publications*: John Gilbert Cooper, *The Tomb of Shakespeare. A Poetical Vision*.

*Art*: Pieter van Bleeck, 'Mrs Cibber as Cordelia in Nahum Tate's Adaptation of *King Lear*'; Hayman, 'Spranger Barry and Mrs Mary Elmy in *Hamlet*'.

**1756**

*Theatre*: Garrick, *Catharine and Petruchio* (adapted from *The Taming of the Shrew*), *Florizel and Perdita* (adapted from *The Winter's Tale*), and *The Tempest: An Opera*. Alexander Sumarokov opens a theatre in St. Petersburg; the repertoire includes versions of *Hamlet* and *Julius Caesar*.

*Publications*: William Harvard, *Ode to the Memory of Shakespeare*; Charles Marsh, *The Winter's Tale* (unperformed); Samuel Johnson, *Proposals For Printing, by Subscription, The Dramatick Works of William Shakespeare*; Domenico Valentini, *Il Giulio Cesare* (unperformed).

**1758**

*Theatre*: Garrick's revival of *Antony and Cleopatra* (adapted in collaboration with Edward Capell).

**1759**

*Theatre*: William Hawkins, *Cymbeline*.

*Publications*: Thomas Wilkes, *A General View of the Stage*; Charles Marsh, *Cymbeline: King of Britain* (unperformed).

**1760**

*Publications*: Robert Lloyd, *Shakespeare: An Epistle to Mr. Garrick*; Capell, *Prolusions; or, select pieces of Ancient Poetry* (including *Edward III*, which Capell thinks could be Shakespeare's).

*Art*: Francesco Zuccarelli, 'Macbeth Meeting the Witches'; Hayman, 'David Garrick as Richard III'; George Romney, 'King Lear in the Tempest tearing off his Robes'.

**1761**

*Theatre*: Garrick, *Cymbeline*.

*Publications*: Charles Churchill, *The Rosciad*; Benjamin Victor, *The History of the Theatres of London and Dublin*, 2 vols.

**1762**

*Theatre*: Garrick, *King Henry the Eighth, With the Coronation of Anne Bullen*; Victor, *The Two Gentlemen of Verona*; Thomas Hull, *The Twins* (adapted from *The Comedy of Errors*).

*Publications*: Henry Home, Lord Kames, *Elements of Criticism*, 2 vols.

*Art*: Johann Zoffany, 'Mr and Mrs Garrick by the Shakespeare Temple'.

**1763**

*Theatre*: Garrick and George Colman, *A Midsummer Night's Dream*.

*Publications*: Anon., *The Three Conjurors, A political interlude. Stolen from Shakespeare* (satire on the arrest of John Wilkes, based on *Macbeth*).

**1764**

*Publications*: David Erskine Baker, *The Companion to the Play House*, 2 vols.

1765

*Publications*: Samuel Johnson, ed., *The Plays of William Shakespeare*, 8 vols.; William Kenrick, *A Review of Doctor Johnson's new edition of Shakespeare*; Thomas Tyrwhitt, *Observations and Conjectures upon Some Passages of Shakespeare* ('Although dated 1766, this pamphlet was in fact published in December 1765', Vickers, 5, 238); Benjamin Heath, *A Revisal of Shakespeare's Text*.

1766

*Publications*: George Steevens, ed., *Twenty of the Plays of Shakespeare*, 4 vols.; James Barclay, *An Examination of Mr. Kenrick's Review of Dr. Johnson's Edition of Shakespeare*.

*Theatre*: Kenrick, *Falstaff's Wedding* (a 'sequel' to *2 Henry IV*, not *The Merry Wives of Windsor*, as stated in Vickers, 5, 182).

*Art*: Thomas Gainsborough, 'David Garrick leaning on a bust of Shakespeare'.

1767

*Publications*: Capell, ed., *Mr. William Shakespeare his Comedies, Histories, and Tragedies*, 10 vols., 1767–8; Richard Farmer, *An Essay on the Learning of Shakespeare*.

*Art*: John Runciman, 'King Lear in the Storm'; Nathaniel Dance, 'Timon of Athens'.

1768

*Theatre*: Colman, *King Lear*; James Love (aka James Dance), *Timon of Athens*; Hannah Pritchard retires.

*Publications*: Richard Warner, *A Letter to David Garrick, Esq., concerning a glossary to the plays of Shakespeare*.

*Art*: Wilson, 'William Powell as Hamlet'; Zoffany, 'David Garrick and Mrs Pritchard in *Macbeth*' and 'Charles Macklin as Shylock'.

1769

*Theatre*: Jean-François Ducis, *Hamlet*; Garrick, *The Jubilee*; Colman, *Man and Wife: or, The Shakespeare Jubilee*.

*Publications*: Elizabeth Montagu, *An Essay on the Writings and Genius of Shakespeare*.

*Other events*: Shakespeare Jubilee at Stratford-upon-Avon.

**1770**

*Publications*: Charles Jennens, ed., *King Lear*; Gentleman, *The Dramatic Censor; or, Critical Companion*, 2 vols.

**1771**

*Theatre*: Richard Cumberland, *Timon of Athens*.

*Publications*: Victor, *The History of the Theatres of London and Dublin*, vol. 3.

*Art*: Nathaniel Dance, 'David Garrick as Richard III'.

**1772**

*Theatre*: Garrick, *Hamlet* (a more radically altered text than the one he has acted before); Ducis, *Roméo et Juliette*; James Goodhall, *Richard II*.

*Art*: Henry Fuseli, 'The Death of Cardinal Beaufort'; Francis Wheatley, 'Elizabeth Younge as Viola, James Love as Sir Toby Belch, James William Dodd as Sir Andrew Aguecheek and Francis Waldron as Fabian' (*Twelfth Night*, 3.4).

**1773**

*Theatre*: Garrick, *The Tempest* (a non-operatic version); Macklin's *Macbeth* in period costume.

*Publications*: *Bell's Shakespeare*, 1773–8 (the 'acting' edition); Johnson and Steevens, eds., *The Plays of William Shakespeare*, 10 vols.; Jennens, ed., *Macbeth*; Jennens, ed., *Othello*; Jennens, ed., *Hamlet*; Tate Wilkinson, *The Wandering Patentee; or, A History of the Yorkshire Theatres, from 1770 to the Present Time*, 4 vols.

**1774**

*Theatre*: Francesco Gritti, *Hamlet* (translated into Italian from Ducis).

*Publications*: Capell, *Notes and Various Readings to Shakespeare*, vol. 1; Jennens, ed., *Julius Caesar*; *Bell's Edition of Shakespeare's Plays, As they are now performed at the Theatres Royal in London*, 9 vols.; William Richardson, *A Philosophical Analysis and Illustration of Some of Shakespeare's Remarkable Characters*; Edward Taylor, *Cursory Remarks on Tragedy, on Shakespeare, and on Certain French and Italian Poets, Principally Tragedians*.

*Art*: James Barry, 'King Lear mourns the Death of Cordelia'; Angelica Kauffmann, 'Elizabeth Hartley as Hermione in *The Winter's Tale*'; Benjamin Vandergucht, 'Henry Woodward as Petruchio in *Catherine and Petruchio*'.

**1775**

*Theatre*: Sarah Siddons acts for one (unsuccessful) season in London, 1775–6.
*Publications*: Elizabeth Griffith, *The Morality of Shakespeare's Drama Illustrated*.

**1776**

*Theatre*: Garrick retires.

*Publications*: Pierre Le Tourneur, *Shakespeare. Traduit de l'anglois*, 20 vol., 1776–83; Anon., *A Lyric Ode on the Fairies, Aerial Beings, and Witches of Shakespeare*.

**1777**

*Theatre*: Colman, *The Sheep-Shearing* (adapted from *The Winter's Tale*).
*Publications*: Maurice Morgann, *An Essay on the Dramatic Character of Sir John Falstaff*; Frederick Pilon, *An Essay on the Character of Hamlet as Performed by Mr. Henderson*; Giuseppe Baretti, *Discours sur Shakespeare et sur M. de Voltaire*; John Collins, *A Letter to George Hardinge, Esq., on the subject of a passage in Mr. Stevens's* [sic] *preface to his impression of Shakespeare*.

*Other events*: Alessandro Verri, *Hamlet* (unpublished and unperformed translation into Italian).

**1778**

*Theatre*: Sarah Siddons and John Philip Kemble, sister and brother, act opposite one another as Desdemona and Othello, in Liverpool.

*Publications*: Steevens, ed., *The Plays of William Shakespeare*, 10 vols. (including 'An Attempt to ascertain the Order in which the Plays attributed to Shakespeare were Written' by Malone); Henry Brooke, unperformed adaptations of *Antony and Cleopatra* and *Cymbeline* in *A Collection of the Pieces formerly published by Henry Brooke, Esq.*, 4 vols.; William Pearce, *The Haunts of Shakespeare*.

**1779**

*Theatre*: Hull, *The Comedy of Errors*.

*Publications*: John Nichols (advised by Steevens), *Six Old Plays, on which Shakspeare founded his Measure for Measure, Comedy of Errors, Taming the Shrew* [sic], *King John, K. Henry IV. and K. Henry V., King Lear*, 2 vols.

**1780**

*Theatre*: William Woods, *The Twins; or, Which is Which?* (adapted from *The Comedy of Errors*); Kemble, *Oh! It's Impossible!* (also adapted from *The Comedy of Errors*; unpublished); Anon., *The Shipwreck* (adapted from the operatic version of *The Tempest* for a puppet theatre).

*Publications*: Malone, *Supplement to the Edition of Shakespeare's Plays published in 1778 by Samuel Johnson and George Steevens*, 2 vols.; Thomas Davies, *Memoirs of the Life of David Garrick Esq.*, 2 vols.

*Art*: Nicolai Abildgaard, 'Richard III before the Battle of Bosworth'.

**1781**

*Art*: Fuseli, 'The Vision of Queen Katharine'.

**1782**

*Theatre*: Siddons returns to London.

*Publications*: Isaac Reed, *Biographia dramatica; or, A comparison to the playhouse*, 2 vols. (based on Baker's *Companion to the Playhouse*).

**1783**

*Theatre*: Ducis, *Le Roi Lear*; Kemble makes his London debut as Hamlet.

*Publications*: Capell, *Notes and Various Readings to Shakespeare*, 3 vols.; Joseph Ritson, *Remarks, Critical and Illustrative, on the Text and Notes of the last Edition of Shakespeare*; Malone, *A Second Appendix to Mr. Malone's Supplement to the Last Edition of the Plays of Shakespeare, containing Additional Observations by the Editor of the Supplement*. By request of the Royal Family, Kemble plays the title role and Siddons plays Constance in *King John*.

*Art*: Fuseli, 'Lady Constance, Arthur and Salisbury' and 'The Weird Sisters'.

**1784**

*Publications*: Thomas Davies, *Dramatic Miscellanies: consisting of Critical Observations on several Plays of Shakespeare*; Richardson, *Essays on Shakespeare's Dramatic Characters of Richard the Third, King Lear, and Timon of Athens. To which are added, an Essay on the Faults of Shakespeare: and Additional Observations on the Character of Hamlet*.

*Art*: Fuseli, 'The Dispute between Hotspur, Glendower, Mortimer and Worcester'.

**1785**

*Theatre*: Siddons makes her London debut as Lady Macbeth; Frederick Pilon, *All's Well that Ends Well*.

*Publications*: Bell's Shakespeare, 1785–8 (the 'literary' edition); Reed, ed., *The Plays of William Shakespeare*, 10 vols.; John Monck Mason, *Comments on the Last Edition of Shakespeare's Plays*; Thomas Whately, *Remarks on Some of the Characters of Shakespeare*; Garrick, *The Poetical Works of David Garrick*, 2 vols.

*Art*: Romney, 'Macbeth and the Witches'.

## 1786

*Theatre*: Hull, *Timon of Athens* (adapted from the version by Shadwell).

*Publications*: Kemble, *Macbeth Re-considered*; Martin Sherlock, *A Fragment on Shakespeare* (English translation of a French translation of an Italian original, published in 1779); Malone, *A Dissertation on the Three Parts of 'Henry VI', tending to shew that those plays were not written originally by Shakespeare* (reprinted in *The Plays and Poems of William Shakspeare* in 1790).

*Art*: Philip James de Loutherbourg, 'Falstaff with the Body of Hotspur'; William Blake, 'Oberon, Titania and Puck with Fairies Dancing'; Joseph Wright of Derby, 'The Tomb Scene: Juliet with the dead Romeo'.

*Other events*: Catherine the Great adapts *The Merry Wives of Windsor* as *This 'Tis To Have Linen and Buck-Baskets*, and conducts further experiments with writing serious drama in a Shakespearian mode.

## 1787

*Theatre*: Kemble, *Cymbeline*.

*Publications*: Andrew Becket, *A Concordance to Shakespeare* ('not a listing of all the words used by Shakespeare so much as an alphabetical collection of quotations on selected topics', Vickers, 6, 460); Samuel Felton, *Imperfect Hints towards a New Edition of Shakespeare*, 2 parts, 1787–8. Nikolai Karamzin translates *Julius Caesar* into Russian.

*Art*: William Hamilton, 'John Philip Kemble as Richard III' and 'The Shepherd's Cot' (*The Winter's Tale*, 4.3); Romney, 'John Henderson as Macbeth'; Abildgaard, 'Richard III Awakening from his Nightmare'; Sir Joshua Reynolds, 'Puck, or Robin Goodfellow'.

## 1788

*Theatre*: Kemble succeeds Thomas Harris as acting manager at Drury Lane; stages a 'lavish' *Henry VIII* (*ODNB*).

*Publications*: Ritson, *The Quip Modest*; Richardson, *Essays on Shakespeare's Dramatic Character of Sir John Falstaff, and on his Imitation of Female Characters*.

*Art*: Joseph Barney, '*The Tempest*, I, 2'; William Hodges, Romney, and Sawrey Gilpin, 'Jacques and the Wounded Stag in the Forest of Arden';

Kauffmann, 'Valentine, Proteus, Sylvia and Giulia in the Forest' (*The Two Gentlemen of Verona*, 5.4); Benjamin West, 'King Lear'.

**1789**

*Theatre*: Kemble, *Coriolanus*.

*Art*: John Boydell's Shakespeare Gallery opens in Pall Mall, London; Fuseli, 'Hamlet and the Ghost'; Reynolds, 'Death of Cardinal Beaufort'; James Gillray, 'Shakespeare Sacrificed,—or—The Offering to Avarice'; Angelica Kauffmann, 'A Scene from *Troilus and Cressida*'; Thomas Stothard, 'The Return of Othello'; Johann Heinrich Ramberg, 'Olivia, Maria and Malvolio' (*Twelfth Night*, 3.4).

**1790**

*Publications*: Malone, ed., *The Plays and Poems of William Shakspeare*, 10 vols.

*Art*: William Hodges, 'Jacques and the Wounded Stag'; Fuseli, 'Titania and Bottom'; Hamilton, 'The Revelation of Olivia's Betrothal' (*Twelfth Night*, 5.1).

**1791**

*Publications*: John Armstrong, *Sonnets from Shakespeare*.

*Art*: Romney, 'The Infant Shakespeare Attended by Nature and the Passions'; Gillray, 'Taming of the Shrew; Katharine & Petruchio; The Modern Quixote'.

**1792**

*Theatre*: Kemble, *King Lear*.

*Publications*: Ritson, *Cursory Criticisms on the edition of Shakespeare published by Edmond Malone*; Malone, *Letter to the Rev. Richard Farmer, Relative to the Edition of Shakespeare*.

*Art*: Hamilton, 'The Carousing of Sir Toby Belch and Sir Andrew Aguecheek'; Robert Smirke, 'The Awakening of King Lear'; West (?), 'Coriolanus Yields to the Pleas of His Mother and Sister'; Henry William Bunbury, 'The Supposed Death of Imogen'; Wheatley, 'The Death of Richard II', 'Parolles ambushed and blindfolded', and 'Valentine Rescuing Silvia from Proteus'.

**1793**

*Publications*: Steevens, ed., *The Plays of William Shakespeare*, 15 vols.

*Art*: Wheatley, 'Helena and Count Bertram before the King of France'; Fuseli, 'Titania, Bottom and the Fairies', 'Gertrude, Hamlet and the Ghost of his Father', 'Macbeth Consulting the Vision of the Armed Head', and 'Macbeth, Banquo and the Witches on the Heath'; Hamilton, 'Isabella Appealing to Angelo'; Matthew William Peters, 'The Death of Juliet'; West, 'King Lear and Cordelia'; De Loutherbourg, '*The Tempest*, Act I scene 1'; Smirke, 'Falstaff under Herne's Oak' (*The Merry Wives of Windsor*, 5.5).

### 1794

*Theatre*: Kemble, *Macbeth, Measure for Measure*, and *All's Well that Ends Well*.

*Publications*: Walter Whiter, *A Specimen of a Commentary on Shakespeare*.

### 1795

*Theatre*: Waldron, *Love and Madness!* (adapted from *The Two Noble Kinsmen*).

*Publications*: Wolstenholme Parr, *The Story of the Moor of Venice . . . With two Essays on Shakespeare, and Preliminary Observations*.

*Art*: Smirke, 'Falstaff Rebuked'; Richard Westall, 'Wolsey Disgraced' and 'Shylock Rebuffing Antonio'; Blake, 'Pity' and 'Hecate' (both inspired by *Macbeth*).

### 1796

*Theatre*: William Henry Ireland, *Vortigern*.

*Publications*: James Boaden, *A Letter to George Steevens Esq.*; Samuel Ireland, *Miscellaneous Papers and Legal Instruments under the Hand and Seal of William Shakespeare*; William Henry Ireland, *An Authentic Account of the Shakspearian Mss.*; W. C. Oulton, *Vortigern under Consideration*; G. M. Woodward, *Familiar Verses from the Ghost of Willy Shakespeare to Sammy Ireland*; James Plumptre, *Observations on Hamlet; and on the motives which most probably induced Shakespeare to fix upon the story of Amleth . . . for the plot of that tragedy: being an attempt to prove that he designed it as an indirect censure on Mary Queen of Scots*.

*Art*: Hamilton, 'Olivia's Proposal'.

### 1797

*Theatre*: Kemble, *The Merry Wives of Windsor* and *Much Ado about Nothing*.

*Publications*: George Chalmers, *An Apology for the Believers*; Samuel Ireland, *An Investigation of Mr. Malone's Claim to the Character of Scholar or Critic*, Waldron, *The Virgin Queen . . . attempted as a sequel to Shakespeare's Tempest*; James Plumptre, *An Appendix to Observations on Hamlet*. The first volumes in *Shakespeare's Dramatische Werke* appear, translated by A. W. Schlegel.

*Art*: Fuseli, 'The Enchanted Island: Before the Cell of Prospero'.

**1798**

*Theatre*: Oulton, *Pyramus and Thisbe* (adapted from *A Midsummer Night's Dream*).

*Publications*: Johann Joachim Eschenburg, *Wilhelm Shakspears Schauspiele*, 12 vols., 1798–1806.

*Art*: Smirke, 'Stephano Confronting the Monster'; Thomas Lawrence, 'John Philip Kemble as Coriolanus'.

**1799**

*Publications*: George Chalmers, *A Supplemental Apology for the Believers*.

**1800**

*Theatre*: Kemble revives *King John* with further cuts and Siddons again in the role of Constance.

*Publications*: G. Hardinge, *Chalmeriana*.

*Art*: Blake, 'Portrait of Shakespeare'.

# Notes

INTRODUCTION

1. Edward Gregg, *Queen Anne* (London: Routledge & Kegan Paul, 1980), 84ff.

2. Gregg, *Queen Anne*, 81, 86–7, 88–9, 97, 127–9.

3. *Oxford English Dictionary*, second edition (Oxford: Oxford University Press, 1989), accessed January 2012.

4. John Downes, *Roscius Anglicanus*, ed. Judith Milhous and Robert D. Hume (London: Society for Theatre Research, 1987), 74.

5. Noting the 'long and acrimonious dispute' about Shadwell's role in creating a new version of *The Tempest*, Milhous and Hume suggest that 'some cuts, a bit of dramatic cobble-work, and the addition of a new song' were all that was required of him. Ibid., 73.

6. David Green, *Queen Anne, 1665–1714* (London: Collins, 1970), 74–5.

7. John Dryden and William Davenant, *The Tempest, or The Enchanted Island*, in *Shakespeare Made Fit: Restoration Adaptations of Shakespeare*, ed. Sandra Clark (London: J. M. Dent, 1997), 1.2.206.

8. Ibid., 2.3.160–4.

9. William Shakespeare, *The Tempest*, ed. Christine Dymkowski (Cambridge: Cambridge University Press, 2000), 12.

10. Tony Claydon, 'William III and II (1650–1702)', in *Oxford Dictionary of National Biography*, accessed November 2011.

11. Gregg, *Queen Anne*, 89.

12. Samuel Johnson, *A Dictionary of the English Language*, 2 vols. (London: J. and P. Knapton et al., 1755), 1, 892; 2, 1,244 and 2,146.

13. Ben Jonson, *Timber: or, Discoveries; Made upon Men and Matter* (1640), quoted in E. K. Chambers, *William Shakespeare: A Study of Facts and Problems*, 2 vols. (Oxford: Clarendon Press, 1930), 2, 210.

14. John Aubrey, *Brief Lives*, ed. Richard Barber (Woodbridge: Boydell, 1982), 285.

15. Margreta de Grazia, *Shakespeare Verbatim: The Reproduction of Authenticity and the 1790 Apparatus* (Oxford: Clarendon Press, 1991), 1–2.

16. Robert D. Hume, 'Before the Bard: "Shakespeare" in Early Eighteenth-Century London', *English Literary History*, vol. 64 no. 1 (Spring 1997), 42–3

17. Lionel Blasney, 'Christening Shakespeare', *The Sewanee Review*, vol. 105, no. 1 (winter, 1997), viii–x.

18. John Dryden, Preface to *Troilus and Cressida, Or, Truth Found Too Late* (1679), quoted in Brian Vickers (ed.), *Shakespeare: The Critical Heritage, Volume 1: 1623–1692* (London: Routledge & Kegan Paul, 1974), 260.

19. Vickers, *Shakespeare: The Critical Heritage*, 6, 16–18.

20. Hazelton Spencer, *Shakespeare Improved: The Restoration Versions in Quarto and on the Stage* (Cambridge, MA: Harvard University Press, 1927), 371, 374, 121.

21. Sonia Massai, 'From *Pericles* to *Marina*: "While Women Are To Be Had for Money, Love, or Importunity"', *Shakespeare Survey, Volume 51: Shakespeare in the Eighteenth Century* (1998), 67–77, 73.

22. Simon Jarvis, *Scholars and Gentlemen: Shakespearian Textual Criticism and Representations of Scholarly Labour, 1725–1765* (Oxford: Clarendon Press, 1995), 11, 15. The other critical works mentioned here are: Gary Taylor, *Reinventing Shakespeare: A Cultural History from the Restoration to the Present* (New York: Grove Press, 1989); Margreta de Grazia, *Shakespeare Verbatim: The Reproduction of Authenticity and the 1790 Apparatus* (Oxford: Clarendon Press, 1991); and Michael Dobson, *The Making of the National Poet: Shakespeare, Adaptation and Authorship, 1660–1769* (Oxford: Clarendon Press, 1992).

23. Jonathan Bate, *Shakespearean Constitutions: Politics, Theatre, Criticism, 1730–1830* (Oxford: Clarendon Press, 1989), 1.

**CHAPTER 1**

1. Colley Cibber, *The Tragical History of King Richard III*, in *The Plays of Colley Cibber, Volume 1*, ed. Timothy J. Viator and William J. Burling (Madison, NJ: Fairleigh Dickinson University Press, 2001), 5.4.240.

2. Hazelton Spencer, *Shakespeare Improved: The Restoration Versions in Quarto and on the Stage* (Cambridge, MA: Harvard University Press, 1927), v.

3. Cibber, *Richard III*, 5.4.204–14.

4. Ibid., 5.4.234–6.

5. Ibid., 5.4.237–40.

6. Christopher Spencer, *Five Restoration Adaptations of Shakespeare* (Urbana: University of Illinois Press, 1965), 27.

7. Arthur Colby Sprague, *Shakespearian Players and Performances* (Cambridge, MA: Harvard University Press, 1953), 151.

8. Cibber, *Richard III*, 4.4.188.

9. Andrew Becket, *Shakspeare's Himself Again* (London: A. J. Valpy, 1815), iv.

10. Robert D. Hume, 'Before the Bard: "Shakespeare" in Early Eighteenth-Century London', *English Literary History*, vol. 64 no. 1 (Spring 1997), 43.

11. Quoted in Brian Vickers, ed., *Shakespeare: The Critical Heritage, Volume 2: 1693–1733* (London: Routledge and Kegan Paul, 1974), 34, 37, 51.

12. Charles Gildon, *Love's Victim: or, The Queen of Wales* (London: Richard Parker, 1701), Preface, A3r.

13. Robert B. Hamm, Jr, 'Rowe's *Shakespear* (1709) and the Tonson House Style', *College Literature*, vol. 31 no. 4 (Summer 2004), 179–205.

14. Vickers, *Shakespeare: The Critical Heritage*, 2, 248–9.

15. François Hédelin, Abbé d'Aubignac, trans. anon., *The Whole Art of the Stage* (London: printed for the author, 1684; facsimile edition, New York: Benjamin Blom 1968), 134–5.

16. Colley Cibber, *The Tragical History of King Richard III* (London: B. Lintott, 1700), A1r.

17. Hume, 'Before the Bard', 53.

18. Colley Cibber, *The Tragical History of King Richard III* (London: Jacob Tonson et al., 1721) and Colley Cibber, *The Tragical History of King Richard III* (London: W. Feales et al., 1736).

19. H. Spencer, *Shakespeare Improved*, 338.

20. Eric Salmon, 'Cibber, Colley (1671–1757)', in *ODNB*.

21. H. Spencer, *Shakespeare Improved*, 335.

22. Scott Colley, *Richard's Himself Again: A Stage History of 'Richard III'* (Westport, CT: Greenwood Press, 1992), 329–30, 91.

23. Judith Milhous, *Thomas Betterton and the Management of Lincoln's Inn Fields 1695–1708* (Carbondale: Southern Illinois University Press, 1979), 113.

24. Colley Cibber, *Venus and Adonis, a masque* (London: Bernard Lintott, 1715), 22.

25. See Chapter 5, 'Cutthroat Competition, 1698–1702', in Milhous, *Betterton*, and Helene Koon, *Colley Cibber: A Biography* (Lexington: University Press of Kentucky, 1986), 34ff.

26. Cibber, *Plays*, 250.

27. Ibid., 330.

28. C. Spencer, *Five Restoration Adaptations of Shakespeare*, 420.

29. Koon, *Cibber*, 38.

30. Ibid., 47.

31. Cibber, *Plays*, 328ff.

32. John Genest, *Some Account of the English Stage: From the Restoration in 1660 to 1830*, 10 vols. (Bath: H. E. Carrington, 1832), 3, 382.

33. Koon, *Cibber*, 36–7.

34. Ibid., 147.

35. Quoted in James T. Hillhouse, *The Grub-Street Journal* (Durham, NC: Duke University Press, 1928), 187.

36. Quoted in *A Biographical Dictionary of Actors, Volume 3: Cabanel to Cory* (Carbondale: Southern Illinois University Press, 1975), 217.

37. Anon., *The Laureat: or, The Right Side of Colley Cibber, Esq.* (London: J. Roberts, 1740), 35.

38. Ibid., 34–5.

39. Judith Milhous, 'Sandford, Samuel' (*fl.* 1661–1698)', in *ODNB*; Koon, *Cibber*, 37.

40. See Milhous, 'Sandford, Samuel', in *ODNB*, for an account of Cibber and other witnesses (Richard Steele and Anthony Aston), to Sandford's acting.

41. Colley Cibber, *An Apology for the Life of Colley Cibber, Comedian, and Late Patentee of the Theatre-Royal*, third edition (London: R. Dodsley, 1750), 109–11.

42. Ibid., 116–17.

43. Cibber, *Plays*, 330.

44. J. P. Vander Motten, 'Iago at Lincoln's Inn Fields: Thomas Porter's *The Villain* on the Early Restoration Stage', in *Studies in English Literature, 1500–1900*, vol. 24 no.3 (Summer, 1984), 415–28.

45. Michael Dobson, *The Making of the National Poet: Shakespeare, Adaptation, and Authorship, 1660–1769* (Oxford: Clarendon Press, 1992), 5.

46. James Boaden, *Memoirs of Mrs Siddons* (London: Henry Colburn, 1827), 1.8; quoted in Jonathan Bate, *Shakespearean Constitutions: Politics, Theatre, Criticism, 1730–1830* (Oxford: Clarendon Press, 1989), 129.

47. Charles Lamb, 'On the Tragedies of Shakspeare, Considered with Reference to Their Fitness for Stage Representation', in Charles and Mary Lamb, *The Works of Charles and Mary Lamb*, ed. E. V. Lucas (London: Methuen, 1903), 1, 113–14.

48. Koon, *Cibber*, 37.

49. Cibber, *Plays*, 340.

50. *Richard III*, 3.4.76 and *3 Henry VI*, 1.4.180.

51. Cibber, *Richard III*, 4.4.504–21.

52. H. Spencer, *Shakespeare Improved*, 338.

53. Milhous, *Betterton*, 144.

54. Nicholas Rowe, *The Tragedy of Jane Shore*, ed. Harry William Pedicord (Lincoln: University of Nebraska Press, 1974), epilogue, 26–9.

55. See Pedicord's introductory discussion of these lines in Rowe, *Jane Shore*, xiii–xiv.

56. For a nuanced account of Rowe's restrained commentary on a sensitive political situation, see Paulina Kewes, '"The State is out of Tune":

Nicholas Rowe's *Jane Shore* and the Succession Crisis of 1713–14', in *Huntington Library Quarterly*, vol. 64, no. 3/4 (2001), 283–308.

57. Brett Wilson, 'Jane Shore and the Jacobites: Nicholas Rowe, the Pretender, and the National She-Tragedy', *English Literary History*, 72 (2005), 823–43, 831.

58. Rowe, *Jane Shore*, prologue, 21–2.

59. Vickers, *Shakespeare: The Critical Heritage*, 2, 208–9.

60. Rowe, ed., *Works*, A1r.

61. Hamm, 'Rowe's *Shakespear*', 187.

62. Don-John Dugas, *Marketing the Bard: Shakespeare in Performance and Print 1660–1740* (Columbia: University of Missouri Press, 2006), 131ff.

63. Ibid., 132.

64. Hamm, 'Rowe's *Shakespear*', 191.

65. Dugas points out the precedent Tonson had himself established by 'attaching' Dryden's name to a series of poetic miscellanies (*Marketing the Bard*, 141), although he does not specify how Dryden's name was attached to these publications. Dryden is certainly the most prominent and frequent contributor to the miscellanies; but his name is not on the title page of the *Miscellany Poems* published in 1684 (not 1683), nor on those of its sequels, *Sylvae* (1685), *Examen poeticum* (1693), and so on. Dryden's presence is not concealed from the reader. Far from it; although *Mac Flecknoe* appears anonymously in *Miscellany Poems*, *Sylvae* begins with a long signed preface. But he is not acknowledged on the title page, as Rowe would be in 1709. These volumes are instead attributed to 'the most eminent hands'.

66. Rowe, *Works*, 1, A1r.

67. Ibid., A2r.–A2v.

68. Ibid., A4r.

69. J. Gavin Paul, 'Performance as "Punctuation": Editing Shakespeare in the Eighteenth Century', *Review of English Studies*, new series, vol. 61, no. 250 (2009), 390–413, 396.

70. Peter Holland, 'Modernizing Shakespeare: Nicholas Rowe and *The Tempest*', *Shakespeare Quarterly*, vol. 51, no. 1 (Spring 2000), 24–32.

71. Rowe, *Works*, 1, xvii.

72. See Barbara Mowat, 'The Form of *Hamlet*'s Fortunes', *Renaissance Drama*, 19 (1988), 97–126, 99ff.

73. Rowe, *Works*, 6, A3v., and 5, 2,196.

74. J. Gavin Paul, 'Performance as "Punctuation"', 396.

75. Stephen Orgel, *Imagining Shakespeare: A History of Texts and Visions* (Basingstoke: Palgrave Macmillan, 2003), 45.

76. Rowe, *Works*, 4, 1,613–4.

77. Fourth Folio, 205.

78. Rowe, *Works*, 4, 1,708–9.

79. J. Gavin Paul, 'Performance as "Punctuation"', 394.

80. Peter Holland, 'Modernizing Shakespeare', 30, 32.

81. Roy Porter, *English Society in the Eighteenth Century*, revised edition (London: Penguin Books, 1991), 217.

82. Rowe, *Works*, 1, ii–xl.

83. Ibid., iii.

84. Charles Gildon, *The Laws of Poetry, As laid down by the Duke of Buckinghamshire in his Essay on Poetry, by the Earl of Roscommon in his Essay on Translated Verse, and by the Lord Lansdowne on Unnatural Flights in Poetry, Explained and Illustrated* (London: J. Morley, 1721), 23, 33, 158, 224.

85. Ibid., 203–7.

86. Rowe, *Works*, 1, xxi–xxii.

87. Samuel Johnson, 'Rowe', in *The Lives of the Poets*, ed. John H. Middendorf, 3 vols. (New Haven: Yale University Press, 2010), 2, 585.

88. The anonymous author of *Royal Remarks; or, the Indian King's Observations on the most Fashionable Follies: Now reigning in the Kingdom of Great-Britain* thought that Rowe had done too much as it was. The book alludes to a 'Critics' Jury' that had lately sat in judgement over 'the body of divine *Shakespeare, lately murdered again by a great poet*, to the inexpressible grief and loss of his executors the booksellers' (Anon., *Royal Remarks; or, the Indian King's Observations on the most Fashionable Follies: Now reigning in the Kingdom of Great-Britain* (London: 'the booksellers', 1710), 19).

89. Peter Martin, *Edmond Malone, Shakespearean Scholar: A Literary Biography* (Cambridge: Cambridge University Press, 1995), 273.

90. Samuel Johnson, 'Rowe', 2, 585.

91. Rowe, *Works*, 1, xxxv.

92. J. Douglas Canfield and Alfred W. Hesse, 'Nicholas Rowe', in *Dictionary of Literary Biography, Volume 84: Restoration and Eighteenth-Century Dramatists*, second series, ed. Paula R. Backscheider (Gale Group, 1989), 262–89, 270.

**CHAPTER 2**

1. Shakespeare, *Richard III*, 5.3.177ff.; as quoted in Richard Steele, *The Tatler*, No. 90 (3–5 November 1709).

2. Sir Thomas Hanmer, ed., *The Works of Shakespear*, 6 vols. (Oxford: Printed at the Theatre, 1747), 6, 361.

3. William Warburton, ed., *The Works of Shakespear*, 8 vols. (London: J. and R. Tonson et al., 1747), 2, 349.

4. Nicholas Rowe, ed., *The Works of Mr. William Shakespear*, 6 vols. (London: J. Tonson, 1709), 5, 2, 319.

5. Alexander Pope, ed., *The Works of Shakespear*, 6 vols. (London: J. Tonson, 1725), 5, 541.

6. Sir Thomas Hanmer, ed., *The Works of Shakespear*, 6 vols. (London: J. and R. Tonson et al., 1745), 1, A2r.

7. See Andrew Murphy, *Shakespeare in Print: A History and Chronology of Shakespeare Publishing* (Cambridge: Cambridge University Press, 2003), 114.

8. Samuel Johnson, *Proposals for Printing, by Subscription, the Dramatick Works of William Shakespeare* (London: J. and R. Tonson et al., 1756), 3–4, 6.

9. Ibid., 7.

10. Alexander Pope, *The Dunciad in Four Books*, ed. Valerie Rumbold (Harlow: Pearson Education, revised edition 2009), 93.

11. Ibid., 95.

12. See *Richard III*, 1597 and 1598 quartos, both Sig. L4v; First Folio, 202; Fourth Folio, 205; Rowe, *Works*, vol. 3, 1,710; Capell, *Comedies, Histories, and Tragedies*, vol. 7, 118; Malone, *Plays and Poems* 1790, vol. 6, 604–5.

13. William Shakespeare, *The Plays and Poems of William Shakspeare*, 21 vols., ed. Edmond Malone and James Boswell (London: F. C. and J. Rivington et al., 1821), 19, 225.

14. Netta Murray Goldsmith, *Alexander Pope: The Evolution of a Poet* (Aldershot: Ashgate, 2002), 165.

15. *Weekly Journal*, 18 November 1721, quoted in Andrew Murphy, *Shakespeare in Print: A History and Chronology of Shakespeare Publishing* (Cambridge: Cambridge University Press, 2003), 64.

16. Goldsmith, *Pope*, 165.

17. Reginald Berry, *A Pope Chronology* (Basingstoke: Macmillan, 1988), 40ff.

18. Alexander Pope, *The Works of Shakespear*, 6 vols. (London: Jacob Tonson, 1725), 1, xxii–xxiii.

19. Lewis Theobald, *Shakespeare Restored, or, A Specimen of the Many Errors as well Committed, as Unamended, by Mr. Pope in his Late Edition of This Poet* (London: R. Francklin, 1726), 137–8.

20. Ibid., 138.

21. See F. W. Bateson, 'Editorial Commentary', *Essays in Criticism*, vol. 5, no. 1 (1955), 91–5, 94.

22. For a sampling of later discussions of Theobald's emendation, see Percy Fitzgerald, 'A Babbled o' Green Fields', *Notes and Queries*, series 7, vol. 6, no. 136 (1888), 84; the two responses to Bateson by Hilda M. Hulme and

Ernest Schanzer, *Essays in Criticism*, vol. 6, no. 1 (1956), 117–21; and Ephim G. Fogel, '"A Table of Green Fields": A Defense of the Folio Reading', *Shakespeare Quarterly*, vol. 9, no. 4 (autumn 1958), 485–92.

23. Theobald, *Shakespeare Restored*, 26–8.

24. Ibid., 93–6.

25. Ibid., 98.

26. Ibid., ii–iii.

27. Ibid., v.

28. Theobald, *Works*, 7, 302.

29. Ibid., 1, lxvi.

30. Tone Sundt Urstad, *Sir Robert Walpole's Poets: The Use of Literature as Pro-Government Propaganda, 1721–1742* (Newark: University of Delaware Press, 1999), 223.

31. Peter Seary, *Lewis Theobald and the Editing of Shakespeare* (Oxford: Clarendon Press, 1990), 145.

32. Theobald, *Works*, 1, vii. Quoted in Brean Hammond, ed., *Double Falsehood or The Distressed Lovers* (London: Methuen, 2010), 93.

33. Seary, *Theobald*, 204.

34. Pope, *Works*, 1, v.

35. Ibid., 1, vii–viii.

36. A 'Stroling Player', *An Answer to Mr. Pope's Preface to Shakespear... Being a Vindication of the Old Actors who were the Publishers and Performers of the Author's Plays* (London: no publisher given, 1729), 4–5.

37. Ibid., 13ff.

38. Ibid., 24–6.

39. Ibid., 46.

40. Ibid., 47–8.

41. Gefen Ben-On Santor, 'The Culture of Newtonianism and Shakespeare's Editors: From Pope to Johnson', *Eighteenth-Century Fiction*, vol. 21, no. 4 (Summer 2009), 593–614, 594–6.

42. Ibid., 598.

43. Theobald, *Works*, 1, xxiv.

44. Pope, *Works*, 1, ii.

45. Theobald, *Works*, 1, iii; Pope, *Works*, 1, iii.

46. Ibid., 602.

47. Brian Vickers, 'The Emergence of Character Criticism, 1774–1800', *Shakespeare Survey 34* (1981), 11–21, 11; John Bligh, 'Shakespearian Character Study to 1800', *Shakespeare Survey 37* (1984), 141–53.

48. Santor, 'Newtonianism', 610.

49. Ibid., 613.

50. Seary, *Theobald*, 132ff.

51. Andrew Murphy, *Shakespeare in Print*, 74. See also Jarvis, *Scholars and Gentlemen*, 94ff.
52. Thomas R. Lounsbury, *The Text of Shakespeare: Its History from the Publication of the Quartos and Folios down to and including the Publication of the Editions of Pope and Theobald* (New York: Charles Scribner's Sons, 1906), 524; quoted in Murphy, *Shakespeare in Print*, 73.
53. Lounsbury, *Text*, 108–9.
54. Ibid., 527–8.
55. Rowe, *Works*, 1, 241.
56. Pope, *Works*, 1, 377; Theobald, *Works*, 1, 366; quoted in Lounsbury, *Text*, 526.
57. Ibid., 109.
58. Theobald, *Works*, 1, xl.

CHAPTER 3

1. Elizabeth Bonhote, *The Rambles of Mr. Frankly*, 4 vols. (London: Thomas Becket, 1772–6), 3, 93.
2. Francis Aspry Congreve, *Authentic Memoirs of the Late Mr. Charles Macklin, Comedian* (London: J. Barker, 1798), 17; quoted in Paul Goring, ed., *Lives of Shakespearian Actors*, 3 vols. (London: Pickering & Chatto, 2008), 2, 15.
3. Aspry Congreve, *Authentic Memoirs*, 18; Goring, 16.
4. Charles Edelman, ed., *The Merchant of Venice* (Cambridge: Cambridge University Press, 2003), 7.
5. Nicholas Rowe, ed., *The Works of Mr. William Shakespear*, 6 vols. (London: J. Tonson, 1709), vol. 1, xix–xx.
6. William Cooke, *Memoirs of Charles Macklin, Comedian* (London: James Asperne, 1804), 90; Goring, 359.
7. Hume, 'Before the Bard', 55, see Table 1.
8. Arthur H. Scouten, 'Shakespeare's Plays in the Theatrical Repertory When Garrick Came to London', *University of Texas Studies in English 1944* (Austin: University of Texas Press, 1945), 257–68, and 'The Increase in Popularity of Shakespeare's Plays: A *Caveat* for Interpretors of Stage History', in *Shakespeare Quarterly*, vol. 7, no. 2 (Spring, 1956), 189–202. For the dates of Charles Fleetwood's Shakespeare revivals and statistics about stock plays at Garrick's Drury Lane and before, see 'The Increase in Popularity of Shakespeare's Plays', 193–4.
9. Hume, 'Before the Bard', 55–6.
10. *BD*, 5.298.
11. Cooke, 91–2; Goring, 360–1.

12. *London Daily Post and General Advertiser*, 11 February 1741, issue 1967. Burney Collection.

13. See 'The Early Illustrators of Shakespeare' by Brian Allen and plates 1 and 2 in Jane Martineau and Desmond Shawe-Taylor, eds., *Shakespeare in Art* (London: Merrell, 2003).

14. Aaron Hill, *The Prompter*, 27 December 1734; quoted in Jane Girdham, 'Thurmond, Sarah (d. 1762)', *Oxford Dictionary of National Biography*, Oxford University Press, 2004.

15. Paul Sawyer, 'The Popularity of Shakespeare's Plays, 1720–21 through 1732–33', *Shakespeare Quarterly*, vol. 29, no. 3 (Summer, 1978), 427–30.

16. For a cautionary tale about the analysis of eighteenth-century theatre finances, as well as a useful consideration of the theatre as a business and all the factors that might go into making a play profitable, see Judith Milhous and Robert D. Hume, 'Theatre Account Books in Eighteenth-Century London', in *Superior in His Profession: Essays in Memory of Harold Love*, *Script & Print* special issue, ed. Meredith Sherlock, Brian McMullin, and Wallace Kirsop, vol. 33, nos. 1–4 (2009), 125–35.

17. Benjamin Victor, *The History of the Theatres of London and Dublin, from the year 1730 to the present time*, 2 vols. (London: Thomas Davies, 1761), 2, 67–8. The *BD* quotes what seems to be a description of Harper adapted by Davies from Victor (7, 119–20).

18. Peter Thomson, 'Harper, John (d. 1742)', *ODNB*, and *BD*, 7, 116ff.

19. Martineau and Shawe-Taylor, eds., *Shakespeare in Art* (London: Merrell, 2003), 52.

20. Jeremy Black, *George II: Puppet of the Politicians?* (Exeter: Exeter University Press, 2007), 80ff.

21. Calhoun Winton, *John Gay and the London Theatre* (Lexington: University Press of Kentucky, 1993), 95.

22. John Loftis, *The Politics of Drama in Augustan England* (Oxford: Clarendon Press, 1963), 128, 130.

23. Winton, *John Gay*, 93.

24. Ibid., 94.

25. John Gay, *The Beggar's Opera*, ed. Bryan Loughrey and T. O. Treadwell (London: Penguin, 1986), 2.3–4.

26. Gay, *The Beggar's Opera*, 2.10.

27. Ibid., 2.10.

28. Cooke, *Macklin*, 54.

29. Ibid., 54–5.

30. *BD*, 3, 225.

31. James T. Hillhouse, *The Grub-Street Journal* (Durham, NC: Duke University Press, 1928; repr., New York: Benjamin Blom, 1967), 169–70.

32. Arthur H. Scouten, 'The Shakespeare Revival', in *The London Stage, 1729–1747* (Carbondale: Southern Illinois University Press, 1968), 1.cxlix ff.

33. Eliza Haywood, *The History of Miss Betsy Thoughtless*, ed. Beth Fowkes Tobin (Oxford: Oxford University Press, 1997), 45–6.

34. Vickers, *Shakespeare: The Critical Heritage*, 3, 13.

35. Loftis, *Politics*, 150ff.

36. Ibid., 142, 152.

37. Emmett L. Avery, 'The Shakespeare Ladies Club', *Shakespeare Quarterly*, vol. 7, no. 2 (Spring, 1956), 153–8, 153.

38. Ibid., 154, 157.

39. Dobson, 148ff.

40. Fiona Ritchie, 'The Influence of the Female Audience on the Shakespeare Revival of 1736–1738: The Case of the Shakespeare Ladies Club', in *Shakespeare and the Eighteenth Century*, ed. Peter Sabor and Paul Yachnin (Aldershot: Ashgate, 2008), 57–70, 60.

41. Ibid., 64–5.

42. Eliza Haywood, *The Female Spectator*, fifth edition (London: T. Gardner, 1755), 1, 265.

43. Dobson, 151ff.

44. Ritchie, 'Influence', 66.

45. David M. Little and George M. Kahrl, eds., *The Letters of David Garrick*, 3 vols. (London: Oxford University Press, 1963), 2, 655.

46. Lewis Theobald, *Shakespeare Restored: Or, A Specimen of the Many Errors, as well Committed, as Unamended, by Mr. Pope In his Late Edition of this Poet* (London: R. Francklin et al., 1727), A3r.

47. Derek Pearsall, 'Chaucer's Tomb: The Politics of Reburial', *Medium aevum*, 64 (1995), 51–73.

48. Ben Jonson, 'To the memory of my beloved, The Author Master William Shakespeare, and what he hath left us', 9–21, in Stanley Wells and Gary Taylor, eds., *The Complete Works*, second edition (Oxford: Clarendon Press, 2005), lxxi.

49. Irby B. Cauthen, 'Thomas May', in *Dictionary of Literary Biography*, vol. 58 (Gale), accessed autumn 2009.

50. See BL Add. 47863, letter from Francis Atterbury to Alexander Pope; and Alfred Jackson, 'Pope's Epitaphs on Rowe', *Review of English Studies*, vol. 7, no. 25 (January 1931), 76–9.

51. John Dart, *Westminster-Abbey: A Poem* (London: J. Batley, 1721), 35–6.

52. Reginald Heber, *An Elegy written among the Tombs in Westminster Abbey* (London: R. and J. Dodsley, 1762), 7–8.

53. Thomas Maurice, *Westminster-Abbey: An Elegiac Poem* (London: printed for the author, 1784), 16.

54. Ibid., 17.

55. Ibid., 19–20.

56. Anon., *An Accurate tho' Compendious Encomium on the Most Illustrious Persons, Whose Monuments are Erected in Westminster-Abbey* (London: printed for the author, 1749), 27.

57. Ibid., 23–5.

58. Bonhote, *The Rambles of Mr. Frankly*, 3, 88–9.

59. Ibid., 90–1.

60. D. M., *Ancient Rome and Modern Britain Compared. A Dialogue in Westminster Abbey* (London: printed for the author, 1793), 10.

61. Anon., *London: A Satire* (London: printed for the author, third edition [1782?]), 28.

62. Haywood, *The Female Spectator*, 1, 266.

63. *London Daily Post and General Advertiser*, 2 March 1741, issue 1983. Burney Collection. When Macklin's Shylock was on his thirteenth performance, *As You Like It* 'Written by Shakespear' was announced for Quin's benefit the following night, while Giffard was staging *All's Well That Ends Well*, also 'Written by Shakespear', and *Harlequin Student* with its representation of Shakespeare's monument was on again (*London Daily Post and General Advertiser*, 9 March 1741, issue 1989).

64. Cooke, *Macklin*, 92; quoted in Goring, *Macklin*, 361.

65. Ibid., 362ff.

66. *London Daily Post and General Advertiser*, 20 February 1741, issue 1975, and 19 March 1741, issue 1998. Burney Collection.

67. *London Daily Post and General Advertiser*, 26 March 1741, issue 2087. Burney Collection.

68. Cooke, *Macklin*, 95; Goring, *Macklin*, 364.

CHAPTER 4

1. Paul Whitehead, 'Verses, dropt in Mr. GARRICK's Temple of Shakespear, at Hampton', in *The Annual Register, or a View of the History, Politicks, and Literature, of the Year 1758*, ed. Edmund Burke (London: Robert Dodsley, 1759), 431–2.

2. Richard Steele, Preface to *The Conscious Lovers*, in *The Plays of Sir Richard Steele*, ed. Shirley Strum Kenny (Oxford: Clarendon Press, 1971), 299.

3. Quoted in Thomas Davies, *Memoirs of the Life of David Garrick, Esq.*, 2 vols. (London: Longman et al., new edition, 1808), 2, 457.

4. George Winchester Stone, Jr and George M. Kahrl, *David Garrick: A Critical Biography* (Carbondale: Southern Illinois University Press, 1979), 206.

5. 25 September 1765, *Public Advertiser*, quoted in Stone and Kahrl, *Garrick*, 325.

6. See Appendix B in Stone and Kahrl, *Garrick*, 656–8.

7. Samuel Johnson, 'Prologue Spoken by Mr Garrick at the Opening of the Theatre in Drury-Lane, 1747', in *The Complete Poems*, ed. J. D. Fleeman (Harmondsworth: Penguin, 1971), 81–2.

8. David Garrick, *Harlequin's Invasion*, 3.2, in Harry William Pedicord and Fredrick Louis Bergmann, eds., *The Plays of David Garrick*, 7 vols. (Carbondale: Southern Illinois University Press, 1980–2), 224–5.

9. *Lethe*, in Garrick, *Plays*, 1, 18.

10. *The Male-Coquette*, in ibid., 1, 136–7.

11. David Garrick, 'Occasional prologue spoken by Mr. Garrick at the opening of Drury-Lane Theatre, 8 September 1750', in David Garrick, *Poetical Works*, 2 vols. (London: George Kearsley, 1785), 1, 102.

12. David Garrick, *An Ode upon Dedicating a Building, and Erecting a Statue to Shakespeare, at Stratford upon Avon* (London: T. Becket and P. A. De Hondt, 1769), 1.

13. *BD*, 6, 92–101.

14. Letter to the Countess of Burlington, 19 September 1749, *The Letters of David Garrick*, 3 vols., ed. David M. Little and George M. Kahrl (London: Oxford University Press, 1963), 1, 128.

15. Stone and Kahrl, *Garrick*, Appendix B, 656–8.

16. Ibid., 505.

17. Ibid., 517.

18. Davies, *Garrick*, 2, 449, 453.

19. Francis Gentleman, *Introduction to Shakespeare's Plays, Containing an Essay on Oratory* (London: J. Bell and York, C. Etherington, 1773), iii.

20. Letter to David Garrick, 27 December 1765, quoted in Stone and Kahrl, *Garrick*, 190.

21. William Cooke, *Memoirs of Charles Macklin, Comedian* (London: James Asperne, revised edition 1806), 107.

22. Arthur Murphy, *The Life of David Garrick*, Esq., 2 vols. (London: J. Wright, 1801), 248–9.

23. As *Lichtenberg's Visits to England*, trans. and ed. Margaret L. Mare and W. H. Quarrell (Oxford: Clarendon Press, 1938).

24. John Taylor, *Records of My Life*, 2 vols. (London: Edward Bull, 1832), 1, 347.

25. Theophilus Cibber, *Dissertations on Theatrical Subjects* (London: printed for the author, 1756), 56.

26. Quoted in John O'Brien, *Harlequin Britain: Pantomime and Entertainment, 1690–1760* (Baltimore: Johns Hopkins University Press, 2004), 231.

27. Deidre Shauna Lynch, *The Economy of Character: Novels, Market Culture, and the Business of Inner Meaning* (Chicago: Chicago University Press, 1998), 73.

28. Letter to Peter Garrick, ante 29 December 1741, in Garrick, *Letters*, 1, 34.

29. 1 January 1795, *St James's Chronicle*.

30. Garrick, *Plays*, 3, 191.

31. Ibid., 4, 2.

32. Quoted in ibid., 4, 396.

33. Letter to George Steevens, [10 January 1775], in Garrick, *Letters*, 3, 982.

34. Letter to David Garrick, n. d. but seemingly also January 1775, in James Boaden, ed., *The Private Correspondence of David Garrick*, 2 vols. (London: Henry Colburn and Richard Bentley, 1832), 2, 122.

35. Garrick, *Letters*, 3, 985.

36. Boaden, *Private Correspondence*, 2, 122.

37. Garrick, *Plays*, 4, 432ff.

38. Harry William Pedicord, '"Ragandjaw": Garrick's Shakespearean Parody for a Private Theatre', *Philological Quarterly*, vol. 60, no. 2 (1981), 197–204.

39. Davies, *Garrick*, 1, 116–17.

40. Gentleman, *Introduction to Shakespeare's Plays*, 8.

41. Garrick, *Letters*, 2, 632.

42. Edmond Malone, ed., *The Plays and Poems of William Shakspeare*, 10 vols. (London: J. Rivington et al., 1790), 1, pt. 2, 283–4.

43. Arthur H. Scouten, 'Shakespeare's Plays in the Theatrical Repertory When Garrick Came to London', *University of Texas Studies in English 1944* (Austin: University of Texas Press, 1945), 257–68.

44. Arthur John Harris, 'Garrick, Colman, and *King Lear*: A Reconsideration', *Shakespeare Quarterly*, vol. 22, no. 1 (winter 1971), 57–66.

45. See Ian McIntyre, *Garrick* (London: Allen Lane The Penguin Press, 1999), 607, and Appendix F in Stone and Kahrl, *Garrick*, 672–3.

46. Memorandum to Sir William Young, 10 January 1776, in Boaden, *Private Correspondence*, 2, 126.

47. Vanessa Cunningham, *Shakespeare and Garrick* (Cambridge: Cambridge University Press, 2008), 157.

48. Garrick, *Plays*, 4, 436.

49. Stone and Kahrl, *Garrick*, 548.

50. Letter to the Rev. Stonehouse, May 1776, in Boaden, *Private Correspondence*, 2, 148.

51. Anon. (sometimes attributed to Charles Gildon), *A Comparison between the Two Stages* (London: 1702), 25, quoted in Judith Milhous, *Thomas*

*Betterton and the Management of Lincoln's Inn Fields 1695–1708* (Carbondale: Southern Illinois University Press, 1979), 131.

52. Quoted in Alan Kendall, *David Garrick: A Biography* (London: Harrap, 1985), 120.

### CHAPTER 5

1. James Boswell, *Life of Johnson*, ed. R. W. Chapman (Oxford: Oxford University Press, 1904; 1980), 350–1.
2. Thomas Seward, 'On SHAKESPEAR's Monument at Stratford upon Avon', in *A Collection of Poems*, 3 vols. (London: R. Dodsley, 1751), 2, 301.
3. Paul Langford, *A Polite and Commercial People: England 1727–1783* (Oxford: Clarendon Press, 1989), 146.
4. Roy Porter, *English Society in the Eighteenth Century* (London: Penguin, revised edition 1991), 311, 364.
5. The difficulties of reaching firm conclusions about literacy and the size of the reading public are concisely discussed in Robin Jarvis, *The Romantic Period, 1789–1830* (Harlow: Pearson Education, 2004), 58–9.
6. Langford, *A Polite and Commercial People*, 94–5.
7. Nancy Copeland, 'The Source of Garrick's *Romeo and Juliet* text', *English Language Notes*, vol. 24, no. 4 (June 1987), 27–33.
8. Edmond Malone, *The Plays and Poems of William Shakspeare*, 10 vols. (London: J. Rivington et al., 1790), 1, 232.
9. *The Works of Shakespear. In which the Beauties observed by Pope, Warburton, and Dodd, are pointed out* (Edinburgh: Alexander Kincaid and Alexander Donaldson et al., 1753), 1, i–v.
10. William Popple, *The Prompter*, no. 57 (27 May 1735), quoted in Vickers, 3, 22–8; Anon., 'Remarks on the Tragedy of the Orphan', *The Gentleman's Magazine*, xviii (November and December 1748), quoted in Vickers, 3, 328–33; and Bonnell Thornton, 'Some Reflections on the Theatres', *Have at You All, or The Drury Lane Journal*, no. 10 (19 March 1752), quoted in Vickers, 3, 463.
11. Henry Felton, *A Dissertation on Reading the Classics, and Forming a Just Style. Written in the Year 1709* (London: Jonah Bowyer, 1713), 212–13, quoted in Vickers, 2, 215.
12. John Dennis, *Original Letters, Familiar, Moral and Critical* (London: W. Mears, 1721), 71–4, quoted in Vickers, 2, 348–51.
13. Eliza Haywood, *The Female Spectator*, book 8 (1745), 2, 90–3, quoted in Vickers, 3, 162–4.
14. Charles Johnson, *The Cobler of Preston* (London: W. Wilkins, second edition 1716), 47.

15. See Katherine West Scheil, 'Early Georgian Politics and Shakespeare: The Black Act and Charles Johnson's *Love in a Forest* (1723)', *Shakespeare Survey, Volume 51: Shakespeare in the Eighteenth Century*, ed. Stanley Wells (Cambridge: Cambridge University Press, 1998), 45–56.

16. See Gerald Kahan, *George Alexander Stevens and the Lecture on Heads* (Athens: University of Georgia Press, 1984), 31ff.

17. *St James's Chronicle*, 6–9 May 1769, quoted in Ian McIntyre, *Garrick* (London: Allen Lane The Penguin Press, 1999), 415.

18. Ibid., 414–32.

19. See Garrick, *Plays*, 2, 108 and 332ff.

20. Jean Benedetti, *David Garrick and the Birth of Modern Theatre* (London: Methuen, 2001), 210.

21. See Martha Winburn England, *Garrick and Stratford* (New York: New York Public Library, 1962), 67–9, 47.

22. Ibid., 11.

23. Quoted in Terry Castle, *Masquerade and Civilization: The Carnivalesque in Eighteenth-Century English Culture and Fiction* (Stanford: Stanford University Press, 1986), 14.

24. Castle, *Masquerade and Civilization*, 2–6.

25. Dobson, 214.

26. Samuel Johnson, *A Dictionary of the English Language*, 2 vols. (London: J. and P. Knapton et al., 1755), 2, 1,615 and 2,125; 1, 393.

27. See Arthur Sherbo, *Samuel Johnson, Editor of Shakespeare* (Urbana: Illinois University Press, 1956), 17ff., and Anne McDermott, 'The Defining Language: Johnson's *Dictionary* and *Macbeth*', *Review of English Studies*, new series, vol. 44, no. 176 (November 1993), 521–38.

28. Samuel Johnson, Preface to *The Plays of William Shakespeare*, 8 vols. (London: J. and R. Tonson et al., 1765), 1, A1r.–A2r.

29. Ibid., A2v.

30. Johnson, *Plays*, B1r–v, B2r, B3r.

31. Ibid., 1, B1r.

32. Ibid., 1, A2v.–A3r.

33. Brian Vickers, 'The Emergence of Character Criticism, 1774–1800', *Shakespeare Survey, Volume 34: Characterization in Shakespeare*, ed. Stanley Wells (Cambridge: Cambridge University Press, 1981), 11–21.

34. Johnson, *Works*, 1, B6v.

35. Ibid., 1, A4v–A5r.

36. Richard Stack, 'An Examination of an Essay on the Dramatic Character of Sir John Falstaff', quoted in Vickers, 6, 479.

37. Vickers, 'The Emergence of Character Criticism', 13.

38. Johnson, *Works*, 1, B8v.

39. Ibid., 1, E4v.
40. Ibid., 1, D1v.
41. Ibid., 1, E5v.
42. Ibid., 7, 465.
43. Ibid., 2, 530.
44. Ibid., 1, 220.
45. Ibid., 8, 236.
46. Ibid., 2, 448.
47. Ibid., 5, 225.
48. Ibid., 6, 159.
49. See T. J. Monaghan, 'Johnson's Additions to His *Shakespeare* for the Edition of 1773', *Review of English Studies*, new series, vol. 4, no. 15 (July, 1953), 234–48.
50. Samuel Johnson, *Proposals for Printing, by Subscription, the Dramatick Works of William Shakespeare* (London: J. and R. Knapton, 1756), 6–7.
51. See Arthur Sherbo, 'The Library of George Tollet, Neglected Shakespearean', *Studies in Bibliography*, 34 (1981), 227–38.
52. Thomas Tyrwhitt, *Observations and Conjectures upon Some Passages of Shakespeare* (Oxford: Clarendon Press, 1766), 12.
53. Edmond Malone, *Supplement to the Edition of Shakspeare's Plays Published in 1778*, 2 vols. (London: C. Bathurst et al., 1780), 1, 373–80.
54. Isaac Reed, ed., *The Plays of William Shakspeare*, 21 vols. (London: J. Nichols et al., 1813), 20, 255.
55. Ibid., 8, 363–4.
56. John Wolfson, 'Bell's Edition of Shakespeare's Plays: A Bibliographical Niughtamre', in *The Book Collector*, vol. 61 no. 4 (Winter 2012), 551–66, 558.

CHAPTER 6

1. Jean I. Marsden, *The Re-Imagined Text: Shakespeare, Adaptation, and Eighteenth-Century Literary Theory* (Lexington: University Press of Kentucky, 1995), 2.
2. Samuel Johnson, Preface to *The Plays of William Shakespeare*, 8 vols. (London: J. and R. Tonson et al., 1765), 1, A3r.–v.
3. William Dodd, *The Beauties of Shakespear: Regularly selected from each Play*, 2 vols. (London: T. Waller, 1752), 2, 219.
4. On 'The Courtship between Romeo and Juliet, in the Garden': 'The elegance and natural simplicity of this scene is enough to recommend it, and must render it agreeable to every reader who hath any taste for tenderness, delicacy, and sincere affection; but when we have seen it so justly performed, and so beautifully graced by some of the best and most judicious actors that ever appeared on any stage, we shall want no comment to enter into its particular excellencies, no chart to guide us

to those beauties, which all must have sensibly felt, on hearing from so feelingly and pathetically expressed, in their own bosoms'. Ibid., 2, 202.

5. Edwin Eliott Willoughby, 'A Deadly Edition of Shakespeare', *Shakespeare Quarterly*, vol. 5, no. 4 (autumn 1954), 351–7. Dodd's desperate financial situation led him to commit forgery, for which the punishment was the death penalty. Protests at the time, including from Johnson, failed to save him, but did lead to the formation of a movement for legal reform.

6. Elizabeth Griffith, *The Morality of Shakespeare's Drama Illustrated* (London: Thomas Cadell, 1775), xii.

7. Ibid., 311.

8. Ibid., 2.

9. Ibid., 358.

10. Ibid., 448.

11. Ibid., 455.

12. In other words, this is the tendency to explain away every error or inconsistency as a mark of Shakespeare's genius. 'A blemish has been rationalized into a beauty, a discrepancy into a subtlety, a numerical error into a "touch of nature"', as Harbage writes of an explanation by Edmond Malone. Alfred Harbage, 'Shakespeare and the Myth of Perfection', *Shakespeare Quarterly*, vol. 15, no. 2 (Spring, 1964), 1–10, 3.

13. Ibid., 358.

14. Griffith, *Morality of Shakespeare's Drama*, 101.

15. Ibid., 107.

16. Ibid., 71.

17. Samuel Johnson, *Proposals for Printing, by Subscription, the Dramatick Works of William Shakespeare* (London: J. and R. Tonson et al., 1756), 8.

18. Arthur Murphy, *The Way To Keep Him*, in *Eighteenth Century Drama: Afterpieces*, ed. Richard W. Bevis (Oxford: Oxford University Press, 1970), 3.1.339.

19. Ibid., 1.2.86; 3.1.358–60.

20. Ibid., 1.2.76–8.

21. Oliver Goldsmith, *She Stoops To Conquer*, in *Poems and Plays*, ed. Tom Davis (London: J. M. Dent, 1975; 1993), 76.27.

22. Ibid.,74.10.

23. Ibid., 93.14–5.

24. Isaac Jackman, *All the World's a Stage* (London: J. Wilkie, second edition 1777), 1.2.

25. Ibid., 2.1.

26. Frances Burney, *Camilla, or A Picture of Youth*, ed. Edward A. Bloom and Lillian D. Bloom (Oxford: Oxford University Press, 1972), 318.

27. Robert Bage, *Hermsprong, or Man As He Is Not*, ed. Peter Faulkner (Oxford: Oxford University Press, 1985), 121.

28. Kate Rumbold, '"Alas, poor YORICK": Quoting Shakespeare in the Mid-Eighteenth-Century Novel', *Borrowers and Lenders: The Journal of Shakespeare and Appropriation*, vol. 2, no. 2 (Fall/Winter 2006), http://www.borrowers.uga.edu/cocoon/borrowers/request?id=781458.

29. Laurence Sterne, *The Life and Opinions of Tristram Shandy*, ed. Graham Petrie (London: Penguin, 1967), 126.

30. John Cleland, *Fanny Hill or Memoirs of a Woman of Pleasure*, ed. Peter Wagner (London: Penguin, 1985), 11–12.

31. Henry Jones?, *The Life and Extraordinary History of the Chevalier John Taylor* (Dublin: D. Chamberlaine, 1761), 156.

32. Tobias Smollett, *The Life and Adventures of Sir Launcelot Greaves*, ed. Robert Folkenflik and Barbara Laning Fitzpatrick (Athens: University of Georgia Press, 2002), xxvi and 203.

33. Tobias Smollett, *The Life and Adventures of Sir Launcelot Greaves*, ed. Peter Wagner (London: Penguin, 1988), 46.

34. Ibid., 63.

35. Ibid., 80–1.

36. Matthew Lewis, *The Monk: A Romance*, ed. Howard Anderson (Oxford: Oxford University Press, 1973), 379–81.

37. Ann Radcliffe, *The Romance of the Forest*, ed. Chloe Chard (Oxford: Oxford University Press, 1999), 44.

38. Ibid., 260.

39. Ibid., 284.

40. Horace Walpole, *The Castle of Otranto: A Gothic Story*, ed. W. S. Lewis (Oxford: Oxford University Press, 1964), 40ff.

41. Clara Reeve, *The Old English Baron*, ed. James Trainer (Oxford: Oxford University Press, 1967), 5.

42. See R. J. S. Stevens, *Recollections of R. J. S. Stevens: An Organist in Georgian London*, ed. Mark Argent (Carbondale: Southern Illinois University Press, 1992), 64ff.

43. Dobson, 2.

CHAPTER 7

1. Samuel Johnson, *A Dictionary of the English Language*, 2 vols. (London: J. and P. Knapton, 1755), 1, 61.

2. Allan Ramsay, *The Gentle Shepherd; A Scots pastoral comedy* (Edinburgh: printed for the author, 1725), 3.4.

3. Jean I. Marsden, *The Re-Imagined Text: Shakespeare, Adaptation, and Eighteenth-Century Literary Theory* (Lexington: University Press of Kentucky, 1995), 2.

4. William King, *Remains of the Late Learned and Ingenious Dr William King, Some Time, Advocate of Doctors Commons, Vicar-General to the Archbishop of Armagh, and Record-Keeper of Ireland*, ed. Joseph Browne (London: W. Mears, 1732), 60.

5. Lurana Donnels O'Malley, *The Dramatic Works of Catherine the Great: Theatre and Politics in Eighteenth-Century Russia* (Aldershot: Ashgate, 2006), 121ff.

6. Linda Colley, *Britons: Forging the Nation, 1707–1837* (New Haven, CT: Yale University Press, 1992), 5.

7. William Shakespeare, *King Henry V*, ed. Emma Smith (Cambridge: Cambridge University Press, 2002), 11.

8. John Brewer, *The Pleasures of the Imagination: English Culture in the Eighteenth Century* (London: HarperCollins, 1997), 84.

9. Voltaire, *Lettres philosophiques* (Amsterdam: E. Lucas, 1734), 210.

10. Ibid., 215.

11. Ibid., 214.

12. Garrick, *Plays*, 6, 381ff.

13. Translated and quoted in A. J. Ayer, *Voltaire* (London: Weidenfeld and Nicholson, 1986), 53.

14. Quoted in John Pemble, *Shakespeare Goes to Paris: How the Bard Conquered France* (London: Hambledon and London, 2005), 5.

15. James Boswell, *Boswell on the Grand Tour: Germany and Switzerland 1764*, ed. Frederick A. Pottle (London: William Heinemann, 1953), 291.

16. Brian Dolan, *Ladies of the Grand Tour* (London: HarperCollins, 2001), 172.

17. Letter from Elizabeth Montagu to Elizabeth Vesey, 7 September 1776, MO 6486, quoted in Elizabeth Eger, *Bluestockings: Women of Reason from Enlightenment to Romanticism* (Basingstoke: Palgrave Macmillan, 2010), 86.

18. Jean François Ducis, *Macbeth, Tragédie en vers et en cing actes* (Paris: P. F. Gueffier, 1790), 2.5.5.

19. Jean François Ducis, *Othello, ou Le More de Venise, Tragédie* (Paris: Barba, 1817), 5.4.6, s. d., second version.

20. Lois Potter, *Othello* (Manchester: Manchester University Press, 2002), 60.

21. Ibid., 61.

22. Quoted in Reeve Parker, *Romantic Tragedies: The Dark Employments of Wordsworth, Coleridge, and Shelley* (Cambridge: Cambridge University Press, 2011), 239.

23. Helen Phelps Bailey, *Hamlet in France: From Voltaire to Laforgue* (Geneva: Droz, 1964), 14.

24. Sir Henry Thomas, 'Shakespeare in Spain', in *Proceedings of the British Academy*, vol. 35, 9.

25. Rafael Portillo and Mercedes Salvador, 'Spanish Productions of *Hamlet* in the Twentieth Century', in *Four Hundred Years of Shakespeare in Europe*, ed. Angel-Luis Pujante and Ton Hoenselaars (Newark: University of Delaware Press, 2003), 180.

26. *The Monthly Magazine, or, British Register*, vol. 14, part 2 for 1803 (London: Richard Phillips, 1803), 615.

27. Ángel-Luis Pujante and Keith Gregor, 'Conservatism and Liberalism in the Four Spanish Renderings of Ducis's *Hamlet*', in *Shakespeare and European Politics*, ed. Dirk Delabastita, Jozef De Vos, and Paul Franssen (Newark: University of Delaware Press, 2008), 304–17, 316.

28. See J. G. Robertson, 'The Knowledge of Shakespeare on the Continent at the Beginning of the Eighteenth Century', *Modern Language Review*, vol. 1 (1905–6), 312–21.

29. Simon Williams, *Shakespeare on the German Stage, Volume 1: 1586–1914* (Cambridge: Cambridge University Press, 1990), 221ff.

30. Karl Philipp Moritz, *Anton Reiser: A Psychological Novel*, trans. by Ritchie Robertson (London: Penguin, 1997), 185.

31. Ibid., 186.

32. Ibid., 190.

33. Johanna Gottfried Herder, *Shakespeare*, trans. and ed. Gregory Moore (Princeton: Princeton University Press, 2008), 48–9.

34. Ibid., xl.

35. Ibid., xxi.

36. Henry Childs Merwin, *Thomas Jefferson* (Boston, MA: Houghton, Mifflin, 1901), 6.

37. Alden T. and Virginia Mason Vaughan, *Shakespeare in America* (Oxford: Oxford University Press, 2012), 11ff., 32.

38. Kevin J. Hayes, *The Road to Monticello: The Life and Mind of Thomas Jefferson* (Oxford: Oxford University Press, 2008), 125.

39. Kevin J. Hayes, 'The Libraries of Thomas Jefferson', in *A Companion to Thomas Jefferson*, ed. Francis D. Cogliano (Oxford: Wiley-Blackwell, 2011), 340.

40. Ibid., 30.

41. Barbara A. Mowat, 'The Founders and the Bard', *Yale Review*, vol. 97, no. 4 (2009), 1–18, 18.

CHAPTER 8

1. Quoted in John Berkenhout, *Biographia Literaria; or A Biographical History of Literature* (London: J. Dodsley, 1777), 399–400.
2. George Bernard Shaw, *Three Plays for Puritans* (London: Constable, 1901), xxx–xxxi.
3. Alexander Pope, ed., *The Works of Shakespear*, 6 vols. (London: Jacob Tonson, 1725), i, xxiii; Lewis Theobald, ed., *The Works of Shakespeare*, 7 vols. (London: Jacob Tonson et al., 1733), i, i.
4. Lucyle Hook, 'Shakespeare Improv'd, or A Case for the Affirmative', *Shakespeare Quarterly*, vol. 4, no. 3 (July 1953), 289–99, 298–9.
5. Terry Belanger, 'Publishers and Writers in Eighteenth-Century England', in Isabel Rivers, ed., *Books and Their Readers in Eighteenth-Century England* (Leicester: Leicester University Press, 1982), 5–25, 18.
6. Edward Capell, ed., *Mr William Shakespeare his Comedies, Histories, and Tragedies* (London: Dryden Leach, 1768), i, 13.
7. See Andrew Murphy, *Shakespeare in Print: A History and Chronology of Shakespeare Publishing* (Cambridge: Cambridge University Press, 2003), 84ff.
8. De Grazia, *Shakespeare Verbatim: The Reproduction of Authenticity and the 1790 Apparatus* (Oxford: Clarendon Press, 1991), 6–8.
9. Simon Jarvis, *Scholars and Gentlemen: Shakespearian Textual Criticism and Representations of Scholarly Labour, 1725–1765* (Oxford: Clarendon Press, 1995), 184.
10. Malone, *Supplement*, vol. ii, 4.
11. Malone, 1790, x, 376.
12. Ibid., vii, 381–2.
13. Joseph Ritson, *Cursory Criticisms on the Edition of Shakspeare Published by Edmond Malone* (London: Hookham and Carpenter, 1792), 78, 56.
14. Edmond Malone, *A Letter to the Rev. Richard Farmer* (London: G. G. J. Robinson et al., 1790), 36, 23.
15. William Henry Ireland, *Miscellaneous Papers and Legal Instruments under the Hand and Seal of William Shakespeare, including the Tragedy of King Lear and a Small Fragment of Hamlet, from the Original Manuscripts in the Possession of Samuel Ireland* (London: J. Egerton et al., 1795), A2v.
16. Bernard Grebanier, *The Great Shakespeare Forgery: A New Look at the Career of William Henry Ireland* (London: William Heinemann, 1966), 36.
17. Ireland, *Miscellaneous Papers*, A4r., A1r., and B1r.
18. Ibid., C4r.–D1v.
19. William Henry Ireland, *Vortigern, An Historical Tragedy* (London: J. Barker et al., 1799), 5.2.

20. Tom Lockwood, 'Manuscript, Print and the Authentic Shakespeare: The Ireland Forgeries Again', in Peter Holland (ed.), *Shakespeare Survey 59: Editing Shakespeare* (Cambridge: Cambridge University Press, 2006), 108–23.
21. De Grazia, 159.
22. James Shapiro, *Contested Will: Who Wrote Shakespeare?* (London: Faber and Faber, 2010).
23. Felicity Nussbaum, *Rival Queens: Actresses, Performance, and the Eighteenth-Century British Theater* (Philadelphia: University of Pennsylvania Press, 2010), 45, 60.
24. Paula Byrne, *Perdita: The Life of Mary Robinson* (London: HarperCollins, 2004), 1.

## CHAPTER 9

1. John Berkenhout, *A Volume of Letters from Dr Berkenhout to His Son at the University* (Cambridge: J. Archdeacon, for T. Cadell, London, 1790), 1, 336–8.
2. See Carol McGuirk, 'Burns and Aphorism; or, Poetry into Proverb: His Persistence in Cultural Memory Beyond Scotland', in *Robert Burns and Transatlantic Culture*, ed. Sharon Alker et al. (Aldershot: Ashgate, 2012), 173–4.
3. Jacques Zonneveld, *Sir Brooke Boothby: Rousseau's Roving Baronet Friend* (De Nieuwe Haagsche: Uitgeverij, 2003), 167ff.
4. Robert Shaughnessy, 'Siddons, Sarah (1755–1831)', *ODNB*.
5. Catherine Bates, 'Pope's Influence on Shakespeare?', *Shakespeare Quarterly*, vol. 42, no. 1 (Spring 1991). 57–9, 59.

# Further reading

## STARTING POINTS

A cluster of books that offer striking approaches to the study of Shakespeare and the eighteenth century are mentioned and discussed briefly in the introduction to this book: Gary Taylor, *Reinventing Shakespeare: A Cultural History from the Restoration to the Present* (New York: Grove Press, 1989); Margreta de Grazia, *Shakespeare Verbatim: The Reproduction of Authenticity and the 1790 Apparatus* (Oxford: Clarendon Press, 1991); Michael Dobson, *The Making of the National Poet: Shakespeare, Adaptation and Authorship, 1660–1769* (Oxford: Clarendon Press, 1992); and Jonathan Bate, *Shakespearean Constitutions: Politics, Theatre, Criticism, 1730–1830* (Oxford: Clarendon Press, 1989). To these must be added an essay, Robert D. Hume, 'Before the Bard: "Shakespeare" in Early Eighteenth-Century London', *English Literary History*, vol. 64 no. 1 (Spring 1997), a book, Jean I. Marsden, *The Re-Imagined Text: Shakespeare, Adaptation, & Eighteenth-Century Literary Theory* (Lexington: University Press of Kentucky, 1995), and an invaluable compendium of Shakespeare-related criticism, alteration for performance, poetry, and editorial commentary: Brian Vickers, ed., *Shakespeare: The Critical Heritage*, 6 vols. (London: Routledge & Kegan Paul, 1974–81).

Paul Baines provides an excellent literary overview in *The Long 18th Century* (London: Arnold, 2004), while John Brewer, *The Pleasures of the Imagination: English Culture in the Eighteenth Century* (London: HarperCollins, 1997) traces the transformation in the status of all the arts across the Georgian period. Anybody interested in the general state of England during that period could learn from the relevant volume in the *New Oxford History of England*, Paul Langford, *A Polite and Commercial People: England 1727–83* (Oxford: Oxford University Press, 1989; new edition, 1992), as well as Roy Porter, *English Society in the Eighteenth Century* (London: Penguin, 1982; revised edition, 1991), H. T. Dickinson, ed., *A Companion to Eighteenth-Century Britain* (Oxford: Blackwell, 2002; 2006), and Frank O'Gorman, *The Long Eighteenth Century: British Political and Social History, 1688–1832* (London: Hodder Arnold, 1997). There are complementary histories of politics and culture, and selfhood and culture in a different era by the same author: Tim Blanning, *The Culture of Power and the Power of Culture: Old Regime Europe 1660–1789* (Oxford: Oxford University Press, 2002) and *The Romantic Revolution* (London: Weidenfeld & Nicolson, 2010).

For further reading on some crucial eighteenth-century ideas, see James Sambrook, *The Eighteenth Century: The Intellectual and Cultural Context* (Harlow: Longman, 1993), Martin Fitzpatrick et al., eds, *The Enlightenment World* (London: Routledge, 2004), Terry Castle, *Masquerade and Civilization: The Carnivalesque in Eighteenth-Century English Culture and Fiction* (Stanford: Stanford University Press, 1986), Linda Colley, *Britons: Forging the Nation, 1707–1837* (New Haven, CT: Yale University Press, 1992), and Janet Todd, *Sensibility: An Introduction* (London: Taylor & Francis, 1986).

## PERFORMANCE

There are helpful general accounts of theatre in the eighteenth century in Peter Thomson, *The Cambridge Introduction to English Theatre, 1660–1900* (Cambridge: Cambridge University Press, 2006), Robert D. Hume, 'Drama and Theatre in the mid and later Eighteenth-Century', John Richetti, ed., *The Cambridge History of English Literature, 1660–1780* (Cambridge: Cambridge University Press, 2005), 316–39, and Jane Moody and Daniel O'Quinn, eds., *The Cambridge Companion to British Theatre, 1730–1830* (Cambridge: Cambridge University Press, 2007). Or see Richard W. Bevis, *English Drama: Restoration and Eighteenth Century 1660–1789* (London: Longman, 1988), Kenneth Richards and Peter Thomson, eds., *The Eighteenth Century English Stage* (London: Methuen, 1972), Allardyce Nicoll, *The Garrick Stage: Theatres and Audience in the Eighteenth Century* (Manchester: Manchester University Press, 1980), or Cecil Price, *Theatre in the Age of Garrick* (Oxford: Basil Blackwell, 1973), all of which have particular strengths.

A good starting point for discovering the works of Shakespeare's eighteenth-century successors and adaptors is James Vinson, ed., *Restoration and 18th-Century Drama* (London: Macmillan, 1980), which includes an introduction by Arthur Scouten summarizing the stage history of the period and over 50 guides to individual dramatists. Much more detail on theatre personnel other than playwrights may be found in Philip H. Highfill, Jr, et al., eds., *A Biographical Dictionary of Actors, Actresses, Musicians, Dancers, Managers, and Other Stage Personnel in London, 1660–1800*, 16 vols. (Carbondale: Southern Illinois University Press, 1973–93). The fullest complete record yet of what actually happened in London's theatres between 1660 and 1800 appears in William van Lennep, et al., eds., *The London Stage, 1660–1800: A Calendar of Plays, Entertainments and Afterpieces Together with Casts, Box-Receipts and Contemporary Comment Compiled from the Playbills, Newspapers and Theatrical Diaries of the Period*, 11 vols. (Carbondale: Southern Illinois University Press, 1960–8), to which a significant update has been added by Judith Milhous and Robert D. Hume, in the form of an online draft of part of a new version of *The London Stage* (http://www.personal.psu.edu/hb1/London%20Stage%202001/), covering 1700 to 1729.

These essential works of reference are supplemented by William J. Burling, *Summer Theatre in London, 1661–1820, and the Rise of the Haymarket Theatre* (Madison: Fairleigh Dickinson University Press, 2000), John C. Greene and Gladys L. H. Clark, *The Dublin Stage, 1720–1745: A Calendar of Plays, Entertainments, and Afterpieces* (Madison: Fairleigh Dickinson University Press, 1993); there are accounts of provincial stages in R. J. Broadbent's *Annals of the Liverpool Stage* (Liverpool: Edward Howell, 1908; repr. New York: Benjamin Blom, 1969) and Sybil Rosenfeld, *Strolling Players and Drama in the Provinces, 1660–1765* (Cambridge: Cambridge University Press, 1939).

Two magnificent resources for historical work on English theatre are to be found in Robert D. Hume and Judith Milhous, eds, *A Register of English Theatrical Documents, 1660–1737*, 2 vols. (Carbondale: Southern Illinois University Press, 1991) and, from the same hands, *Vice Chamberlain Coke's Theatrical Papers, 1706–1715* (Carbondale: Southern Illinois University Press, 1982). A single volume of documents, David Thomas, ed., *Theatre in Europe: A Documentary History, Restoration and Georgian England 1660–1788* (Cambridge: Cambridge University Press, 1989), offers a more concise account of the essential developments, while Charles Beecher Hogan, *Shakespeare in the Theatre, 1701–1800*, 2 vols. (Oxford: Clarendon Press, 1957) remains a valuable resource.

Milhous and Hume are also the co-authors of *Producible Interpretations: Eight English Plays, 1675–1707* (Carbondale: Southern Illinois University Press, 1985), which explores in detail how plays might have been staged in that period, from *The Country Wife* to *The Beaux' Stratagem*, while Hume has also edited a comprehensive collection of essays, *The London Theatre World, 1660–1800* (Carbondale: Southern Illinois University Press, 1980). A later complement to these publications is Tiffany Stern, *Rehearsal from Shakespeare to Sheridan* (Oxford: Oxford University Press, 2000). Some authoritative essays on various aspects of eighteenth-century theatre, from farce to stage design to prompt-books, appear in the period in George Winchester Stone, Jr, ed., *The Stage and the Page: London's 'Whole Show' in the Eighteenth-Century Theatre* (Berkeley: University of California Press, 1981).

What was happening to the genres of dramatic writing in general during this period is incisively analysed in Laura Brown, *English Dramatic Form, 1660–1760: An Essay in Generic History* (New Haven, CT: Yale University Press, 1981). And for the stage history of some individual plays, see Scott Colley, *Richard's Himself Again: A Stage History of Richard III* (New York:

Greenwood Press, 1992), John Ripley, *Coriolanus on Stage in England and America, 1609–1994* (Madison: Fairleigh Dickinson University Press, 1998), David L. George, *A Comparison of Six Adaptations of Shakespeare's Coriolanus 1681–1962: How Changing Politics Influence the Interpretation of a Text* (Lampeter: Edwin Mellen Press, 2008).

Katherine West Scheil, *The Taste of the Town: Shakespearean Comedy and the Early Eighteenth Century* (Lewisburg, PA: Bucknell University Press, 2003) studies a range of alterations and their reception, while George C. Branam, *Eighteenth-Century Adaptations of Shakespearean Tragedy* (Berkeley: University of California Press, 1956) provides some enlightened discussion of these adaptations and a checklist of them. Theatre's place in the political scene, across the century, becomes clearer thanks to John Loftis, *The Politics of Drama in Augustan England* (Oxford: Clarendon Press, 1963), Marc Baer, *Theatre and Disorder in Late Georgian London* (Oxford: Clarendon Press, 1992), and George Taylor, *The French Revolution and the London Stage, 1789–1805* (Cambridge: Cambridge University Press, 2000). David Worrall examines a wide range of theatrical activity and government attempts to control it in *Theatric Revolution: Drama, Censorship, and Romantic Period Subcultures 1773–1832* (Oxford: Oxford University Press, 2006). Sybil Rosenfeld, *Temples of Thespis: Some Private Theatres and Theatricals in England and Wales, 1700–1820* (London: Society for Theatre Research, 1978) includes a scattering of direct information about Shakespeare plays in non-professional productions, but there is a rich first chapter on that subject in Michael Dobson, *Shakespeare and Amateur Performance: A Cultural History* (Cambridge: Cambridge University Press, 2011). A contrasting form of professional activity is carefully assessed in Jane Moody, *Illegitimate Theatre in London, 1770–1840* (Cambridge: Cambridge University Press, 2000), while Dane Farnsworth Smith and M. L. Lawhon, *Plays about the Theatre in England, 1737–1800 or, The Self-conscious Stage from Foote to Sheridan* (Lewisburg, PA: Bucknell University Press, 1979) gives a taste of the self-referential, Shakespeare-quoting strain in plays of the period. A further challenge to complacent ideas about conventional theatre history and historiography lies in Jacky Bratton, *New Readings in Theatre History* (Cambridge: Cambridge University Press, 2003), especially in its study of the battle over theatre history in the early 1800s through to the mid-century Reform Acts.

GARRICK

On the life and career of one eighteenth-century actor in particular—on his acting, his directing, his play-writing, his Shakespeare Jubilee—a great deal has been written, both during and after his lifetime. Long and useful entries on David Garrick may be found in both the sixth volume of the *Biographical Dictionary* and the *Oxford Dictionary of National Biography*; the author of the latter, Peter Thomson, has also written some interesting related essays on Garrick, such as 'Celebrity and Rivalry: David [Garrick] and Goliath [Quin]' in *Theatre and Celebrity in Britain, 1660–2000* (Basingstoke: Palgrave Macmillan, 2005), edited by Mary Luckhurst and Jane Moody, and 'David Garrick: Alive in Every Muscle' in his collection *On Actors and Acting* (Exeter: Exeter University Press, 2000).

Ian McIntyre's *David Garrick* (London: Allen Lane, The Penguin Press, 1999) takes a chronological approach to its subject, while George Winchester Stone, Jr, and George M. Kahrl, in *David Garrick: A Critical Biography* (Carbondale: Southern Illinois University Press, 1979), divide this substantial book into thematic sections such as 'The Apprentice', 'The Manager', 'The Private Man', and 'The Actor'. There are separate book-length studies of some of those themes in Elizabeth P. Stein's *David Garrick, Dramatist* (New York: Modern Language Association of America, 1938) and Kalman A. Burnim's *David Garrick: Director* (Pittsburgh: University of Pittsburgh Press, 1961), which draws on the surviving promptbooks, among other sources, to show how Garrick staged *Macbeth*, *Romeo and Juliet*, *King Lear*, and *Hamlet*, as well as one play not by Shakespeare, *The Provoked Wife* by Vanbrugh. Vanessa Cunningham's *Shakespeare and Garrick* (Cambridge: Cambridge University Press, 2008) argues for the literary side of Garrick's endeavours, emphasizing his contribution to the scholarly study and appreciation of Shakespeare; like Cunningham's study, Kahrl, *The Garrick Collection of Old English Plays: A Catalogue with an Historical Introduction* (London: British Library, 1982) testifies to Garrick's influence beyond the stage and interest in sixteenth- and seventeenth-century drama. His correspondence has been published as David M. Little and George M. Kahrl, eds., *The Letters of David Garrick*, 3 vols. (London: Oxford University Press, 1963), and his plays, including 12 adaptations of Shakespeare, as well as relevant dramatic pieces such as *Harlequin's Invasion* and *The Jubilee*, appear in Harry William Pedicord and Fredrick Louis Bergmann, eds., *The Plays of David Garrick*, 7 vols. (Carbondale: Southern Illinois University Press, 1980–2).

Of the books mentioned immediately above, several devote space to Garrick's Shakespeare Jubilee in Stratford-upon-Avon. But there are also book-length studies of that by J. M. Stochholm, *Garrick's Folly: The Stratford Jubilee of 1769* (London: Methuen, 1964), Christian Deelman, *The Great Shakespeare Jubilee* (London: Michael Joseph, 1964), and Martha Winburn England, *Garrick's Jubilee* (Columbus: Ohio State University Press, 1964).

OTHER ACTORS

The empowerment of women as actresses during the eighteenth century is superbly analysed by Felicity Nussbaum in *Rival Queens: Actresses, Performance, and the Eighteenth-Century British Theater* (Philadelphia: University of Pennsylvania Press, 2010). Later eighteenth-century acting is examined in Celestine Woo, *Romantic Actors and Bardolatry: Performing Shakespeare from Garrick to Kean* (New York: Peter Lang, 2008), and Reiko Oya has some interesting things to say about Garrick in the context of some of his most celebrated peers, in *Shakespearean Tragedy: Garrick, the Kembles, and Kean* (Cambridge: Cambridge University Press, 2007), although a better introduction to the same group of star performers appears in the Great Shakespeareans series, Peter Holland, ed., *Garrick, Kemble, Siddons, Kean* (London: Continuum, 2010). Facsimiles of biographies, periodical reviews, poems, and more relating to Garrick, Charles Macklin, and Margaret Woffington may be found in Gail Marshall, series ed., *Lives of Shakespearian Actors, Part 1*, 3 vols. (London: Pickering & Chatto, 2008) and to Sarah Siddons in *Lives of Shakespearian Actors, Part 2* (2009). The image and the celebrity of the actor has also been fruitfully studied in publications such as Shearer West, *The Image of the Actor: Verbal and Visual Representation in the Age of Garrick and Kemble* (London: Pinter Publishers, 1991), Gill Perry, *Spectacular Flirtations: Viewing the Actress in British Art and Theatre, 1768–1820* (New Haven, CT: Yale University Press, 2007), and, in a broader context, Joseph Roach, *It* (Ann Arbor: University of Michigan Press, 2007). Linda Kelly, *The Kemble Era: John Philip Kemble, Sarah Siddons and the London Stage* (London: Bodley Head, 1980) is an enjoyable 'dual biography' of Siddons and her brother Kemble; a refreshing approach informs Judith Pascoe, *The Sarah Siddons Audio Files: Romanticism and the Lost Voice* (Ann Arbor: University of Michigan Press, 2011), which goes in search of ways to understand what Siddons sounded like and why her voice had such a powerful effect on audiences.

Actresses other than Siddons have attracted biographers who often, understandably, have had less to say about their performances in Shakespeare than in anything in their offstage lives that might be called 'sensational'. An exception is Anthony Vaughan, *Born To Please: Hannah Pritchard, Actress, 1711–1768: A Critical Biography* (London: Society for Theatre Research, 1979), which claims her as one of the great actresses of the century.

TEXT

Over several chapters, Andrew Murphy's *Shakespeare in Print: A History and Chronology of Shakespeare Publishing* (Cambridge: Cambridge University

Press, 2003) offers a thorough and fair account of the publication of Shakespeare during the eighteenth century, including the numerous disputes over who 'owned' Shakespeare and how his editors treated his texts. Murphy also contributes a concise account of 'The Birth of the Editor' to a useful volume of essays he has edited, *A Concise Companion to Shakespeare and the Text* (Oxford: Wiley-Blackwell, 2007). There are closer readings, as it were, of the culture and practice of textual criticism in Simon Jarvis, *Scholars and Gentlemen: Shakespearian Textual Criticism and Representations of Scholarly Labour, 1725–1765* (Oxford: Clarendon Press, 1995), Marcus Walsh, *Shakespeare, Milton and Eighteenth-Century Literary Editing: The Beginnings of Interpretative Scholarship* (Cambridge: Cambridge University Press, 1997), and Joanna Gondris, ed., *Reading Readings: Essays on Shakespeare Editing in the Eighteenth Century* (Madison, WN: Fairleigh Dickinson University Press, 1998).

When it comes to individual editors of Shakespeare, coverage is uneven: there is a long overdue act of redress in Peter Seary, *Lewis Theobald and the Editing of Shakespeare* (Oxford: Clarendon Press, 1990), and a careful consideration of Edmond Malone's career as a whole in Peter Martin, *Edmond Malone, Shakespearean Scholar: A Literary Biography* (Cambridge: Cambridge University Press, 1999). *Pope's Literary Legacy: The Book-Trade Correspondence of William Warburton and John Knapton*, ed. Donald W. Nichol (Oxford: Oxford Bibliographical Society, 1992) includes a scattering of relevant material, such as Warburton's agreement over the copyright of his editorial contributions in 1747. On Warburton, there is also Robert M. Ryler's critical overview *William Warburton* (Boston, MA: Twayne, 1984); and in his multiple studies of various others, Arthur Sherbo has sought to cover the rest of the ground: his books include *The Birth of Shakespeare Studies: Commentators from Rowe (1709) to Boswell-Malone (1821)* (East Lansing, Michigan: Colleagues Press, 1986), *Isaac Reed, Editorial Factotum* (Victoria, BC: English Literary Studies, 1989); *The Achievement of George Steevens* (New York: Peter Lang, 1990); *Shakespeare's Midwives: Some Neglected Shakespeareans* (Newark: University of Delaware Press, 1992), and *Richard Farmer, Master of Emmanuel College, Cambridge: A Forgotten Shakespearean* (Newark: University of Delaware Press, 1992). Some of the most influential critics and editors of Shakespeare are considered in Claude Rawson, ed., *Dryden, Pope, Johnson, Malone* (London: Continuum, 2010).

Sherbo has also edited the seventh and eighth volumes in the Yale Edition of the Works of Samuel Johnson, *Johnson on Shakespeare* (New Haven, CT: Yale University Press, 1968), offering abundant examples of Johnson's critical commentary on the plays. A better introductory selection to this key encounter between writer and critic would be *Samuel Johnson on Shakespeare*, ed. H. R. Woudhuysen (Harmondsworth: Penguin, 1989). There is a bold reading of Johnson's notes to Shakespeare as 'naked criticism' in Edward Tomarken, *Samuel Johnson on Shakespeare: The Discipline of Criticism* (Athens: University of Georgia Press, 1991), a staunch defence of Johnson in G. F. Parker, *Johnson's Shakespeare* (Oxford: Clarendon Press, 1989), and a wide range of subjects in *Comparative Excellence: New Essays on Shakespeare and Johnson*, ed. Eric Rasmussen and Aaron Santesso (New York: AMS, 2007).

CRITICISM

*Shakespeare Survey, Volume 51: Shakespeare in the Eighteenth Century*, ed. Stanley Wells (Cambridge: Cambridge University Press, 1998) contains some fascinating pieces on, for example, Shakespeare and early Georgian politics, race, and *Double Falsehood*; the same might be said of two collections of essays with similar titles: Fiona Ritchie and Peter Sabor, eds., *Shakespeare in the Eighteenth Century* (Cambridge: Cambridge University Press, 2012) and Peter Sabor and Paul Yachnin, eds., *Shakespeare and the Eighteenth Century* (Aldershot: Ashgate, 2008). There are also some perceptive and useful essays in Jean I. Marsden, ed. *The Appropriation of Shakespeare: Post-Renaissance Reconstructions of the Works and the Myth* (Hemel Hempstead: Harvester Wheatsheaf, 1991).

Samuel Schoenbaum, *Shakespeare's Lives* (Oxford: Oxford University Press, 1991) devotes about 100 pages out of 600 to retracing the footsteps of Shakespeare's biographers from Nicholas Rowe to Edmond Malone. Don-John Dugas, *Marketing the Bard: Shakespeare in Performance and Print 1660–1740* (Columbia: University of Missouri Press, 2006) is full of information about the early years of the Shakespeare 'brand', while Peter Dávid-házi, *The Romantic Cult of Shakespeare: Literary Reception in Anthropological Perspective* (Basingstoke: Macmillan, 1998) explores the Shakespeare craze at the other end of the century. Although some of the findings of Robert Gale Noyes, *The Thespian Mirror: Shakespeare in the Eighteenth Century Novel* (Providence, RI: Brown University, 1953) are now seen to be open to question, it remains a standard work for studying Shakespeare in relation to the emerging genre of the novel. A single chapter in Elizabeth Eger, *Bluestockings: Women of Reason from Enlightenment to Romanticism* (Basingstoke: Palgrave Macmillan, 2010) usefully summarizes the achievements of three female Shakespearians—Elizabeth Montagu, Charlotte Lennox, and Elizabeth Griffith—putting them in the context of an intellectual culture under the constraints of gender politics.

A great deal has been written about the Ireland forgeries, including: Patricia Pierce, *The Great Shakespeare Fraud: The Strange, True Story of William-Henry Ireland* (Stroud: Sutton Publishing, 2005), Doug Stewart, *The Boy Who Would Be Shakespeare: A Tale of Forgery and Folly* (Boston, MA: Da Capo, 2010), and a novel by Peter Ackroyd, *The Lambs of London* (London: Chatto & Windus, 2004), in which the Lambs of the title are, of course, Charles and Mary. In *Reforging Shakespeare: The Story of a Theatrical Scandal* (Bethlehem, PA: Lehigh University Press, 1998), Jeffrey Kahan suggests that William Henry's *Confessions* had been too readily trusted, and that the whole Ireland family was implicated in a knowing attempt to fake their way into a central, and enriching, position in the Shakespeare industry—the latest incarnation of a long-held suspicion, but not one that seems to have found many modern supporters. Bernard Grebanier, *The Great Shakespeare Forgery: A New Look at the Career of William Henry Ireland* (London: Heinemann, 1966) is a more entertaining and informative account, while Tom Lockwood offers a more recent theoretically nuanced response in 'Manuscript, Print and the Authentic Shakespeare: The Ireland Forgeries Again', *Shakespeare Survey 59: Editing Shakespeare*, ed. Peter Holland (Cambridge: Cambridge University Press, 2006), 108–23. Robert Miles puts the affair into the context of emerging ideas about authorial personality and nationalism in *Romantic Misfits* (Basingstoke: Palgrave Macmillan, 2008).

When modern critics need to cite a precursor who either got it all wrong or who was thinking along the right lines, a number of older studies of the eighteenth century and Shakespeare present themselves for praise or belated castigation. Especially helpful in this regard is *Shakespeare Improved: The Restoration Versions in Quarto and on the Stage* (Cambridge, MA: Harvard University Press, 1927), in which Hazelton Spencer considers (and disapproves of) each Restoration and early eighteenth-century alteration of Shakespeare in turn. Other pioneers include David Nichol Smith, *Shakespeare in the Eighteenth Century* (Oxford: Clarendon Press, 1928; 1967), which handily presents the prefatory material from eighteenth-century editions by Rowe, Pope et al. in a single volume, and G. C. D. Odell, *Shakespeare from Betterton to Irving*, 2 vols. (London: Constable, 1920–21), which takes a long view of the plays on stage. F. E. Halliday, *The Cult of Shakespeare* (London: Duckworth, 1957) seems to be the first post-war book devoted to what now might be called Shakespeare's afterlife.

As well the books on the Stratford Jubilee, the mid-1960s produced Robert Witbeck Babcock, *The Genesis of Shakespeare Idolatry 1766–1799: A Study in English Criticism of the Late Eighteenth Century* (New York: Russell & Russell, 1964) and Louis Marder, *His Exits and His Entrances: The Story of*

*Shakespeare's Reputation* (Philadelphia: J. B. Lippincott, 1963), a story told with a good eye for amusing detail. A flavour of late nineteenth-century criticism may be caught in Ernest Walder, *Shakesperian Criticism: Textual and Literary, from Dryden to the End of the Eighteenth Century* (Bradford: Thomas Brear, 1895; New York: AMS, fasc. repr., 1972) and Thomas R. Lounsbury's 'Shakespeare Wars' trilogy (all New York: Charles Scribner's Sons): *Shakespeare as a Dramatic Artist: With an Account of His Reputation at Various Periods* (1901), *Shakespeare and Voltaire* (1902), and *The Text of Shakespeare: Its History from the Publication of the Quartos and Folios down to and including the Publication of the Editions of Pope and Theobald* (1906).

### ILLUSTRATIONS

Beautifully illustrated, with essays from Jonathan Bate and others, Jane Martineau and Desmond Shawe-Taylor, eds., *Shakespeare in Art* (London: Merrell, 2003) is a gallery in itself. Two books by Stuart Sillars—*Painting Shakespeare: The Artist as Critic, 1720–1820* (Cambridge: Cambridge University Press, 2006) and *The Illustrated Shakespeare, 1709–1875* (Cambridge: Cambridge University Press, 2008)—offer guides to the 'visualisation' of the plays from Hogarth to the Boydell Shakespeare Gallery, and illustrated editions of Shakespeare, respectively. A thorough account of a single play as it has been put into images is supplied by Alan R. Young, *Hamlet and the Visual Arts, 1709–1900* (Madison: Fairleigh Dickinson University Press, 2002).

### SHAKESPEARE ABROAD

Much has been written about Shakespeare's relationship with Germany in the late eighteenth and early nineteenth centuries; critical coverage of his spread to other parts of the world has been more uneven. John Pemble, *Shakespeare Goes to Paris: How the Bard Conquered France* (London: Hambledon and London, 2005) is a partially successful guide to Shakespeare's progress through French culture and on the French stage, while, as a succinct account of how he became a cult writer in the German-speaking states, the introductory essay to Johann Gottfried Herder, *Shakespeare*, trans. and ed. Gregory Moore (Princeton: Princeton University Press, 2008) is difficult to beat. On the same subject, see also Samuel L. Macey, 'The Introduction of Shakespeare to Germany in the Second Half of the Eighteenth Century', *Eighteenth-Century Studies*, vol. 5, no. 2 (Winter 1971–2), 261–9.

For good accounts of the beginnings of Continental performances of Shakespeare, see Simon Williams, *Shakespeare on the German Stage, Volume*

*One: 1586–1914* (Cambridge: Cambridge University Press, 2004), Keith Gregor, *Shakespeare in the Spanish Theatre 1772 to the Present* (London: Continuum, 2009), and Gaby Petrone Fresco, *Shakespeare's Reception in 18th Century Italy: The Case of Hamlet* (New York: Peter Lang, 1993). For information on some of the key figures beyond the stage, see Roger Paulin, ed., *Voltaire, Goethe, Schlegel, Coleridge* (London: Continuum, 2010) in the Great Shakespeareans series. And for an enlightened view of 'Bardolatry' from north of the border, see Robert Crawford, 'The Bard: Ossian, Burns, and the Shaping of Shakespeare' in *Shakespeare and Scotland*, ed. Willy Maley and Andrew Murphy (Manchester: Manchester University Press, 2004). The initial chapters in Alden T. and Virginia Mason Vaughan, *Shakespeare in America* (Oxford: Oxford University Press, 2012) succinctly and judiciously cover the uncertain subject of the first performances of Shakespeare both before and after Independence, as well as the close ties between the received canon of English literature and the colonies. See Chapter Four of Lurana Donnels O'Malley, *The Dramatic Works of Catherine the Great: Theatre and Politics in Eighteenth-Century Russia* (Aldershot: Ashgate, 2006) for an account of the 'Shakespearean Influence' on the plays of Catherine the Great.

# Index